Design history:
fad or function?

Design History Society

Design Council

Design history: fad or function?

First edition published in the United Kingdom 1978 by
Design Council
28 Haymarket London SW1Y 4SU

Edited by Terry Bishop
Designed by Gill Streater
Cover illustration by Derek Blois, Brighton Polytechnic
Typeset by Castle Printers (London) Ltd
Printed and bound in the United Kingdom by
The Whitefriars Press Limited
Tonbridge, Kent

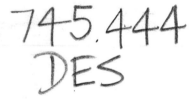
ISBN 0 85072 089 3

Contents

Introduction

The newly emergent discipline of design history has by now spread its roots quite thickly and established itself firmly enough to show that it is here to stay. This is clearly evidenced by the number of new BA courses based in faculties of art and design in British polytechnics that include it in their syllabuses; by the growing number of exhibitions that include designed objects; and by a general desire to understand objects from the past within their context. As an academic discipline it is undoubtedly the child of the art schools, where the increasing number of design students need a historical perspective more relevant to their immediate needs than the one provided by traditional fine art history, and it is largely within their confines that it has blossomed and yielded fruit.

The Department of Art History in the Faculty of Art and Design of Brighton Polytechnic has, for five years, been pursuing a programme of research into twentieth-century British design. It was pleased, therefore, to see signs of encouragement of the discipline on a national scale, and very willing to follow Newcastle and Middlesex Polytechnic in hosting a design history conference in September 1977.

The subject of the conference was design history itself and the approach was a pluralistic one, demonstrating that there are in fact many design histories – ones that emphasise links with the history of technology, others more strongly allied to social history and sociology, and others that use terminology borrowed from the history of the fine and decorative arts. This interdisciplinary nature of the subject was reflected in the range of lectures, which were in three main sections that focused in turn on the designer, the consumer and the object. They covered, among others, such varied historical topics as railway design, relations between the designer and the law, wallpaper design, early American industrial design, and the professional structures available to graphic designers. These topics instantly laid bare the bones of such burning aesthetic and socio-cultural issues as taste, style, individualism versus anonymity in design, the social and economic restraints on the design process, the relevance of quality judgements in design history and, more fundamentally, what is design history and for whom is the discipline being developed?

Discussions at Brighton were wide ranging and they showed the diversity of backgrounds from which people have moved into design history – a diversity that added richness to the proceedings and encouraged a feeling of mutual respect among the delegates.

The predominant theme that emerged from the conference was one of 'unity in diversity', with a feeling that initial forays were gradually being consolidated and built upon. It was generally agreed that design history certainly has a function to fulfil and cannot be dismissed as a passing 'fad'. It is hoped that the papers in this collection will reinforce this view.

One positive step into the future achieved by the conference was the formation of the Design History Society which, as a formally constituted body with a committee of seven at present, will serve to encourage the development of Design History at all possible levels and in every possible direction.

The Design History Society defines itself as a means of facilitating communication between members and as a focus for the interchange of ideas, information and resources. This will be achieved by arranging a programme of meetings to coincide with exhibitions of design; by compiling a list of unpublished research projects in design history from educational sources, museums and private individuals; by arranging annual conferences at which a variety of papers will be presented; by securing the publication of papers on design history presented by members at conferences and meetings; and by holding joint conferences and meetings with other organisations with similar or complementary interests.

It is hoped that, through the work of the committee and with the help of the Society as a whole, the Brighton Conference will be followed by even larger and more varied and stimulating events that will help to establish Design History as a serious and well researched discipline.

Penny Sparke
Lecturer in Design History
Brighton Polytechnic

The historian, the critic and the designer

James Holland
Education Officer, SIAD

In preparing this paper on the historian, the critic and the designer, I found that some of what I wanted to say had already been said with considerable authority a good many years ago. I shall quote from this distinguished precedent without disclosing the name of its author until I finish, though you may guess it before then. As a foretaste, let me offer you this: 'From our historians we must expect a more exact analysis of the social conditions which have produced art in the past.' And in this context we may include design.

My purpose is to review the changing part that the art historian has played during the post-Coldstream years of design education; to welcome the emergence of the design historian; to examine his function and how far this must involve critical attitudes; and to speculate a little on the future of design history, which clearly is not going to flourish in a vacuum, but will need to be related to other design-centred activities. I am rather conscious that design history has developed rapidly and I hope I will not provide too many glimpses of the obvious.

In welcoming the growing recognition of the design historian I do so with a number of reservations. The historian observes and deduces from a predetermined standpoint in time. He is not a roving reporter; unlike a terrestrial explorer, he cannot wander about. He is more like an astronomer – limited to the view from his observatory, but able to make what deductions he may from what he can see. The analogy may not be exact, but it does require the observer – whether historian or astronomer – to take his own standpoint into account. Other than in compiling lists of dates of births and deaths, history can never be entirely objective. 'We do not glean wisdom from historical facts but only from our interpretation of their significance. It is the conclusions which the historian draws from these facts that we find stimulating, even though we may disagree violently with his point of view.' The events and circumstances of which history is comprised cannot be approached from all directions at once, and cannot be encompassed by the historian from his fixed observation post.

I do not think that the historian is to be regarded as little more than a scavenger of data, though of course historical research will always be the basis of his work. But to assemble the detritus of the past into ever larger heaps is not enough, and if the historian is to sort the significant from the trivial he must to some extent become the critic.

I have suggested that history cannot be approached from all directions at once; it is an art more than a science. I realise in my own lifetime that events, people and environments that I have known very well at first hand are almost never reconstructed or re-created on radio, television or in print, to convey the real feeling of the occasion. 'It was not like that at all', one must insist, in spite of the archives and all the available research facilities. Costumes may be original, the period slang accurately revived, all the theatrical setting most carefully restored, but still it was not like that at all. So it seems important that the historian himself must be fully aware of where he stands – not necessarily to advertise his position so much as to realise what slant, what bias, is likely to colour his deductions. While I do not expect a purely objective and entirely impersonal picture from the historian, I do expect him to approach his theme from a carefully considered, deliberate direction – though I do not want this approach to be so doctrinaire and dogmatic that all unfavourable evidence is suppressed. Least of all does one welcome history re-written by the political or religious extremist – there is no such thing as Marxist history, or for that matter Catholic or Fascist history, though there are interrelations. So I want the historian to be prepared to say sometimes 'I don't know. I can't reconcile this evidence with that. Over to you, dear listener or reader, for your own interpretation.' For the intelligent listener will eventually detect and reject the dogmatic critics, who in the end are left performing only for one another.

So having made these considerable reservations, I turn to examine the growing appreciation of design history, and a reasonable starting point might be the Coldstream Council and its reports. These, with the setting up of NCDAD and DipAD, marked something of a watershed in the history of art and design education – if only because, by implication and almost for the first time, art and design education was regarded as something more than training in limited skills, and the need for the artist and designer to acquire a breadth of understanding of other and complementary skills and values was recognised. I say 'by implication', because as this new approach developed there were some voices raised against this liberal attitude. In fact, only a few weeks ago David Hockney produced this: 'When a group of middle-class intellectuals takes over the Royal College of Art and introduces what they call general studies, which in effect downgrade the act of painting, it takes 15 years for people to see that it was a mistake.' It seems to me that this must be one of the most inconsequential remarks of 1977, and it can be contrasted with Richard Hoggart: 'I am not greatly persuaded by the view that budding artists are easily maimed by being made intellectually self-conscious. In my experience, most talented people have their own, built-in prophylaxis against that risk. In general, greater self-awareness seems useful for any of us; it is a considerable stay against self-delusion.'

Two features of DipAD were, I think, particularly significant: the entry requirement of five O-levels or an acceptable equivalent in general education; and the original insistence, later modified, on an injection of fine art into all design studies – a sort of aesthetic additive for which the dosage, if not the precise method and point of injection, was firmly specified. One might now be pardoned for suspecting that the prescription could have been more for the benefit of the doctor than the patient. It certainly reflected an attitude epitomised by a famous principal of the Royal College of Art who threatened wayward fine art students, 'If you can't do better than that, you'll find yourself in the Design School.'

It would be tempting to trace precisely how and when this

Fine Art snobbism developed in this country. I imagine it was almost entirely a by-product of the Industrial Revolution and the social patterns this imposed. I quote again: 'A hundred years ago a humble workman could buy a Staffordshire pottery figure and put it on his mantelpiece. He can no longer afford to buy Staffordshire figures, or anything like them, but the State will buy a picture for him and hang it in the local art centre.' And now charge him to look at it, I might add. There is little evidence to suggest that this snobbism existed in a marked form in pre-Victorian days, but this again is territory for the design historian's attention. It is significant that the DipAD general educational requirement – modest as it was – was resented most vociferously by a fine art lobby, one of whose battle cries, I remember, was 'How many O-levels did van Gogh have?', though a careful reading of his life suggests that he could have had quite a handful had they then existed. The myth of the artist as Inspired or Holy Fool, with all its many *vie de bohème* variants, is of course closely linked with the fine art snobbism. The artist was to be regarded as something between remittance man and an eremitic monk – demanding the handouts of society as a right, but in no sense admitting an obligation to it. I quote again: 'I see no civic difference between the poet and the painter; each is an individual giving expression to a personal vision which may or may not be of great social importance, but in one case Society can ignore the creative gift with impunity, in the other it is now to be bullied into accepting it and paying for it out of public revenue.'

This concept of the artist was urged as one reason against incorporating some art colleges within polytechnics. What is now worth noting is the extent to which the concept has become modified during the two decades since Coldstream, and though there are many who regret the old days of the wholly independent art college, and there have been some notable shotgun marriages between art colleges and technical colleges where the recriminations have not yet died down, the feeling that we are all in the contemporary maelstrom together, and that we might as well try to come to terms with our fellows and their skills, is now much more widely accepted.

There is of course no precise line beyond which fine art ceases to be fine art and becomes, say, decorative illustration or ceramic sculpture or interior design, and there is no virtue in trying to establish formal boundaries, but I have little doubt that under today's conditions artist and designer are pursuing appreciably different paths which, so far as one can see, are unlikely to converge. Another quotation: 'When a painter painted for the Catholic Church or for the court of a king, he had a fairly exact idea of what was expected of him; he was faced by a definite task…Before the sixteenth century the orders which the Church gave the glass painter were as detailed as a modern contract for building a factory. All the great medieval painters and renaissance painters right down to the time of Michelangelo were craftsmen carrying out formal contracts.' But the authority whom I quote was something of a voice crying in the wilderness, and fine art interests were very loth to abandon their claim to be supported by society while being in no way responsible to their benefactors. I quote for the last time, to show that what I am saying is not a new heresy: 'As for painting easel pictures – well, why not, if you, a useful citizen, feel so inclined? You might paint a great picture in your spare time, just as T. S. Eliot wrote a great poem in his spare time. But you will not any longer, of you are a reasonable person, expect your fellow-taxpayers to support you while you indulge in an activity which no longer has any economic sanction.'

I would not want what I have said about fine art in relation to design studies to be interpreted as any denigration of the practice of fine art. Nor have I anything but respect for the many art historians I have known. It is the official reluctance to recognise that fine art and design are today on separate tracks – and in particular that design is not an inferior brand of fine art, to be practised by those of lesser talents and blunter sensibilities – that I believe is to be condemned.

It is no sort of recognition of fine art to impose it, in the way that religious instruction was imposed on general education, as something that can do no harm and just conceivably might do some good in an indefinable way. However, though fine art and design education must pursue different paths, I would find it very depressing if design became so identified with systems and technological considerations that the intuitive and, to use an old-fashioned word, inspirational approaches could only be associated with fine art. If history is an art rather than a science, how much more true this is of design. Young designers, and some not so young, can be seduced by all the sophistication, all the hardware and software, of contemporary technology; but arguably, all the spectacular advances and breakthroughs in design applications have had something of the unpredictable, of intuition, even of inspiration, in them. I think particularly of Paxton's blotting-pad sketch for the Crystal Palace and of Brunel's innovations. And of course it is true that there is a large sector of the design spectrum – including textile design, decorative building elements and poster and publicity design – which acknowledges the intuitive and the inspirational, and into which systems and automation can make only limited inroads.

One reflection of the disparate status of art and design studies is in their respective literatures, as can be seen in college libraries. Many shelves will be filled with historical and critical works on artists of every school from the Cro-Magnon on, and many more such studies appear every year. By comparison, the history of design is still sparsely covered and areas of specialised design have virtually no historical literature.

Various reasons for this suggest themselves. Much design is necessarily transient, with a much more ephemeral life than the gallery or mural painting. Often the design quality is only to be appreciated fully in terms of materials, processes and demands which themselves are transient. In spite of all our enjoyable nostalgia and sentiment, the design of the steam locomotive was only fully significant to its own age of steam – although I admit that there is some prospect of this returning as we head back eventually to the caves or the treetops.

It is incidental that this transience can often make studies in design history more complete in themselves, though they can never be completely self contained. In my own lifetime the aeroplane has developed from the first powered flights at Kitty Hawk, and given a few more years I may well witness its replacement by the hot air balloon and the hang glider. Equally, the water or wind driven mill, the galleon and the three-decker, the stagecoach and the tram, are all only to be assessed in terms of their contemporary technologies. Design is largely problem-solving, and until the problems themselves are fully appreciated, the rightness and elegance of any solution cannot be fully estimated.

The design historian, as we have seen, must be a social historian in the widest sense, able to relate the design to the problems it attempts to solve, whether these concern energy sources, materials, or markets and demands. And if circumstances can explain design, design itself can often tell us something about historical circumstances – in particular when the design is not the inspiration of one designer but has been evolved anonymously as the result of generations of trial and selection by makers and users. The familiar English garden fork and spade might illustrate this, shaped as they have been by generations of gardeners and farm workers. Compare these with their Mediterranean equivalents – how much they tell us about the environments in which they are used, the workers who use them, their clothing and footwear, the climate and the soil. I think we would all agree that in trying to define the scope of design history, it must not be reduced to the level of a history of ornament or decoration. In my student days there were still in circulation some admirable dictionaries of ornament, the fruits of Victorian eclecticism. Egyptian, Greek, Roman, Renaissance, assorted Gothic, they offered a choice of appropriate motifs for every purpose – a sort of primitive Letraset service. If superficial familiarity with the period trimmings has been replaced by a more profound appreciation of design, there is little to regret; to understand Gothic architecture as an aspect of western medieval society and its structural aspect is more valuable than being able to mock up an Early English crocket or finial at short order.

But at one time the art student was required to learn the Classical Orders in such detail that, if commanded to draw, say, the Corinthian Order of the Temple of Minerva at Rome correct to scale, he could do so with no reference to the published plates. I am not sure that the disappearance of such a discipline is entirely a gain. In looking today at the work of graphic designers in particular I am often surprised at what little reserves of background knowledge they seem to possess, and how dependent they have become on photo references. It should be said, however, that in some colleges both staff and students have recently shown increasing interest in reviving such studies as formal perspective, anatomy and, above all, drawing from the life model, and it may be that many a plaster cast of the Venus de Milo or Antinous is being dusted off or scraped down against the return of antique drawing.

I believe there are some currently accepted design concepts that the historian and critic may come to challenge. One is the belief that if a thing looks right, it most probably is right – that the most functionally successfully will automatically be the most aesthetically rewarding. I wonder, and I am interested that the theme of your conference suggests that you may be questioning this yourselves. As one instance, the racing car of the 1930s and 1950s was a smooth, elegant, streamlined affair that was aesthetically pleasing. The contemporary Formula 1 car looks rather like a discarded iron bedstead, but can one say with conviction that it answers its contemporary problems less adequately than the elegant machines of the 1930s?

From what I have said, it follows that the design historian must expect to do much of his own research; the art library will only be helpful to a limited extent. He must search in catalogues and technical journals, manufacturers' files, in patent offices and archives, in industrial museums and in the junkyards of the older industrial undertakings. I am sure that in our earliest industrial centres – the Midlands and the Black Country, Lancashire, Yorkshire and Durham – there are still records and evidence of design development back to the beginning of the Industrial Revolution. I know that some years ago lecturers at Birmingham discovered that one long-established firm which produced those heraldic and pictorial devices that decorated the sides of trams and trains was throwing out sackloads of transfers for long-extinct undertakings –

South American tramways, the Kowloon Light Railway – evidence of the days when this country really was the workshop of the world.

The design historian, in common with most other academics, operates at two levels, exercising both intake and output – researching and developing his selected subjects on the one hand and, on the other, as lecturer or tutor, imparting a more panoramic view of design history to students who are themselves more likely to become practising designers than historians. Professor Galbraith has said that 'the historian should not sit crowing on his own little dunghill, but should be able to cover anything from Beowulf to Virginia Woolf'. It is this output to the student that mostly concerns me.

I have urged for many years that design history deserves to be treated more seriously in professional design education, and I welcome the present indications that this is now happening. But I would be alarmed by any evidence that this was creating a new mystique with its own vocabulary and values, remote from the daily practice of design. The young designer needs to be able to understand and acknowledge the traditions of his skill and to possess a frame of historical reference – it is almost always the charlatan and the ignoramus who boast of rejecting or ignoring tradition – but the sure way to divert the student from the enjoyment of design history is to detach it from his own practice. When, in the early days of DipAD, I joined the staff of a large college – later a polytechnic – I was surprised and rather saddened by the reluctance of many students to attend the required history of art lectures because, they said, they found them dull, boring and uninteresting. Remembering my student days at the Royal College I recalled how much everybody looked forward to the weekly art history lectures then being given by Professsor Wellington – urbane, sensitive, not without wit, and in themselves modest works of art. There were other admirable lecturers, not that we agreed with all that was said, but I found it difficult to understand how such an enriching subject could ever be boring. Perhaps I underestimated the capacity of less accomplished lecturers to impart dulness to any subject, though it is more likely that I expected too much response from students who had arrived on their courses with very much less of a struggle than earlier generations. But surely art and design history should be a delight and not a penance for the committed student, stimulating speculation and discussion long after the lectures themselves.

A further matter for surprise was the narrowness of the slice of design history chosen for study. I appreciate that one must choose between breadth and depth in defining areas for study, and that only by restricting the field will one be able to penetrate to those aspects that yield only to study in depth. In the case of the professional design student, I would expect his main study to be of this nature, restricted to what can be studied in depth, rather than superficial and dilettantish encounters with an unlimited range of design skills. But as regards the history of art or design considered as a complementary study, it seems to me to be important that the student should be able to take a panoramic view, and be able broadly to relate one culture or tradition to another, rather than be profoundly involved within narrow limits of time or space. If I may offer an example from the early days of DipAD: in one instance students were required to compare the work of Bernini and Borromini – a fascinating assignment for anyone who had spent days in Rome examining their work at first hand, but arguably over-specialised and remote for students who were still unfamiliar with the very important eighteenth-century developments in British design that had taken place in the very town where they worked.

We have to acknowledge that we have come a long way from those early days of DipAD, and it is no longer considered that a proportion of fine art studies is needed to make design courses academically respectable.

You will know that, after an unusually prolonged period of ruminaton, the DES has made some decisions about the future of the many non-degree or vocational design courses, which since the days of NDD have lacked any national structure or national award, but have somehow endured, and very often flourished exceedingly. The perhaps rather misnamed Technicians Education Council, TEC, which has been given the responsibility for these courses, has realistically enough acknowledged its need of support in dealing with this hitherto unfamiliar area, and has appealed to the educational and professional bodies experienced in this field for help in planning the future of these courses, including my own society, SIAD. This is reasonable, since our assessments for probationary membership have been widely adopted by colleges as a national award. In assessing courses and students we have given the same weight to technical and professional understanding as to creative skills, and certainly professional understanding should include historical awareness of the development of those skills. Today we are seeing, in the present state of the British printing industry, what can happen when a craft or skill lacks pride in its past and spirit to face the future. For if there is one thing that the embryo designer can learn from the history of design, it is that there is no future for Luddite attitudes, and that while materials and processes, media and markets will inevitably change, the designer who foresees this and is prepared to re-assess the new demands and the problems they will present will always have a function in industry and in society. If for no other reason, I believe that this is why the teaching of design history must be on a broad and comparative basis.

These rather random thoughts, which I have tried to weave into some sort of pattern, I think amount to both a welcome and a plea to the design historian from the standpoint of the practising designer and the student of design. A welcome partly because there are so many areas of past design activity yet to be explored and expounded, and we shall be greatly interested in all that you can uncover and tell us about the environments in which they developed. In doing this you will be imposing a pattern, an ordered picture, selecting and exercising your critical functions, and this will often require you to put a name or 'handle' to trends or broad movements in retrospect. It is not uncommon to meet students who are more concerned with dropping individual designers into the correct period slot than in appreciating their work, but many of these apparently clearly labelled categories were undefined and nameless in their day. We know, for example, that Manet, Degas, Monet, Pissarro and Sisley never got together under a common banner of Impressionism; and Art Deco was not, I believe, in common usage as a term during its original manifestations. There were, of course, exceptions when manifestos were being issued and movements declared their principles, but I think that often we need reminding that movements which now appear tidy, conscious and compact were at the time vague and unformed, even to the participants.

In your important critical role do not, I beg, become doctrinaire or assume the omniscience of the Sunday Supplement journalist. Students, and particularly the more sensitive and responsive ones, can be more immediately influenced than we imagine by sweeping generalisations and ready-made criteria, and in my time I have had to turn candidates away from certain foundation courses because they arrived so overloaded with newly acquired prejudices that they would have been unreasonably handicapped on a senior course and would have held their fellow students back. For what you will not be imparting is 'taste' – least of all 'Good Taste', and the title and presentation of this conference makes it clear, at least to me, that you have no illusions about this. *Chacun à son mauvais goût.*

I suppose I encounter as many professional design students as any one person could expect to do, and in various capacities. In my experience a fair proportion of students who get to senior courses – say three out of four – acquire a reasonable working competence, enough to be able to sustain current standards. A small number give one that rewarding impression that here is something more – not just the capacity to keep abreast, but to add something and to advance the practice of their chosen skills. I find the new interest in design history particularly significant for such pacemakers, since they will be the real custodians of the tradition in the future.

Need it live? 'History is bunk', said Henry Ford. Happy the land that has no history, and one can understand the disillusionment behind this. Is there not a case for pulling down the shutters and turning our backs on the past, meeting today's problems – design problems included – from scratch? But I don't believe that any culture of significance has ever emerged fully fledged, by virgin birth or spontaneous combustion as it were, and the continuing fallacy of a return to prelapsarian innocence is for neither the historian nor the designer. However dim the torch, it must still be handed on.

Since design, in its widest sense, is an abstraction that is as widely manifest as order or chaos, the question must arise as to how one can approach the history of anything so diffuse and discover any sequence or pattern in its many and varied forms. Two possibilities occur to one. The first is by selecting a limited range of related skills and their applications and pursuing these through the years – as, for instance, the history of costume, or furniture, or transport, or visual communication. The other is to start from defined historical periods and seek all the contemporary design manifestations – design in pre-Conquest Saxon England, or from 1800 to 1850 in Britain, for example. These would be alternative approaches, and it might be hoped that eventually the one could broaden enough to embrace the other. While the former might be something that the practising designer and design tutor would undertake within their specialist skills, the comprehensive approach through a historical period seems to me to be much more the province of the design historian.

But this is speculation and you will develop your own attitudes on this. What I do believe is that the design historian has a responsibility to the designer – and particularly to the embryo designer – to encourage a comparative and critical approach; to demonstrate that the roots of design skills go very deep in the evolution of society; and to show that the considerations and factors that determined design solutions in the past may change in detail, but will still in principle shape the successful designs of the future.

Finally, I remind you of my earlier quotations. They come from an article – 'The Fate of Modern Painting' – published in *Horizon* number 95 in 1947. The author was Herbert Read.

From a lipstick to a steamship

the growth of the American design profession

Penny Sparke
Brighton Polytechnic

Little attention has been paid, in the study of the history of design, to the changing nature and status of the designer – be he craftsman or applied artist, architect or interior designer, product or graphic designer. There has been a tendency to emphasise the social context of the object and of consumer taste while neglecting the necessary analysis of the structure that supports the designer and which must determine, to a great extent, the nature of his work.

The main purpose of this paper is to show how strong commercial factors affected the early development of industrial design in the United States and how questions of artistic creativity were largely subordinated to such concerns.

As soon as the division of labour, necessitated by industrialisation, broke down the unity of craft production, the 'designer' (as he came to be called) found himself part of a system whose ends were those of technology and commerce rather than art. There were several instances of this marriage between art and technology in the nineteenth century, and the work of Peter Behrens for AEG in Germany at the turn of the century provided a twentieth-century prototype of the new hybrid character known later as the 'industrial designer', but it was in the United States in the 1920s that the first substantial wave of self-conscious, self-modelled 'designers for industry' emerged. A study of the particular conditions that engendered them and of the primary determining factors that moulded their role will help to provide an understanding of the early meaning of the term 'industrial designer' which has remained a constant in the twentieth century.

The reason for the alliance of visually trained individuals with mass production was first and foremost a question of economics, stemming from the need for increased sales on the part of the newly established companies in the 1920s. In the five boom years that followed the end of the First World War, technological innovations aided the expansion of industrial production, and more and more companies were establishing themselves in the American market with new products of a technological nature for the home and the office, directed at the newly affluent consuming public. Fierce competition meant that the functional efficiency of the new goods and extensive graphic advertising could no longer act as the only selling tools and inevitably the choice between a number of similar articles began to be determined by appearance – a factor that had hitherto been given only minimal attention, either by engineers employed by the firms or by members of the executive staff who 'had a good eye'.

By 1926 the market was glutted by the huge number of new goods, and in 1927, the year in which the first effects of economic recession were felt in the United States, the main problem for industry began to be one of distribution rather than manufacture. The designer played an important part in industry from this time onwards, through the Wall Street Crash of 1929 and into the early depression of the 1930s, by giving objects visual 'sales appeal' which made them more desirable than those of their competitors, and by lowering the costs of retooling and labour and therefore of the article itself. The industrial designer emerged, therefore, in a period of economic growth followed by one of economic recession, and thrived in both as the 'silent salesman'[1] of the new, mass-produced consumer goods.

Advertising in general expanded greatly in the 1920s[2] and it was from its ranks and from other areas of commercial design that most of the pioneer industrial designers emerged. In *Art in Industry* of 1922 – a report of an industrial art survey conducted under the auspices of the National Society for Vocational Education and the Department of Education of the State of New York – Charles R. Richards describes the field of graphic advertising, which was expanding rapidly at this time:

'The element of design may be said to enter the field of printing and graphic advertising through two channels, one represented by the compositor or layout man who deals with typographical design including ornament, and the other by the commercial artist, so called, who deals with all kinds of pictorial and decorative compositions, whether in line or mass, which are to be printed by any of the reproductive processes.'[3]

A designer called Joseph Sinel coined the name 'industrial design' in 1919 to describe the same kind of work that Richards is documenting – work that often involved, in the words of Richards, 'representations of machinery, shoes, automobiles, and other subjects requiring great accuracy of delineation'.[4]

Advertising agencies, headed by art directors, liaised with the business organisation in which the general scheme of an advertisement was planned and with the artist who was selected to develop the design – whether he was freelance, employed by service studios, or on the staff of the agency itself. Large advertisers employed their own advertising managers and department stores often employed their own artists for mail advertising.

It was within this structure that many of the early industrial designers gained their first experience of working for industry, for instance as part of a sales team that included salesmen, statisticians and economists. When the new industries decided their goods needed styling they turned to the art directors of the advertising agencies to select appropriate individuals to design their goods for them and inevitably the graphic illustrators were among the first to be approached.

The extent to which they were already integrated into the business and commercial interests of American industry is made clear by Richards: 'Advertising is an art that we have carried further than any other country. Our consumption of goods is largely effected through its medium. Its volume and diversity have become synonymous with American business methods.'[5]

The visually trained individuals who moved into the new profession of industrial design were not, therefore, painters, sculptors or architects, but rather a disparate group of men, who, moving around the periphery of the fine arts world, were more concerned with the application of art to commerce, particularly in the field of graphic advertising.

Walter Dorwin Teague, frequently nominated as 'the dean of industrial design',[6] came to New York in the early part of the century and in the evenings attended the Art Students' League – an art school where, in addition to classes in drawing, painting, modelling and composition, there were classes in illustration, lithography and etching, and which trained a large majority of the new commercial artists. Teague worked as a typographer and advertising illustrator in New York from 1908 onwards, working first for the Calkinsa and Holden Advertising Agency and later for Community Plate and Phoenix Hosiery campaigns on a freelance basis.[7] His graphic work soon became renowned and some of his famous 'Teague borders' were exhibited in one of the Metropolitan Museum of Art's annual exhibitions of Industrial Art in the early 1920s.

Teague put a deliberate end to these pursuits, however, as more and more requests came from clients, not only to design their advertising campaigns and their packaging, but also to give them ideas for styling the products themselves. In the mid-1920s he sketched some new lines for cars and grand pianos and decided that after the 30 June 1926 he would devote his office to product design only. The request in 1927 by Eastman Kodak for him to restyle the Brownie camera – a project which began on the 1 January 1928 – consolidated his determination to become an industrial designer.

1 *A sales slip register designed by Walter Dorwin Teague in the early 1930s*

Among other early industrial designers who moved through the two-dimensional field were Lurelle Guild and Raymond Loewy. As a result of a sketch of a lady passenger which he did on his voyage over from his native France in 1919, the latter was encouraged to move into the field of fashion illustration and, deserting his early experience in engineering, Loewy was employed by the Condé Nast publishing corporation drawing advertisements for them in his early years in New York City. He also designed some costumes for Florenz Ziegfeld, but wrote later that 'magazines were more to my taste'.[8]

In 1927, the bumper year for industrial design, Loewy met Horace Saks, who was about to open his Fifth Avenue store, and drew some advertisements for him. This was soon to develop into a larger design commitment as he went on to design the elevator operators' uniforms. Loewy's move from two to three dimensions came in 1929 with a request from Sigmund Gestetner for an improved design for his duplicating

machine, and in 1930 to design a car for the Hupp Motor Company. In 1933 Loewy decided that he wanted more than just cars and opened an office with two designers, a secretary and a business manager, thus establishing his own industrial design service.

Other pioneer industrial designers whose early experience came from commercial graphic design were John Vassos and Donald Deskey. Deskey counted the position of art director of an advertising agency among the many jobs he held in the early years of his career.

Among the numerous effects that this training had on subsequent industrial design was that of shaking off the influence of Europe, and particularly France, which was felt in the other 'Art Industries'. Richard writes again: 'Europe exercises very little influence upon the character of lithographic or other advertising design in this country largely because of what is

2 *Gestetner duplicating machine before and after redesign by Raymond Loewy in 1929*

considered to be the unsuitability of foreign designs to American advertising needs.'[9]

Another preparation ground for industrial design lay in the profession of stage design. Norman Bel Geddes, the pioneer industrial designer who combined practical projects with fantastic visions for the future, evolved his expressive ideas about 'space, sound and light'[10] in designing sets for the theatre.

He began his career as a portrait painter, which proved unprofitable, and then moved into advertising illustration designing, among other things, posters for Packard and General Motors. He was dismissed from this work because of time spent with the theatre and subsequently took up stage design, first in California and then in New York, where he designed sets for over 90 operas and plays. He was the first stage craftsman to use spotlights for general illumination, and he created highly dramatic effects with simple props and expressive lighting. Among his most successful sets were those for the 'Divine Comedy' in 1921 and Max Reinhart's production of 'The Miracle' in 1923.

Bel Geddes called theatre design his 'fickle mistress',[11] however, and changed direction again in 1927: 'I decided that I would no longer devote myself to the theatre but would experiment in designing motor-cars, ships, factories, railways – sources more akin to life today than the theatre.'[12]

His first off-stage design was nevertheless not very far removed from his earlier pursuit and provided an example of yet another common point of entrance into industrial design.

This was the area of store window dressing and store design which constituted yet another kind of selling tool, this time for the retailer rather than the manufacturer. Bel Geddes was asked by the Franklyn Simon store in New York to design their windows for them and he approached the task as a set designer, producing some startling, dramatically lit, stark windows of which he wrote, 'the window is the stage and the merchandise the players.'[13] After his experience in window display Bel Geddes moved into industrial design proper with a commission from the Toledo Scale Company to design a new scale for them. The company did not in fact produce the designs that Bel Geddes came up with and the commission went to Harold Van Doren, another of the early industrial designers.

After advertising agencies, contact with stores was the most important way into industrial design and once more emphasised the strong links with commerce. It provided a means of combining 'beauty with profit'[14] – the primary aim of the new American designers. Raymond Loewy designed a window for Saks of Fifth Avenue which John Kobler described: 'Working behind drawn shades one night, Loewy tossed aside all the mannikins but one, a female in a chaste evening gown, and with studied insolence dropped at her feet a mink coat. When the management recovered from the shock sharp words were exchanged after which he quit.'[15]

This incident characterises the daring with which these strong individuals helped create the striking image of the new industrial design profession. Richards writes that, in the world of freelance design, 'personality, special talent, and imaginative quality count for so much'.[16]

Henry Dreyfuss also came from the world of stage design. He worked on Broadway from the age of 18 designing scenery, costumes and trick effects. Both his father and his grandfather had worked in a theatre equipment shop and, after studying at the Ethical Culture School, Dreyfuss enrolled as a pupil apprentice of Bel Geddes and helped on effects for, among other productions, 'The Miracle'. He was hired by J. F. Plunkett, the manager of the Strand Theatre in New York, in the mid-1920s, but moved into industrial design in 1929 because of the insecurity of stage design and the need to earn a regular wage: 'Why, some of the most beautiful sets I have ever seen lasted only a few nights if the show was a flop. Besides, I wanted to get married and have a family.'[17]

In 1927 Dreyfuss was invited by Oswald Knauth at Macy's to become the store's display designer, to walk around the store and redesign anything that he didn't like. He turned the job down as he wanted to be his own boss and instead opened his own office and began work on some industrial projects under his own steam. His first job was a cigarette lighter made of a new material called catalin and his second the redesign of the mason jar. It was with a commission from the Bell Telephone Laboratories to design a new mouthpiece/receiver combination that Dreyfuss moved into product design proper, and it provided him with his first encounter with 'human engineering', which was to preoccupy him for 40 years.

Store design became an important focus for several artists who wanted to move into the commercial arena. Frederick Kiesler, a latter-day European constructivist who had come to America in the 1920s, wrote a book, published in 1930, entitled *Contemporary Art as applied to the Store and its Display*, in which he combined illustrations of Modernist shop-fronts with American designs by himself for Saks, by Bel Geddes, and by Donald Deskey. A distinction emerges between the work of the two continents as Bel Geddes and Deskey added futuristic expressiveness to the bare bones of the constructivist aesthetic, thus encapsulating the American spirit of faith in the future of technology.

The three main areas of commercial design that I have outlined as forming the professional basis for industrial design – advertising graphics, stage design, and store design – all formed a very strong part of the American environment in the early 1920s. Richards bears witness to this when he writes in 1922: 'The ever-present spectacle of the street, the theatres . . . with the rich display of the department stores, with the eye-catching advertisements in the magazines, the public press and other commercial literature.'[18]

The pioneer designers' feel for the nerve centres of modern life, already evident in their early careers, anticipated their fantastic visions of the 1930s and marks the final break with European 'purism', which never moved into the streets on such a large scale.

Donald Deskey stands apart from the industrial designers mentioned so far as he, along with Russel Wright and Gilbert Rhode, emerged from the area of furniture design. This had tended to be bracketed with the 'Art Industries' – among them textiles, fashion, pottery and jewellery – which had a tradition of concern with the problem of appearance and all of which had studios on the premises. A writer in *Fortune* magazine exclaimed that 'now it was the turn of washing machines, furnaces, switchboards and locomotives'.[19]

Deskey spent an adventurous youth travelling around America and doing many jobs, several of which were involved with advertising and illustration. He gradually moved towards fine art and went to Paris to study, returning in 1923 to teach design in Pennsylvania and going back to Paris in 1925 to see the exhibition of Decorative Arts. It was after this experience that he moved into furniture and interior design, and his first success was in 1926 with some screens that appeared in the background of a window at Saks. He designed windows for Franklyn Simon which demonstrated his interest in unusual materials – in this case iron, copper, and brass – and in 1927 he did the cork and metal window for Saks which Kiesler illustrated. This developed into an interest in using aluminium and tubular steel in furniture and he quickly saw the possibility of producing and selling furniture by modern methods. The peak of the early phase of his career came with designs for the interior of Radio City Music Hall in 1931, a commission he obtained through the Rockefeller family whose apartment he had designed in 1930. Deskey made sallies into industrial design, but remained predominantly an interior designer with strong industrial connections.

The question of which industries called the commercial artists into their ranks is an interesting one. One of the very first firms to decide that appearance was a selling point was the Ford Motor Company, negating its earlier principle of sticking fast to a single design. In 1927 Henry Ford closed the plant for several months in order to develop a new line and the Model A quickly superseded the Model T as a result. S. and M. Cheney wrote in 1936: 'Ford has shown that all mass production is crude in its early stages and that a standard of quality is introduced gradually as the processes are perfected.'[20]

3 A Franklyn Simon store window designed by Norman Bel Geddes in 1929

4 Big Ben alarm clock designed by Henry Dreyfuss in the early 1930s

5 Washing-machine designed by Donald Deskey in the mid 1930s

6 Interior design for Radio City Music Hall by Donald Deskey 1931

This change of heart on the part of one of the first mass-producers encouraged other companies to think along the same lines. Firms like Eastman Kodak and the Gestetner Company employed, the new freelance designers on a consultancy basis, through advertising agencies, whereas others, like the electrical firm of Westinghouse, employed a designer to work within their ranks. In their case, Donald Dohner, who had been on their staff for some years as a product engineer, became the designer in residence. George Sakier worked as the director of the Bureau of Design on the American Radiator and Standard Sanitary Corporation.

The public images that these pioneer industrial designers created for themselves and had created for them were as much a selling point as the streamlined styling they gave to products. Bel Geddes was frequently referred to as the P. T. Barnum of design, Teague was the rational businessman who read a lot, and Raymond Loewy was the exuberant, stylish Frenchman who rode in the cabs of the locomotives he designed. The first profiles of them were written in the *New Yorker* magazine in the early 1930s, [21] and *Life* frequently mentioned them, including as much about their private lives as about their designs. Cartoons appeared in *Fortune* which charted their success with such captions as 'Gentlemen, I am convinced that our next biscuit must by styled by Norman Bel Geddes'.[22] They were projected by the popular press as archetypal creative artists for whom intuition and inspiration were paramount. This was in spite of the fact that most of the work they did in the area of 'consumer engineering'[23] was organisational and rationally conceived. Bel Geddes was frequently called 'the man who cost American industry a billion dollars',[24] because of his fantastic projects like the revolving restaurant conceived for the Century of Progress exhibition in Chicago in 1933, but most of the designs that went into production were realistic and safe in sales terms.

However professional and business-like the industrial designer was, he was also seen as a sculptor in his making of prototype designs in clay or Plasticine or even life-size mock-ups. The artistic side of their role was emphasised by the designers themselves in their autobiographical treatises on design – among them Bel Geddes's *Horizons* of 1932, Teague's *Design This Day* of 1940, and Van Doren's *Industrial Design – a Practical Guide,* also of 1940 – and by several contemporary commentators, particularly those who came from the field of art criticism.

The great majority of the 25 or so individuals who constituted the industrial design profession in 1930 had received a formal art education – W. D. Teague at the Art Students' League in New York, Donald Deskey at the University of California, and Bel Geddes at the Cleveland School of Art and the Chicago Art Institute – and they knew about avant-garde European ideas. Bel Geddes, in *Horizons,* makes reference to Cézanne and Picasso; Teague makes more general reference to organic forms in nature; and S. and M. Cheney in *Art and the Machine* put the industrial designers into a continuum of machine-inspired art in the avant-garde tradition from Cézanne onwards, pinpointing Brancusi, Helion and Archipenko as the formal inspirators behind object styling.

Several of the designers had travelled to Europe and seen Modernism at first hand. Teague had gone during 1926, the year of his conversion into product design, had apparently been impressed by the works and ideas of Le Corbusier. As a result he had decided to eliminate all the traces of the past from his office. Dreyfuss travelled in Europe at the same time

7 *Archipenko's 'Boxing', which was illustrated in S. and M. Cheney's* Art and the Machine, *published in 1936*

8 *A photograph by Margaret Bourke-White used in S. and M. Cheney's* Art and the Machine

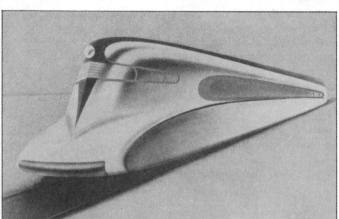

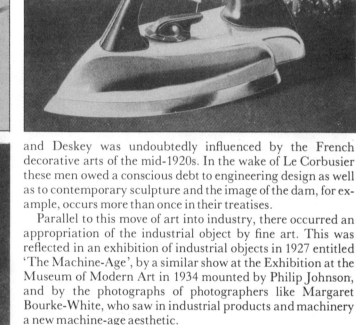

9 *Three designs by Raymond Loewy: a locomotive for the Pennsylvania Railroad (early 1930s); the Fast Commuter train (sketch design early 1930s); and a Westinghouse iron (sketch design 1932)*

10 *An SGE gas stove designed by Norman Bel Geddes in 1932*

and Deskey was undoubtedly influenced by the French decorative arts of the mid-1920s. In the wake of Le Corbusier these men owed a conscious debt to engineering design as well as to contemporary sculpture and the image of the dam, for example, occurs more than once in their treatises.

Parallel to this move of art into industry, there occurred an appropriation of the industrial object by fine art. This was reflected in an exhibition of industrial objects in 1927 entitled 'The Machine-Age', by a similar show at the Exhibition at the Museum of Modern Art in 1934 mounted by Philip Johnson, and by the photographs of photographers like Margaret Bourke-White, who saw in industrial products and machinery a new machine-age aesthetic.

This adoption by high culture of the aesthetic of the machine was a move away from the direction of industrial design itself, which tended instead towards public taste, working as it did on ideas framed to fit the public imagination. This was nowhere more evident than in the designs for transportation. Loewy's Hupmobile and work for the Pennsylvania Railroad, together with Teague's 'Marmon', Dreyfuss's 'Mercury' train, Otto Kuhler's locomotives and Bel Geddes's visionary transport designs, all employed the visual vocabulary of streamlining which broke away from the aesthetic of Purism and captured, symbolically, the optimism in technology. These designs developed a visual idiom that moved quickly into smaller consumables – irons, drink-dispensers, and sticky-tape dispensers among others.

The minimal purist element in American industrial design of the 1920s and 1930s was offset by the commitment to commerce and to the consumer. Their byword – 'beauty plus profit' – owed more to their experiences with advertising agencies than to their knowledge of the European avant-garde or to organic sculpture. Van Doren describes their main preoccupations when he writes in 1940 that 'The Bauhaus lacks...the realistic qualities that we Americans, rightly or wrongly, demand. It will be difficult, I believe, to acclimatize the esoteric ideas of the Bauhaus in the factual atmosphere of American industry'.[25]

The fundamental link with commerce that characterised the designers and distinguished them from their purist counterparts both in Europe and the United States was clear in the way they set up their consultancy agencies, in which pure business played a very strong part. Teague employed from the beginning a man called Brophy whom he had met at the YMCA when he first arrived in New York and who took care of the business side of things. As early as 1928 Bel Geddes had a staff of 10 working with him, of whom some were businessmen and others 'beautifers'. Loewy had from the start a partner called William Snaith who was simply a business executive.

The way in which they related to the industries that called upon their services was strictly by a business arrangement in which contracts were drawn up. An example of the kind of transactions that were made is that of Bel Geddes with Mr W. Frank Roberts, the president of the Standard Gas Equipment Corporation, who wanted a new stove design and planned to pay 1500 dollars for about two weeks' work. Bel Geddes said that the job would take a year and would cost 50,000 dollars. First he put an engineer in the Standard Gas Plant and set others of his staff to studying rivals' methods. The field reports made a book of 300 pages.[26]

Although many of the designs the new industrial designers developed were visually spectacular and rejected historicism in favour of the new streamlined aesthetic, the designers' first concern was for the market and they worked alongside sales researchers and economists – demonstrating the fact that they were not self-sufficient, creative artists who could follow their own whims but, in the words of Van Doren, 'one of the gears in the train which includes management, sales promotion, advertising, engineering and research'.[27]

The truth of this is reinforced by the backgrounds from which the pioneers emerged and from their shared experience in the various commercial fields in which they worked, and it is only by an examination of these structures that a realistic picture of the industrial designer, and subsequently of industrial design, will emerge.

1 Henry Dreyfuss is quoted as saying that 'Design is a Silent Salesman' by Radcliff, J. D. 'Designer for Streamlined Living' in *Coronet* June 1947

2 The American Tobacco Company spent more than one million dollars in a month in 1929 advertising Lucky Strike cigarettes

3 Richards, C. R. *Art in Industry* New York, 1922, 227

4 *Ibid* 228

5 *Ibid* 242

6 'W. D. Teague: Dean of Design' in *Printers' Ink* January 1959

7 The biography of W. D. Teague can be found in an article 'The Industrial Classicist' in *The New Yorker* December 1934

8 Loewy, R. *Never Leave Well Enough Alone* New York, 1951, 60

9 See Richards, C. R. *op cit* 230

10 'Bel Geddes' in *Fortune* July 1930, 57

11 Bel Geddes is quoted by Pulos, A. J. 'The Restless Genius of Norman Bel Geddes' in *Architectural Forum* July/August 1970

12 Bel Geddes, N. *Horizons* New York, 1932

13 See *Fortune op cit* 31

14 *Ibid*

15 Kobler, J. 'The Great Packager' in *Life* 2 May 1949, 120

16 Richards, C. R. *op cit* 232

17 Henry Dreyfuss is quoted in an article in *Fortune* May 1951

18 Richards, C. R. *op cit* 242

19 'Both Fish and Fowl' in *Fortune* May 1951

20 Cheney, S. and Cheney, M. C. *Art and the Machine* Whittlesey House/ McGraw Hill, New York, 1936

21 Articles appeared in *The New Yorker* on Deskey, Teague and Dreyfuss in the early 1930s

22 See *Fortune op cit* (19) 40

23 The term 'consumer engineering' was used as the title of a book written by Sheldon, R. and Arens, E., New York, 1932

24 Freedgood, S. 'Odd Business, This Industrial Design' in *Fortune* February 1959, 131

25 Van Doren, H. *Industrial Design – A practical Guide* New York, 1940

26 See *Fortune op cit* (19)

27 See Van Doren, H. *op cit*

Streamlined expresses of the LNER

Alan Self
ICI Plastics Division

The streamlined expresses designed and built by the London & North Eastern Railway in 1935-37 and run until the outbreak of war have received a considerable amount of coverage in railway enthusiasts' publications. Among the engineering and performance details that make up most of this literature, there are some clues to the methods and intentions of the designers. The purpose of this paper is to abstract from the recorded data a story that may help to show how engineers use form, not simply to fulfil functional needs, but for style also.

Before the First World War there were a dozen major British railway companies and many smaller ones, each with its own very recognisable style of design and decoration. There were competing services to many towns, such duplication of routes having been officially encouraged to avoid abuse of the virtual monopoly which railways at first enjoyed. The companies set out to assert their individuality and impress their passengers with a memorable, favourable 'brand image' that would influence them to choose the same service next time. Engines and coaches were expensively finished and considerable effort was devoted to keeping them clean and polished. Even after the government-sponsored grouping of 1923, which reduced the number of companies to four, an element of rivalry remained and so did distinctive company styles of design and colouring.

Every company had a Chief Mechanical Engineer (often abbreviated to CME) who, in addition to his legal responsibility for the safe condition of trains, usually controlled their design and construction, since the major railways built most of their equipment in their own works. This contrasted with the situation in America, where most of the locomotives were made by three independent, specialist firms and railway managements were already becoming highly cost-conscious during the nineteenth century, so restricting the scope of the companies' mechanical engineers to develop skills as stylists.

In Britain, however, a Chief Mechanical Engineer was expected to provide trains that were not only reliable and economical, but distinctively styled to impress passengers and the technical and popular press. Many CMEs had their own instantly recognisable 'line', sometimes even transplanted to another company when the engineer changed jobs. Others relied to a greater or lesser extent on their draughtsmen to create a distinctive product, which was nevertheless always credited to the Chief by name. Whoever did the styling, he was always a railway employee; there appears to be no case of an industrial design consultant being employed on locomotives in Britain until 1957.

The basic form of the steam locomotive owes much to the predominance of flat sheet and plate materials in its construction. Sheet is relatively easy to bend into shapes of single curvature, but requires much more energy to form into double-curved shapes since stretching then becomes necessary. A typical British steam locomotive had frames of flat steel plate arranged vertically inside the wheels, carrying a cylindrical or slightly coned boiler made by bending flat

1 *A non-streamlined LNER express locomotive under construction c1925 designed by Sir Nigel Gresley with careful detailing for smooth outline and finish*

plates. Normally the only visible double-curved sheet components were the steam dome cover, which had a hemispherical top, and the smokebox door, which was domed slightly. Both these parts were essentially decorative since they did not follow the cruder forms of the functional parts beneath.

Castings and forgings were used for most of the rotating and sliding parts, while considerable quantities of tubing were used in the boiler and for conveying steam, water and oil. In Britain, external runs of tubing were avoided whenever possible for the sake of appearance.

The chimney, with its complex double curves produced by casting, was acknowledged to have a profound effect on the appearance of an engine. The actual flue was generally a plain conical tube, but most chimneys had subtle compound shapes and external rims which were part of the designer's individual hallmark of style.

Other elements of personal style appeared in the shapes of the wheel-splashers and cab, in the relative overall proportions of the design, and in the painting and lettering. Locomotive design in Britain was a consciously applied art and the smooth lines of most of the engines set them apart from those of many other countries, to the extent that one American writer has recently described ordinary British engines as 'semi-streamlined'.

Deliberate attempts to reduce the resistance to motion through the air by fitting fairings date back well into the nineteenth century. The largest such experiment was on the PLM in France, where many express locomotives were so fitted in the 1890s in an attempt to reduce the effects of the Mistral on trains running along the Rhône valley. The fairings had sharp leading edges like boat hulls, on the mistaken assumption that the form evolved over centuries for low drag in a hull floating on water would also be correct for moving through air. No improvement was found in the running of the trains and some crews thought that the fairings made matters worse. On later PLM engines only the wedge-fronted cab was perpetuated; it helped to deflect smoke out of the driver's line of sight and reflections in the glass at night were reduced.

The rapid development of powered aircraft led to the discovery that the lowest drag in air was achieved with fish-like forms having a smoothly rounded leading edge and a sharp trailing edge. In a wind-tunnel, it could be seen that the air flowed round such bodies almost without turbulence, which could be detected by looking at 'stream lines' made visible by injecting fine streams of chemical smoke into the moving air. Hence the term 'streamlined' was coined to describe a shape developed by this method to have low drag.

In 1929 an express locomotive (No 10,000) appeared on the LNER with a boiler of novel design derived from the type used in ships. Because of the height of this boiler, there was no room within the permitted overall height for a chimney to project above the casing. To ensure that the smoke would not be drawn down over the cab, an aerodynamicist was engaged as a consultant for the design of the external shape. The result, which was officially described as 'aerodynamic screening' and not as streamlining, was a blunt wedge-shaped form rising in a convex curve from the front buffers to the chimney, enclosed in a forward extension of the boiler casing open at the top to create a strong upward airflow past the chimney. Visually, it was a radical change from existing designs, but the principle of a smooth sheet steel casing, fitting closely over the actual boiler and with the minimum of double curvature, was retained. Only the wedge at the front was different in principle, and that had been developed to fulfil a new need.

This blend of traditional standards and methods of finish with forms appropriate to newly identified needs was typical of the work of the LNER designers under the Chief Mechanical Engineer, Sir Nigel Gresley, and his Principal Assistant, O. V. S. Bulleid. Although responsible for 10 works with 100,000 employees, Gresley maintained an active personal interest in design, particularly of the larger locomotives. Bulleid was also deeply interested in all aspects of design and in 1937, when he became CME of the Southern Railway, he was responsible for some highly original locomotives of unique appearance, in defence of which he revealed his approval of Modern Movement architecture. Like Gresley, he had entered the railways as a premium apprentice on leaving public school, but unlike many railway engineers he had also accumulated experience elsewhere during and after the First World War.

Gresley had always kept himself well informed about developments in other countries; his next express locomotive (No 2001, built in 1934) was designed to try several features that had given high power with economical use of coal when applied in France. The appearance of No 2001 was, however,

poles apart from that of the typical French product, which carried drums, pumps and their associated pipework all over the outside of the boiler casing. No 2001 followed the LNER tradition of an uncluttered, smooth exterior, flowing curves, and careful attention to the overall line and proportions. The boiler casing was made in an elliptical cross-section so that the drums could be placed between it and the boiler, completely out of sight. The 'aerodynamic screening' as applied to No 10,000 was redesigned and tested in a wind-tunnel by the City and Guilds College, but this time the Press described the new engine as 'streamlined', which in technical terms it was not.

The use of this term reflected the fast-growing fashion for 'streamlining' most things that moved and many that did not – a fashion that was the stock-in-trade of the American industrial design consultants who had by now risen to fame and fortune. Blunt, curved forms, often decorated with 'stream lines' as ridges or painted stripes along their sides – a visual

2 Gresley's experimental locomotive No 10000, built in 1939. 'Aerodynamic screening' at the front was designed to deflect smoke over the cab (Crown Copyright: National Railway Museum)

3 Locomotive No 2001, designed by Gresley and Bulleid in 1934. The 'aerodynamic screening' is blended into a traditional locomotive shape (Crown Copyright: National Railway Museum)

4 Ettore Bugatti's railcar in France c1934. The wedge-shaped ends were developed by trial and error for low drag (H. G. Conway)

4

style evidently suggested by the wind-tunnel photographs with their smoke trails – were all the rage for everything from vehicles to food mixers.

Prominent among the designers of external cladding and colour schemes for American locomotives and coaches were Otto Kuhler, Henry Dreyfuss and Raymond Loewy. Almost all the steam locomotives had the boiler turned into a projectile by placing a blunt nose on the smokebox, and the chassis enclosed to make a box with a curved apron round the front to meet the legal requirement for a cow-catcher. Many carried decorative 'whiskers' radiating from a point low on the front and continuing along the sides as straight 'streamlines', sometimes as corrugations reminiscent of Junkers aircraft.

The 'projectile on a box' formula and the bright colouring that went with it certainly sold seats, but probably did little to reduce fuel consumption. Wind-tunnel tests were carried out in some cases, but probably with the main object of curing the problem of smoke being drawn down over the cab, to which these designs were prone in a crosswind. The high speeds achieved were more the result of refined mechanical design and higher power than of streamlining. However, the craze spread to Europe and a number of related designs appeared in Germany, France and Britain during the mid-1930s.

Gresley was evidently unimpressed because when he initiated the design of a streamlined steam locomotive late in 1934 he proceeded along a different path, for which some reasons may be conjectured. Considerable trouble had always been taken on the LNER to produce elegant engines with a high standard of finish, so Gresley would have felt no need of any help from outside, nor is it likely that the expense would have been accepted lightly amid the post-depression stringency. The idea of covering one of his designs in a purely

theatrical cladding designed by someone else, for no good functional reason, would have been offensive to him. Even when his own streamlined engines had been built, he sometimes made disparaging remarks in private about their 'tin casings', despite the care that had been taken to achieve some useful benefits from the streamlining.

The form decided on by Gresley for his streamlined 'A4' locomotive was a blunt wedge without the enclosing side-sheets which had characterised the two designs already mentioned, rising from the buffers to the chimney in a curve of constant large radius. This was blended into a boiler cladding having a elliptical curve at the top, and vertical sides which flared out above the wheels to meet a valance of aerofoil shape. This valance, the top of which was flat to afford a much safer foothold than on most other streamlined engines, is said to have been the result of an on-the-spot inspiration which came to Bulleid while looking at the partly-completed casing. Gresley is reported to have insisted that a real aerofoil section should be used instead of a freehand line – a rather revealing illustration of his preference for 'real' forms with functional respectability, even where, as in this case, there could be no detectable difference in performance. The casing was designed with single curvature almost throughout, for assembly from sheets of steel which could be bent with existing machinery.

Aerodynamically, the crucial part of the design was the wedge-shaped front. It was based on the front of the Bugatti petrol railcar operating on the PLM, which had been evolved by Ettore Bugatti by the simple method of fitting bodies of different shapes to a car and comparing the petrol consumption at constant speed. As a method of getting results in the rather complex case of a vehicle moving through the air over the surface of the ground, as opposed to the easier case of a free airstream as in flight, it had much to recommend it. Some changes were in fact made to the shape for Gresley's locomotive after tests in a wind-tunnel with smoke blown from the chimney of a model, resulting in a final shape which was efficient for drag reduction at high speeds and outstandingly successful for smoke deflection above the cab. The net value of the drag reduction at the normal maximum speed of 90 mph when set against the 3½ tons extra weight for the casing and the reduced accessibility for maintenance was, however, open to question.

To illustrate the contrast between this approach to design and some others, the response of the Great Western Railway's CME to an instruction from his Board to beat the rumoured LNER streamliner into service was as follows. He took a paperweight model of an existing express engine and proceeded, with tongue firmly in cheek, to smooth out the projections with Plasticine to make 'aerodynamic' blunt-nosed, sharp-tailed shapes determined by pure guesswork. The model was then handed to a draughtsman with orders to detail the fairings for production in sheet metal. After the scheme had received due publicity, which emphasised fuel saving, the fairings were gradually removed as their practical disadvantages in causing overheating and hindering maintenance became apparent.

The LNER's first streamlined express was named the 'Silver Jubilee' and entered service in September 1935, construction of the first locomotives and the seven special coaches having been authorised to start only in March of the same year. The experiments with No 2001 and a more conventional version built at the same time had given the design team much useful information, which enabled them to select for the A4

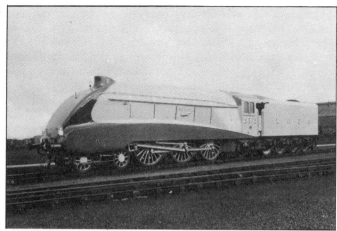

7

5 *One of four locomotives built for the 'Silver Jubilee', 1935, in its original grey livery. Designed by Gresley and Bulleid using the Bugatti wedge front for streamlining and smoke deflection (Crown Copyright: National Railway Museum)*

6 *The 'Silver Jubilee' train showing the flexible fairing between the coaches and the deep valances below, both for drag reduction. The covering is aluminium Rexine with stainless steel trim. Designed by LNER engineers in 1935 (Crown Copyright: National Railway Museum)*

7 *The first-class carriage interior of the 'Silver Jubilee', designed by White Allom Ltd and finished in Rexine, maple veneer and blue moquette (Crown Copyright: National Railway Musem)*

streamlined locomotives only those novel features that worked well under British conditions. Thus, despite the short time available for design and construction, the A4 had an excellent performance straight from the drawing board.

The original colour scheme was a departure even from colourful British tradition and consisted of pale grey over most of the superstructure, with mid grey on the aerofoil valances and charcoal grey on the wedge-shaped nose (which was likely to collect the most dirt since it had to be opened frequently to shovel char from the smokebox). It is said to have created a sensation among railway enthusiasts, although one lady whom I interviewed was unimpressed, and recalled that on seeing the train pass on its inaugural trip, she thought 'that old grey thing' to be less attractive than the apple green which was standard on the LNER.

For the coaches an even more striking finish was adopted – Rexine in an aluminium colour was applied up to roof level, with trim strips of stainless steel in a rather severe rectangular arrangement which, together with the generally hard, pale appearance, gave a Bauhaus flavour. The most obvious reason for choosing silver was the verbal association with the Jubilee itself. Other likely inspirations were the stainless steel coaches produced by the Budd company for several American

railroads, which would have been far too expensive for the LNER, and the current imagery of powered flight with its smooth, shiny aluminium-doped fabric and unpainted aluminium sheet surfaces. In several contemporary railway publicity photographs, airliners were shown flying low alongside expresses. The choice of such pale finishes for steam trains presupposed the means of keeping them clean – in the case of the Silver Jubilee and its successors on the LNER, the whole exterior was washed by hand with soap and water after each journey.

Sir Nigel Gresley was a personal friend of Sir Charles Allom, whose firm White Allom Ltd designed, made and fitted interiors for an impressive clientele including the Royal Family, high society and Cunard. Gresley employed this firm for the interiors of several trains including the Flying Scotsman and Silver Jubilee. There seems to be no record or recollection of their having been consulted on the exterior of the streamlined locomotives or coaches, although it is possible that Gresley might have discussed the subject informally with his friend.

White Allom's interiors for the Silver Jubilee were rather plain and even austere, although expensive materials were used including maple and quartered teak veneers, Rexine instead of paint on walls and ceilings, and jazz-pattern moquette upholstery. The seats were blue in the first class and green in the third, the latter being a departure from the traditional red or brown.

When White Allom were employed, the LNER gave details of the accommodation required and the consultants subsequently presented their scheme as a series of coloured perspectives with samples of the proposed materials. The coaches, completely finished externally, would then be handed over to White Allom as empty shells. Sometimes they would be handed over in sidings at Kings Cross and sometimes at Doncaster Works. White Allom then moved in with their own staff and materials to fit the interior. Woodwork and soft furnishings were made by White Allom in their own workshops, while metalwork was usually made by Comyn Ching Ltd or Morris Singer Ltd, and lighting fittings by Dernier and Hamlyn Ltd.

Mr W. B. Best, who is still with Holloway White Allom Ltd,

In regular service, the Silver Jubilee proved very successful and was often completely full. The capital cost of £34,000 for seven coaches and the first of the locomotives is said to have been recovered in two years from the fare supplements alone (equivalent to 25p first class and 15p third class on fares of around £3.50 and £2 respectively). The running of the train was not only fast but punctual, a strong point with the businessmen who were the customers the LNER most wanted to attract. The journey time of four hours from London to Newcastle, including a stop at Darlington, was only 27 minutes longer than today's non-stop time.

The Silver Jubilee seemed to show that by providing such new standards of service, emphasised by the obvious novelty of the train's appearance, the LNER would be able to strengthen its passenger business against the competitive threats of the internal combustion engine both on the road and in the air –

8 *The observation cars of the 'Coronation', 1937, under construction showing the wooden roof with partial steel cladding and curved windows of Perspex. Designed by LNER engineers (Crown Copyright: National Railway Museum)*

9 *The 'Coronation' train from the rear. Finished in blue paint with stainless steel trim (Crown Copyright: National Railway Museum)*

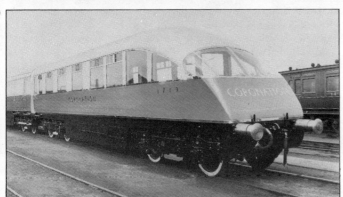

recalls how as a young man he was present at Kings Cross during some of the LNER coach fitting jobs. Frequent visits were made by the LNER staff to check that the work was up to the agreed specification. O. V. S. Bulleid was often there, and was very approachable. From time to time, Sir Nigel Gresley appeared in person. His considerable presence and his close attention to detail made him a formidable person to deal with, and he would 'blow his top' when dissatisfied, but once things were put right any displeasure was soon forgotten.

threats which were beginning to look very real by the mid-1930s. In 1937 the streamlined services were expanded with the introduction of two new trains, the Coronation, running from London to Edinburgh in six hours with one stop, and the West Riding Limited, running from London to Leeds and Bradford in three hours and five minutes.

Externally, these new trains were similar to the Silver Jubilee except for the colours. From a collection of special colours promoted by the British Colour Council to celebrate the Coronation of George VI, the LNER chose Garter Blue for the engines and the coach sides up to window level, with Marlborough Blue for the upper side panels, a scheme very similar to the current British Rail style. The construction pictures show the hybrid structure of the coaches with their teak frames, plywood interior partitions and steel skin with applied stainless steel strips to cover the joins in the skin. The double-curved roof over the rear windows of the streamlined observation car was a real boat-building job with tapered and steamed planks, although the paint finish was so good as to give the impression that the whole surface was metal.

Internally the new trains were more conspicuously expensive in their furnishings than the Silver Jubilee, particularly in the first-class saloons with their partitioned alcoves having

10 *A first-class saloon in the 'Coronation',
probably designed by James P. Smith of
White Allom Ltd. Anodised aluminium
brightwork with a green colour scheme in
Rexine and moquette (Crown Copyright:
National Railway Museum)*

only two seats across the whole width of the coach. The decor
in 'Kensington Odeon' style, with deeply fluted upholstery in
moquette and aluminium wall trimmings enclosing cloth panels with elaborately stitched patterns, bore the distinctive
hallmark of James P. Smith, a designer in White Allom's
studio. The name of Acton Surgee Ltd has also been mentioned in connection with the Coronation; this firm was started by
two designers from White Allom, who continued to work in co-
operation with their old employers on some projects.

These flamboyant interiors were certainly different from the
usual rather dingy finishes of the period, and much less austere
than the Silver Jubilee's decor, but no doubt the LNER's well-
to-do customers would have felt at home in them, and would
have been thankful for surroundings that did not remind them
of a railway carriage. As the trains ran for only two years until
the outbreak of war, we do not know how the elaborate fittings
and finishes would have stood the test of time, but Mr Best
says that the quality of the fittings and materials would have
been such that they would have become unfashionable before
wearing out.

How essential was streamlining to the success of the LNER
trains? Gresley's version of the current design craze was more
functional than most, and its valuable smoke-lifting qualities
must have been among the reasons why the 34 A4 locomotives
that survived the war carried their original streamlined
casings almost complete (except for the panels covering the
wheels) until the end of steam on British Rail in the mid-1960s.
By this time, all casings and fairings had long been removed
from the ex-LMS and GWR streamlined engines, while a start
had been made on the conversion of Bulleid's SR express
locomotives to a more conventional form without their casings.

The cash value of streamlining to the railways lay much
more in its visual appeal to passengers than in the reduction of
air resistance. Shortage of maintenance staff during and after
the war emphasised the extra time needed to service and repair
enclosed working parts, while steam in general came to be

associated in the public mind, not with power and speed, but
with grimy obsolescence.

The special coaches for the LNER streamliners were stored
intact during the war, but they never ran again as complete
trains, being dispersed around the system afterwards as
ordinary express stock. Soon their distinctive colours dis-
appeared beneath BR red and cream; with their fairings and
valances removed they became recognisable only to
enthusiasts, and all were eventually scrapped except the two
observation cars from the Coronation, which still survive in
modified form on private lines. The A4 locomotives continued
to pull the principal East Coast expresses to Scotland until the
diesels came, and no fewer than six have been preserved in
Britain, America and Canada – some indication of the magic
of LNER design, performance and publicity in the brief years
from 1935 to 1939.

Much of the LNER's fame rested on the record runs which
were organised on several occasions, culminating in the still
unbroken world record for steam of 125 mph achieved by the
A4 locomotive Mallard in July 1938, beating by a very narrow
margin the previous record set up by a German streamlined
locomotive. The LNER was more fortunate than the other
British companies in having on its principal main line a
straight stretch of track ideal for such attempts, being some 20
miles long with a moderately falling gradient and no
restriction at the far end. Among the other records for steam
power attained by A4 locomotives were a continuous run of
more than 25 miles at over 100 mph on the Press trip of the
Silver Jubilee, and in 1936 a maximum of 113 mph on a train in
regular passenger service (most other records being set on test
or demonstration runs). Gresley had planned another attempt
to raise the world record by a more significant margin, believ-
ing that an ultimate speed of 130 mph was possible, but as this
run was scheduled for September 1939 the opportunity was
lost, never to return. In these attempts, which bore little
relation to ordinary railway running, it is likely that the

streamlined casing did play an essential part, although no comparative maximum speed tests with unstreamlined locomotives were ever attempted.

Comparing Gresley's unique locomotives with the numerous examples in many countries derived visually from the American industrial designers' projectile-on-a-box formula, one may sympathise with the British engineers who had confidence in their combined skills as functional designers and as stylists, and did not feel any need to engage consultants.

The role of styling in the design of technical products has often been overlooked, particularly by Modern Movement apologists looking for a 'machine aesthetic' supposedly flowing from purely functional considerations. In many cases the shape of a functional part could vary within certain limits without affecting its performance to any practical extent. Modern products and their circumstances of use are often so complicated that a compromise is necessary when trying to satisfy a number of conflicting design criteria, and several different compromises could be as good as one another. Even if there is one ideal form, it may be impossible to find it within prevailing constraints of time, money and information.

Nevertheless, the designer has to draw something, and what he draws will in such circumstances depend, not only on the technical data available to him, but also on his knowledge of what has worked before, on his judgement of the ability of the works to manufacture it, and on his personal aesthetic. It is this last factor that deserves greater recognition in the work of engineering designers. The British steam locomotive designers had long been encouraged to develop their skills in that direction, and among their products there are many examples to suggest that the architect and the industrial design consultant are by no means the only people to have bridged the gap between fine art draughtsmanship and product design draughtsmanship.

It was not really engineering products themselves that Le Corbusier and other Modern Movement pioneers had fallen in love with, but the design skills so similar to their own that had brought these products into being.

The books listed below have provided much of the factual information for this paper. Where page numbers are not shown, there are many relevant references throughout the book.

Further information and assistance were kindly given by Mr W. B. Best and Mr F. R. Lodge of Holloway White Allom Ltd; Mrs V. E. Coleman, an eyewitness of the Silver Jubilee's inaugural run, whose grandfather and uncle were LNER drivers; Mr J. N. P. Rowe, an engineer and model-maker; National Railway Museum, York; and Steamtown, Carnforth.

Allen, C. J. *The Coronation and Other Famous LNER Trains* Nicholson & Watson, 1938, 31–52, 144–163, 170

Allen, C. J. *The Locomotives of Sir Nigel Gresley* Longmans, 1945, 82–85, 115–139

Allen, G. F. (ed) *History of Railways* New English Library, 1972 (partwork), 121–125

Anon *The World's Railways and How They Work* Odhams, nd c 1947, 6, 38, 75, 118–130, 242–266

Beavor, E. S. *Steam was My Calling* Ian Allan, 1974, 48–69

Boughton, T, *The Story of the British Light Aeroplane* John Murray, 1963, 229

Brown, F. A. S. *From Stirling to Gresley* Oxford Publishing Co, 1974, 144–146

Brown, F. A. S. *Nigel Gresley, Locomotive Engineer* Ian Allan, 1961

Bulleid, H. A. V. *Bulleid of the Southern* Ian Allan, 1977, 31–41

Bulleid, H. A. V. *Master Builders of Steam* Ian Allan, 1963, 56–87, 143–145, 153

Cheney, S. and Cheney, M. C. *Art and the Machine* Whittlesey House/McGraw Hill, 1936, 128–129

Clay, J. F. and Cliffe, J. *The LNER 2-8-2 and 2-6-2 Classes* Ian Allan, 1973, 7–16, 29–54

Cox, E. S. *British Railways Standard Steam Locomotives* Ian Allan, 1966, 43, 70, 92–94, 109, 200

Cox, E. S. *Speaking of Steam* Ian Allan, 1971, 13–16, 84–86, 101, 107

Day-Lewis, S. *Bulleid, Last Giant of Steam* Allen & Unwin, 1968, 75, 108, 166

Haresnape, B. *Railway Design since 1830* Ian Allan, 1968/1969 (2 vols), vol 1 105, vol 2 11–44, 93

Harris, M *Gresley's Coaches* David & Charles, 1973, 11–25, 96–105

Holcroft, H. *An Outline of Great Western Locomotive Practice 1837–1947* Ian Allan, 1971, 84, 96, 101

Holcroft, H. *Locomotive Adventure* vol 2, Ian Allan, 1965, 171 307–310

Mercer, F. A. *The Industrial Design Consultant* Studio, 1947, 62–64

Nock, O. S. *The British Railway Steam Locomotive* vol 2, Ian Allan, 1966, 106–109, 134–146

Nock, O. S. *Railways at the Zenith of Steam* Blandford, 1970, 5–7, 162–164

Nock, O. S. *The Gresley Pacifics* vol 2, David & Charles, 1974

Nock, O. S. *The GWR Stars, Castles and Kings* vol 2, David & Charles, 1973, 26

Railway Correspondence & Travel Society *Locomotives of the LNER* part 2A, 1973, 92–135, 206–208

Reed, R. C. *The Streamline Era* Golden West Books (USA), 1975

Rogers, H. C. B. *Chapelon, Genius of French Steam* Ian Allan, 1972, 10, 42–43, 113–114

Schaefer, H. *The roots of modern design* Studio Vista, 1970, 22–45

Schapiro, A. H. *Shape and Flow* Heinemann, 1961, 102–157

Scott, R. and Reed, B. *Gresley A4s* Profile Publications, 1971

Tuplin, W. A. *Great Northern Steam* Ian Allan, 1971, 80–111

Tuplin, W. A. *The Steam Locomotive, its form and function* Adams & Dart, 1974, 138—142

Turner, P. St John and Nowarra, H. J. *Junkers* Ian Allan, 1971, 22–23, 55

Vuillet, G. *Railway Reminiscences of Three Continents* Nelson, 1968, Plate 5 and 303

Winchester, C. and Allen, C. J. (eds) *Railway Wonders of the World* Amalgamated Press, 1935–1936 (partwork), 33–39, 88–92, 173–176, 400–406, 1037–1045, 1281, 1409, 1436–1442

The designer and the law

a historical perspective

Dr Mary Vitoria
Queen Mary College, University of London

The designer has always sought protection, not only against plagiarism and commercial exploitation of his work by others but also against unauthorised alterations and possible mutilations of his work. English law provides three distinct forms of protection against unauthorised commercial exploitation – patents, registered designs and copyright – but remains relatively unconcerned with what is recognised in other jurisdictions as the 'droit moral' – ie the artist's right to the integrity of his work. This is a result of the historical development of the various forms of intellectual and industrial property protection.

The law regards the investment of labour and skill that goes towards the creation of a design, be it functional, aesthetic or both, as a form of property. Yet it is a rather peculiar form of property as 'from its immateriality it can be stolen through a window without cutting a pane of glass and it can be carried off by the eye without being found on the person'.[1] The earliest form of industrial property protection was the patent system, which was introduced in 1623 by the Statute of Monopolies. The basic intention of the patent system has always been the encouragement of new and improved industries. In return for disclosing his invention to the public by means of a patent the inventor is granted a monopoly for 20 years.[2] A designer can only obtain patent protection for his design if it is functionally new; the patent system does not provide protection for designs whose novelty is purely aesthetic. For example, a two-spouted teapot, assuming it is novel, may receive patent protection as it has the novel function of allowing two cups of tea to be poured out simultaneously. A teapot having a new and differently designed spout would not be susceptible of patent protection unless the spout performed a function hitherto unknown for spouts to perform, such as trapping the tea-leaves in a U-bend. For most designers patent protection is probably not appropriate and they must rely on registered design and copyright for protection.

Before dealing with the history of design protection it is worth while considering the nature and scope of the protection provided by registered designs and by copyright. Indeed, one of the most fascinating features of the history is the progressive abandonment of reliance on registered designs in favour of copyright. In registered design law the term 'design' has a very specific meaning. A design means: 'features of shape, configuration, pattern or ornament applied to an article by any industrial process or means being features which in the finished article appeal to and are judged solely by the eye but does not include a method or principle of construction or features of shape or configuration which are dictated solely by the function which the article to be made in that shape or configuration has to perform.'[3]

As can be seen, the intention is to protect aesthetic features and not functional ones which are the province of patents. A registered design, like a patent, confers a monopoly, known as design copyright, on the proprietor of the design for 15 years.[4] During this period the proprietor has the exclusive right to make and sell or import for sale any article in respect of which the design is registered. Once a design is registered the monopoly is absolute and the proprietor can prevent anyone from infringing his rights, even if they themselves devised the design independently. Although the protection conferred by a registered design is referred to as design copyright it is, in fact, a true monopoly right and not just a right to prevent copying. A design must be new and original to be capable of registration.

Copyright subsists in artistic works such as drawings, paintings, sculptures, engravings and photographs irrespective of artistic quality, and in works of artistic craftsmanship such as, for example, a mackintosh chair or a Bernard Leach pot.[5] The duration of copyright is the author's (ie the orginator's) lifetime plus 50 years. This is far longer than the 15 years provided by registered designs, but on the other hand the protection against infringement is not absolute and is a weapon only against copyists. Those who independently arrive at the same design are not caught by copyright, but a work to attract copyright protection need only be original in the sense of not being copied from someone else; it need not be absolutely novel as must a registered design. It is also important to realise that copyright does not protect ideas, but only the tangible form in which they are expressed. So, if A describes in detail to B a new design for wallpaper and B manufactures wallpaper embodying A's design, A has no remedy in copyright against B, although he may have a remedy in breach of confidence.

The history of design protection is the history of the response of Parliament to those whose commercial interests were under threat from widespread copying and price under-cutting. Protection is only needed when piracy is advantageous. There was no need for literary copyright – the first to receive protection – until after the advent of printing. The first *copyright* Act was in 1709, in the reign of Queen Anne; prior to that, unauthorised printing had been controlled by a series of largely ineffective Licensing Acts and by the rules and regulations of the stationers Company.

The first protection given to any works of art was by the Engraving Copyright Act of 1734 – the so-called Hogarth Act. Hogarth was, perhaps, the first engraver whose works had a mass middle-class appeal and the popular nature of his subjects made price the only limit to the market. Piracy of engravings consequently became profitable for the first time. In response to Hogarth's pressure for protection against loss of revenue through sales of pirate prints, the Act gave to any person who 'invented and designed, engraved, etched or worked in mezzotint or chiaroscuro',[6] or from his own designs caused others to do so, the sole right of printing and selling the same for 14 years. It did not provide protection for the engraver who worked from the original drawings of others or who engraved from classical subject matter. Such protection came by an amending Act in 1767.

Ornamental design became the subject of legal rights in

1787 under the Designs Copyright Act. Such rights had first been established in France in 1737 for the benefit of the silk manufacturers of Lyons. Protection in Britain was at first given only to those who designed new and original patterns for printing linen, cotton, calico and muslin, these being the only decorative arts prolific enough to require protection. It is important to note that the right given was a monopoly right: the sole right of printing, reprinting and selling the patterns for two months after the design was published – ie copies issued to the public. In 1794 the period was extended to three months. Rival manufacturers who infringed were liable to pay damages and to forfeiture and destruction of the offending blocks and plates. Sellers of pirated designs were not liable unless they knew the designs had been printed without the consent of the proprietor.

In 1839 the Act was extended to include other woven fabrics such as wool, silk and hair. The only formality required of the proprietor of the design was that his name was to be attached to the end of each piece of fabric. Later in 1839 a much more extensive revision of the law took place. The Designs Copyright Act 1839 extended protection, which hitherto had been restricted to fabrics, to designs for articles of manufacture by whatever means the designs were applied provided that the designs were merely ornamental as opposed to being useful. It also gave protection, not merely to the ornamentation placed on an article, but also to the shape in which it was made. More important still the Act introduced a system for registering designs at a Design Office. The benefits conferred by the Act could only be secured if the proprietor had registered his design before publishing it, and every article had to bear the name of the first registered proprietor and the number and date of registration. Registration was a completely new principle and differed fundamentally from the earlier design copyright Acts under which the proprietor acquired protection as soon as he issued copies of his design to the public. This principle has never been departed from in the case of industrial designs. Designs for lace were excluded, possibly because applications for registration of lace designs would have overwhelmed the new Designs Office; lace became protected in 1842. Members of the public were not allowed to inspect the copies of the designs at the Designs Office except with the consent of the proprietor. This was in accordance with the wishes of the textile manufacturers who feared that if the designs were open for inspection, new designs would be copied or imitated in a way that would be difficult to prove was a piracy and their headstart in the market would be lost.

This period was obviously one of immense activity as in 1842 the whole of the previous legislation on designs was swept away and an amending and consolidating Act, the Copyright of Designs Act 1842, was passed. The period of copyright protection was extended in many cases to three years, and again the Act was confined to ornamental designs. The remedies against piracy were practically the same, but fraudulent imitation of designs was now forbidden in express terms. In the following year protection was extended to useful designs by the Copyright of Designs Act 1843. This, in fact, legitimised a practice that had been going on previously: inventors deterred by the enormous expense of obtaining a patent were in the habit of registering their inventions as ornamental designs. Despite the fact that the registration was probably invalid it was commercially preferable to have an invalid registration with which to threaten competitors than none at all – anything to retain the headstart in the market.

By 1843 our system of modern design registration had become established in more or less its modern form. Further major repeals and consolidations took place in the Patents, Designs and Trade Marks Act 1883, which removed the distinction between ornamental and useful designs, and in the Patents and Designs Act 1907. The present law is the Registered Designs Act 1949. A curious feature of the design legislation up to the 1949 Act was the tautologous definition of design: '...a design means any design applicable to an article whether the design is applicable for the pattern or shape or configuration or for ornament thereof...'[7] It was left to judicial interpretation to establish guidelines, a much relied on example being the case of *Re Bayers Design*[8] where Lord Justice Fletcher-Moulton said: 'Designs apply to nothing but that which the eye can tell entirely. Nothing in my opinion is a good design but that of which full knowledge is given when once you have shown to the eye what your design is.'

This judicial view eventually became the statutory definition in the 1949 Act where 'design means features... [that] appeal to and are judged solely by the eye...'[9] It was not until as late as 1971 that some further meaning was given to what constitutes a design capable of registration. In *Amp Incorporated v Utilux Proprietory Ltd*[10] the House of Lords decided that where the features of shape or configuration of an article, in this case an electric terminal, were dictated solely by the function which they had to perform and there was neither the purpose nor the result of making an appeal to the eye then the design was not capable of registration. This case is of seminal importance in considering the protection given by copyright to many industrial articles, a topic to be discussed later.

It was not only of whether a design was capable of registration that the eye was to be the sole judge: it alone was to be referred to in considering the question of infringement – whether the defendant's design was an obvious or fraudulent imitation of the plaintiff's. In *Holdsworth v McCrea*[11] it was said by the House of Lords that: 'In the case of those things as to which the merit of the invention lies in the drawing or in the forms that can be copied, the appeal is to the eye, and the eye alone is the judge of the identity of the two things; whether, therefore, there by piracy or not is referred to an unerring judge, namely, the eye, which takes the one figure and the other figure and ascertains whether they are the same.' Three examples will suffice. In *Staples v Warwick*[12] the defendants' crenellated helter-skelter tower was held not to infringe the plaintiff's lighthouse design (see Figure 1). In *Holden v Hodgkinson Bros*[13] the defendant, although he had designed his tombstone from an idea suggested by seeing the plaintiff's tombstone, had successfully altered the design sufficiently as not to infringe (see Figure 2). In *Oliver v Thornley*[14] infringement of a lace design was found established as the essential features had been taken and the differences which were differences in detail did not prevent the two designs from being essentially the same (see Figure 3).

The use of copyright to protect industrial designs is a twentieth-century phenomenon and so only a brief outline of the older law need be given. As previously stated, the first protection given to the arts was to etchings and engravings by the Hogarth Act of 1734 and its amending Act of 1767. Sculpture was first protected in 1798, but this Act only covered human and animal figures. The Act was very badly drafted, one commentator remarking rather acidly 'that we must infer that the Act was the production of an artist who wielded his pen less dexterously than his chisel'.[15] There was a second Act

1 *Staples v Warwick (1906). The plaintiff's lighthouse helter-skelter tower is on the left, with the alleged infringement on the right*

2 *Holden v Hodgkinson (1904). The plaintiff's tombstone design is on the left, with the alleged infringement on the right*

3 *Oliver v Thornley (1896). The plaintiff's lace design (left) was held to have been infringed by the design on the right*

in 1814 to 'amend and render more effectual' the first. The last classes of works to receive statutory protection were paintings, drawings and photographs. These received protection under the Fine Arts Copyright Act in 1862. This Act purported to give protection for the term of the life of the author plus seven years. It, too, was badly drafted and produced the remarkable effect that copyright was lost altogether on the first sale of the work unless on that occasion there was a written document expressly assigning the copyright to the purchaser or expressly reserving it to the author. Further, the Courts gave a restricted meaning to infringement and generally speaking restricted it to reproduction of the copyright work in a medium similar to that of the original work. For example, in *Hanfstaengl v Empire Palace*[16] it was held that although the Act of 1862 gave the author the sole right to reproduce a painting and the design thereof 'by any means and of any size', nevertheless reproduction of a painting in the form of a tableau vivant did not amount to infringement; however the painted canvas background placed behind the living figures did! Unlike the protection given to industrial designs, which conferred a monopoly on the proprietor, the protection given to artistic works by the nineteenth-century legislation was a protection against copying. Confusingly, the term 'copyright' is applied to the two different forms of protection. To make the position clear: design copyright, sometimes referred to as industrial copyright, is a monopoly right while artistic copyright is a right only to prevent copying.

From 1862 onwards each form of artistic endeavour was protected by its own Act. A major revision did not occur until 1911 when the Copyright Act of that year swept away all the old artistic copyright Acts and gathered all forms of artistic copyright within its ambit. It also extended the scope of artistic copyright to cover reproduction in any material form whatsoever.[17] In certain cases this had the result that the extended artistic copyright could overlap design copyright to give double protection. For example, a design for a teapot could be registered under the Act then in force for registered designs, the Patents and Designs Act 1907. Anyone who made a teapot of that or a closely similar design would infringe the design copyright in the registered design. If the manufacturer of the teapot had also made drawings of the teapot before going into production, artistic copyright would subsist in those drawings. Since the artistic copyright could be infringed by reproduction in any material form, the mere making of a teapot copied from those drawings would infringe that copyright. (This was in contrast to the earlier Acts under which the copyright in the drawing of a teapot could only be infringed by copying and making another drawing of the teapot.) Further, the copying could be indirect and in most cases would be; for instance, the artistic copyright in the drawing could be infringed by copying an actual teapot based on those drawings. It was considered desirable that the protection given to industrial designs should be limited to that provided by the registered design system so that the design would enter the public domain after 15 years and other manufacturers would then be free to copy and to compete in the market. An attempt was therefore made to minimise the possibility of overlap of artistic with industrial copyright. This was done by inserting a special section, section 22, into the Copyright Act 1911. Its intention was to exclude from artistic copyright protection those designs which were capable of registration under the 1907 Act and which were used or intended to be used industrially – that is, applied to mass-produced products. The intention of the section was that the industrial designer should rely on the 1907 Act and receive a monopoly for 15 years and the non-commercial artist should rely on the 1911 Act and receive protection against copying for his lifetime plus 50 years. As will be seen, despite many attempts by the legislature, this separation has never been successfully achieved.

The most important case to test the meaning of section 22 was the House of Lords case of *King Features Syndicate Inc v O & M Kleeman Ltd*[18] where, for a time at least, 'Popeye the Sailor' was captured by a pirate. 'Popeye' had originally appeared in a series of cartoons published in an American newspaper and later in films. The alleged infringement consisted of reproductions of Popeye in the form of dolls and brooches. The author

at the time he made the drawings had no intention of commercially exploiting them except in the form of comic strip and, so far as the 1907 Act was concerned, this did not constitute industrial application. Some years later he licensed certain manufacturers to make articles in the form of design such as toys, brooches etc. The defendants denied that the author (and hence the Syndicate to whom he had assigned the copyright) had any rights to enforce. They argued that as the author had authorised the reproduction of the work in forms that were registrable as designs (the brooches and the toys) then by section 22 of the 1911 Act such designs were excluded from artistic copyright protection. Furthermore, as the author had not registered the designs the defendants argued that he was not entitled to registered design protection either. The Court rejected this argument and held that the use or the intention to use specified in section 22 was only to be considered at the time the work was created. Since when he first drew Popeye the author had no intention of applying the design industrially, his drawings were not excluded by section 22 from copyright protection. Lord Wright said: '…a picture produced by an artist, or a piece of statuary produced by a sculptor, does not lose its copyright under the Act of 1911 merely because at some later date it or some portion of it is used as a model or pattern for the multiplication by industrial methods of objects of commerce, for instance for wallpapers or figures in relief or three-dimensional figures.'

This decision was of great importance to artists, especially those who drew characters in cartoons and comics, whose work acquired popularity at some time later than the original conception. More important still, manufacturers realised that they could rely on copyright, with its long period of protection, to prevent copying of their designs.

A further result of the Popeye case was that it was after all still possible to obtain double protection. If the author of a cartoon figure protected by the Copyright Act had registered the figure of the cartoon as a design for a doll or a brooch (he would, of course, have had to do this before publication of the cartoon otherwise the design would not have satisfied the statutory requirement of novelty) he would get protection for the doll or brooch under both Acts. The result would have been that when his registration under the 1907 Act had expired after 15 years, the manufacture of the doll or brooch by others would still have infringed his artistic copyright. Thus the designs would not have entered the public domain on the expiry of the registration. This possibility of double protection was removed by the Copyright Act 1956.[19] Under this Act artistic copyright subsists and continues to subsist in all works that are original artistic works, irrespective of whether the intention of the author when he creates it is to use the work as an industrial design and irrespective of whether the work is so used. If the proprietor applied the work later as an industrial design then the protection of the Copyright Act 1956 ceased as regards articles made to that particular design and 'associated designs'. The original work continued to enjoy protection against direct copying under the 1956 Act. So, for example, if the author of Popeye later granted a manufacturer a licence to make Popeye dolls without first securing registration, anyone would be free to make Popeye dolls, but the author could still restrain the unauthorised reproduction of any cartoons using Popeye as a character. If the copyright owner applied for registration before applying the work industrially he would again lose the protection of the 1956 Act but would, of course, have protection for his design under the Registered Designs

Act 1949, which had replaced the 1907 Act. He could not be met with the objection that his design was not novel and therefore not capable of registration because he had previously published it as a cartoon, as the 1956 Act specifically provided that a design was not to be treated as other than new by reason only of any use previously made of it as an artistic work.[20]

Not everyone was satisfied with the 1956 Copyright Act. The toy and brooch manufacturers were not happy with the protection provided. The problem lay in that many of their designs were naturalistic in origin, for example, brooches having a floral or an insect design, and toy soldiers and model aeroplanes correct in every detail. Such designs were denied the possibility of registration as they did not satisfy the novelty requirement. Worse still, any copyright protection was lost as soon as the design was applied industrially. As a result of their lobbying, a private member's Bill was introduced which became the Design Copyright Act 1968.[21] This Act, which is the Act currently in force, has radically changed the position of industrial designs and has once more resulted in double protection being available. The position now is that an artistic work receives full artistic copyright protection for the author's lifetime plus 50 years. If a corresponding design is applied industrially copyright protection for that design and associated designs ceases after 15 years, whether or not the design is registered. If the design is registered it receives double protection of copyright and registered design for 15 years when both cease; if it is not registered it is protected only by copyright for 15 years when the protection ceases.

Already the 1968 Act has its critics. The Courts have interpreted the word 'design' as used in the Act to exclude drawings of purely functional articles,[22] so that the full copyright period of the artist's lifetime plus 50 years is retained even when articles manufactured in accordance with the drawings are sold. It has also been held that the copyright in the drawings is infringed by a manufacturer who copies the articles.[23] For this reason most manufacturers of spare parts for cars must have a licence from the car makers as the latter have the original drawings for those parts and can enforce the copyright in those drawings to prevent unauthorised manufac-

ture. On the other hand, drawings that result in designs having aesthetic appeal lose all protection after 15 years. An anomalous position is thus reached in that purely functional items receive far greater protection than those having aesthetic appeal. The Whitford Committee, which reported in March 1977, again grappled with the problem of finding a satisfactory form of protection for industrial designs.[24] It recommended dividing designs into category A and category B designs. Category A designs are those which consist only of surface pattern and the shapes of three-dimensional articles of which the aesthetic appearance will influence the purchaser in making the purchase. Category B designs are the shapes of three-dimensional articles where the appearance of the article does not influence the purchaser, who buys the article in the expectation that it will do the job for which it was intended. (This is somewhat reminiscent of the 'ornamental' and 'useful' designs of the nineteenth-century legislation.) Category A designs would receive copyright protection without the need for registration and the term of protection once the design had been industrially applied would be 25 years from the first marketing of the design. With regard to category B designs the nine members of the Committee could not reach agreement. Two wished to exclude such designs from protection altogether. Of the remaining seven, four wished to accord the same protection to category B as to category A designs while three favoured the introduction of a design copyright system for a period of protection between 15 and 25 years. There has been no legislation yet to implement any aspect of the report.

Finally a word about the artist's 'moral rights' in his work. These are his rights to his reputation and in most continental jurisdictions take the form of a right to claim authorship of the work, sometimes called the right of paternity, and the right to object to any distortion or modification of the work if this prejudices the author's honour or reputation, sometimes called the right of integrity. The only similar provision in English law is section 43 of the Copyright Act 1956 which makes the false attribution of authorship actionable. As can be seen from its history, English industrial property law has concerned itself almost wholly with the protection of economic interests.

1 From Turner, T. *On Copyright in Design in Art and Manufactures* London, 1849

2 *Patents Act 1977* Section 25(1)

3 *Registered Designs Act 1949* Section 1(3)

4 *Registered Designs Act 1949* Section 8

5 *Copyright Act 1956* Section 3

6 *Engraving Act 1734*

7 *Patents and Designs Act 1907* Section 93

8 (1907) *24 RPC* 65

9 *Registered Designs Act 1949* Section 1(3)

10 [1972] *RPC* 105

11 1867 *Law Reports 2 House of Lords* 380

12 (1906) *22 RPC* 609

13 (1904) *22 RPC* 102

14 (1896) *13 RPC* 391

15 Turner, T. *op cit*

16 (1894) *2 Chancery* 1

17 *Copyright Act 1911* Section 1(2)

18 (1941) *58 RPC* 207

19 *Copyright Act 1956* Section 10

20 *Copyright Act 1956* Section 44(1)

21 This amended Section 10 of the Copyright Act 1956

22 Amp Incorporated v Utilux Proprietory Ltd [1972] *RPC 105*

23 British Northrop Ltd v Texteam Blackburn Ltd [1973] *Fleet Street Patent Law Reports* 241

24 *Report of the Committee to consider the Law on Copyright and Designs* (The Whitford Committee) 1977 Cmnd 6732 HMSO

Professional organisations

stricture or structure for graphic design?

Jude Freeman
Brighton Polytechnic

I was prompted to write this paper by a realisation that the majority of historical advertisements that are reproduced, talked or written about today were originally the work of known freelance designers.

Rather than attempting to measure the relative quality and success of designs produced by freelance designers and advertising agencies, which is, strictly speaking, impossible, I would like to focus on contemporary attitudes to the status and changes in the graphic designer's work in Britain during the years 1925–55, this being a period of more radical change in British graphic design than any other the profession had experienced.

In the inter-war years, commercial artists, as they were then called, operated in a variety of ways, just as they do today. They could work for an advertising agency as a business employee; on an equal co-operative basis with several other designers in a studio practice; or freelance either completely independently, both producing and seeking their own work, or by enlisting the services of an agent to act on their behalf at a go-between with the 'art buyer'.

The number of advertising agents grew rapidly between the two world wars. Whereas only a handful existed before the Great War, 651 agencies advertised their services in the *Advertisers Annual* of 1940. Several of these British agencies ran successful European offices. The Institute of Incorporated Practitioners in Advertising[1] which was set up in 1927, formerly existing as the Association of British Advertising Agents (founded in 1917), acted as the professional body defining advertising standards and ethical practice. The Institute admitted only carefully vetted agencies to its ranks, on application. In addition to a dividing line between professional and other agencies, there existed a further delineation between run of the mill/hack agencies and the reputedly creative ones. The London Press Exchange under Reginald Sykes, S. H. Bensons Ltd, W. S. Crawford & Co Ltd, Charles Highams and certain other agencies were recognised for the employment of talented designers. Ashley Havinden, for instance, who joined Crawfords in 1922 and went on to become its managing director and one of Britain's most progressive graphic designers, is an excellent example of a committed individual working within agency practice.

The smaller commercial art studios also flourished during these years, since for the designer they offered an attractive compromise between agency and freelance work. It was quite customary for a group to join together working non-competitively, sharing studio costs and work. The Bassett-Gray Studio,[2] founded in 1922 by Milner Gray and Henry Bassett, was probably the prototype for later enterprises such as The Crichton Studios, The Clement Dane Studio, and Carlton Studios, each producing very capable advertisements which demonstrated, according to *Posters and Publicity*, 'teamwork instead of individual prowess'.[3] The annual *Commercial Art* commented that, though excellent '...their work does not attain such celebrity as that of the first-rate individual

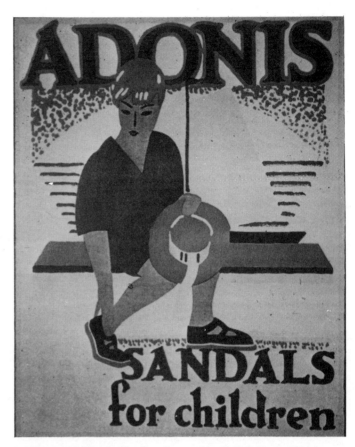

1 *Edward McKnight Kauffer, showcard for C & J Clark, 1924*

designers – whose fame once established, enables them to design independently...'[4]

It was thus assumed that the best designers usually worked freelance and because of this, many young recruits to the profession naturally aspired to this enviable position. As an experienced artists' agent, Donovan Candler, remarked sardonically in 1937, 'almost every young artist...when he leaves art school thinks he is an embryonic McKnight Kauffer'[5] (Figure 1). It was Kauffer's position as a famous freelance designer that they imitated as much as his progressive style. The year after he died in 1955, *Graphis* noted that he had only ever designed three posters for purposes of direct sale, a remarkable fact which it attributed to the blindness of business men.[6] On the contrary, though, it surely indicated his ability to choose what he designed which, along with the obvious lure of general independence, was the main attraction of freelance work.

In addition to the positive reasons for going solo, there were significant negative aspects of agency practice. Rightly or wrongly, many agencies and large studios were associated with drudgery; repetitive work as a member of a team on long-standing contracts often meant anonymity and hence failure for many designers by contemporary standards. Nevertheless, many freelance designers started off in agency or studio work. When Tom Eckersley and Eric Lombers, working as partners (Eckersley Lombers), came down from Manchester in 1935 to launch themselves on the London advertising world, they received what was considered to be standard advice given to all beginners by advertising agents and art agents – 'Go into a studio – your type of work is not what is wanted'[7] – advice which they, in fact, successfully disproved. While their graphic work was sufficiently confident for them to equate freelancing with the opportunity to do original work, other young designers welcomed an informal apprenticeship with an agency in order to gain practical experience before going freelance. Reginald Mount, for example, who has been freelance for most of his life, originally worked for Lintas, Greenlys and Odhams Press before the Second World War in order to acquaint himself with working methods and find out his particular specialism before freelancing.

Although the advising experts varied as to the desirable length of stay – ranging from six months to six years[8] – they were unanimous that after going through the agency mill the designer should leave before becoming stereotyped, and henceforward 'plough his own furrow through the field of commercial art'.[9] Plenty of additional advice about ploughing straight and avoiding bumps was offered in pursuit of the glorious goal – the harvest of success. There is no accurate way of estimating the number of freelance graphic designers in Great Britain before the Second World War, but there were certainly many more who followed this pattern than after it. They undoubtedly saw agency work as second best, a restriction on their originality.

For the many who did branch out alone, such as Abram Games, who has freelanced since 1936, work came from various sources. Printers who carried a stock of speculative designs which could be adapted to one of a variety of commodities often hired the designer's services in order to secure print orders. Agencies, frequently contracting out much creative work, also used them on an ad hoc basis and some large advertisers such as the GPO, Shell Mex and BP Ltd, and London Passenger Transport Board, who preferred to deal directly with the designer in order to communicate their requirements, avoiding the middle men, also provided work. In his *Enquiry into Industrial Art in England,* Pevsner referred to the quality of design work by 'the best commercial artists in London' and he, in fact, urged manufacturers to 'take advantage of these artists, not only for advertising, but also for industrial design'.[10] Vital requirements for successful freelancing were speed and originality, but above all, in order to build up a reputation, the freelance designer needed to be a specialist. This could take various forms, either in style, subject matter, or – as tended to occur most frequently – in the concentration on a particular medium.

The freelance designer in Britain between the wars was recognised not only for his specialist ability, whether it lay in figure drawing, fashion illustration or photography, but also, as often as not, he became associated with poster design. This medium more than any other attracted the finest graphic design talents. By the 1930s several advertising agencies (such as LPE, Crawfords and Bensons) were offering poster services, but although agencies had long progressed beyond their original function in the previous century as space-brokers who received their discount from the Press, they had, nevertheless, maintained this traditional link with press advertising. In terms of expenditure, press advertising (which included journals and magazines as well as national and local papers) was by far the major advertising medium. By 1938, poster advertising (which also included outdoor signs and transport ads) accounted for 8.3 per cent of the total annual advertising expenditure, whereas the press share accounted for 85 per cent[11] (of £59 million). Although total advertising figures vary considerably and earlier sums are unsubstantiated, it can be fairly safely assumed that this expenditure ratio had existed between press and poster publicity throughout the 1930s – the press share amounting to ten times that of the outdoor medium. The 1920s may have witnessed a slightly different financial relationship when in 1925 for instance an expenditure of £7 million [12] was suggested by the Department of Overseas Trade for poster advertising alone, but media monitoring was then only in its infancy and these amounts must be treated as approximations (if not wild guesses). Despite this phenomenal financial difference, the poster medium was considered by many to be superior to press advertising. Various commentators in the 1920s had singled out the poster as the finest means of capturing the public imagination. At the Advertising Convention in 1926 it was stated that poster advertising was more 'universally useful than any other system of advertising', and the author went as far as to state categorically that 'definite results can be obtained with a small expenditure'[13] (a rather outlandish statement even for 1926) (Figures 2 and 3). Not only was the poster the central feature of many advertising campaigns backed up in the press, but it also attracted the most comment and was widely written about. While it was recognised rather begrudgingly that agencies had their organisational part to play in advertising, as in America where they were said to 'wield great power towards the advancement of art in publicity',[14] this contribution paled in contrast to the fêted freelance designers who were respected as the aristocrats of the profession. The cream of the creative talent in design for print was undoubtedly attracted to poster work: Fred Taylor, Tom Purvis, F. C. Herrick, Austin Cooper, Harold Sandys Williamson, George Sheringham, Gregory Brown, Dora Batty and Pat Keely were all great individualists specialising in poster work (Figure 4).

British travel posters in the 1920s and 1930s were highly rated as some of the best ever designed, and in 1937 A. Defries pronounced the British poster display at the Paris exhibition 'Arts et Techniques de la Vie Moderne', 'in regard to printing and variety, easily the best the world had to show…'[15] The 'creative individualism' she remarked upon was indeed essentially that of British freelance designers.

Poster design was by nature a far less standardised procedure than design for press advertisements, which were bound to conform to newspaper regulations, not only in size, but also in content. Perhaps because of its flexibility, the poster was more suited to individual design work than that of a team. Just as there was an historical reason for the connection between press advertising and the agencies, so the freelance link with the poster medium had its roots. Many of the first pictorial posters in the late nineteenth century had been designed by painters who were drawn to the medium because of both its mass audience and also its capacity for making them some ready money. If not actually by painters, then posters were often copies of their work (Figures 5 and 6). The modern British poster had existed since its inception in a hinterland between art and commerce. Roger Fry, who thought that advertising was 'hynoptism on a large scale'[16] had noted this

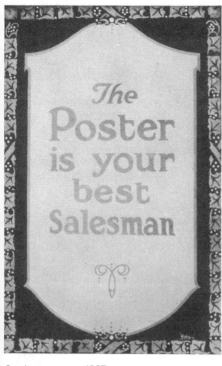

2 *Anonymous, c1927*

3 *Poster hoardings, Willenhall, Staffordshire, 1930*

4 *Tom Purvis for LNER, 1926*

5 *Fred Walker ARA 'The Woman in White', 1871*

6 *Sir John Millais, 1886*

7 *'Poster Street' at the Empire Exhibition, Wembley, 1924-5*

ambiguity in 1926, when he delivered his lecture *Art and Commerce* based on a visit to a poster exhibition. Interestingly enough, at the Wembley Empire exhibition of 1924/5 the outdoor poster display was symbolically sandwiched between the Palaces of Art and Industry, on neutral ground (Figure 7).

This schism became particularly pronounced in the 1930s, and the freelance designer's role as the poster creator was also affected by this confusion. In their manual *Commercial Art Practice* (1927), Knights and Norman had stated that the professional advertiser was 'inclined to make a fetish of originality'.[17] It was certainly true that the biggest advertisers during this period sought this originality above all from freelance designers. The 'pictures by famous artists' attitude indeed lasted well into the 1930s in Great Britain. Shell and London Transport, who employed both renowned and aspiring artists for their extensive advertising campaigns, were said to be 'patrons' of contemporary arts fulfilling the twentieth-century equivalent of the Medici patronage in the quattrocento (Figures 8 and 9). The terminology is revealing: poster designs were 'commissioned' and when the Empire Marketing Board[18] initiated the Government's first large peace-time campaign in 1926 it had special hoardings erected around the UK called 'picture frames', which was exactly their function, as out of the five units three were for pictures and two for copy – separating the accepted fusion of copy and picture. The EMB was christened the Royal Academy of the Poster World. Similarly, Jack Beddington, who, as publicity manager to Shell, is said to have been 'a man in love with talent',[19] while using a succession of agencies to do his press advertising, always regarded poster design as a job for an artist. In the mid-1930s he launched a scheme using lorry bills instead of commercial hoardings. He commissioned a series of paintings with the slogan 'These Men Use Shell' (Figure 10) which were conceived above all as paintings with lettering added below and above by the printers. Paul Nash, Graham Sutherland, John Armstrong and Ben Nicholson worked alongside Clive Gardiner, McKnight Kauffer and Hans Schleger (alias Zero) on these picture posters, which were

available to the public, the intention being that they should be cut out and framed for the home. Beddington's rather esoteric lorry bill scheme and Pick's advertising programme, which concentrated on the destination rather than the service itself (which Pick after all had every reason to be proud of) helped to pioneer the cause of high-quality publicity. Their tremendous support in wider contexts is today fully recorded, but it is not fully recognised that they inadvertently cemented the rift between 'art publicity' and standard commercial work. Instead of legitimising advertising as an important modern design area in its own right, the use of artists perhaps unintentionally only elevated the status of the work they were specifically involved with.

The advertising agencies also realised that poster design required a specialist and that the freelances were the most creative specialists available. Of the several breeds available, however, they preferred the avowed 'poster designer' or 'modern publicity artist' rather than the 'water colour and poster artist' type of designer. Very few agencies had a large or capable enough creative section to cater for every design aspect and so they often used outside freelances, sometimes unacknowledged, for their poster work. Bensons, for instance, which was an unusual agency in that it used posters quite extensively, employed freelances very often and Gilroy, who designed many of the Guinness posters for Bensons, was always freelance (Figure 11). This poster work would be supported by a strong press campaign, and the overall credit would of course go to the agency, not to the freelance. Although the art directors and freelance designers worked together generally on a basis of mutual respect – recognising their different skills – the poster versus press argument had, at times, been quite bitter. One of the contributors to E. McKnight Kauffer's treatise on *The Art of the Poster* (1924) had been exttreme enough to claim that 'anyone can produce a press advertisement after a fashion, rough and imperfect though it may be; but it takes an artist to create a poster'.[20] Similarly, the freelances were sometimes criticised for unreliability and temperamental behaviour. Press advertising was, however, rapidly outgrowing its crude antecedents – the original lettered insertions – and although this was a slower metamorphosis than that from the bill to the pictorial poster, the tide was turning. When the annual *Posters and Publicity* reappeared in 1930 as *Modern Publicity*, it had dropped the word 'Posters' from its title in deference to press advertising. Under the championship of a unique agency designer such as Ashley, press advertisements began to display a greater awareness of layout principles and gradually came to be recognised as a potentially artistic medium that had been overshadowed by the poster.

These, then, are some of the tendencies and inconsistencies underlying the production of British graphics before the war. Designers do seem to have flourished particularly well in a flexible working set-up, especially in poster design, which it was recognised emerged most successfully from an individual rather than a team. The freelance designer enjoyed a certain prestige that the agency employee did not, but the freelance position was gradually being eroded towards the end of the 1930s. In 1937, *Gebrauchsgraphik* dedicated a special issue of their magazine to a survey of London's advertising scene in which they drew attention to the 'mechanization, over-organization and excessive commercialization' of British advertising in practice. Their conclusion, that 'the Creative Spirit was been sacrificed to business methods, and routine and set forms have taken the place of human imagination and daring excursions into fresh territory',[21] was perhaps over-generalised, but it pointed to the future.

This development was postponed when the outbreak of war decimated commercial advertising. George Begley recalls that the agencies 'fired many of their staff, cut the pay of the survivors and prepared for years of misery. At the same time they looked round the countryside for premises unlikely to be bombed.'[22] The number of UK advertising agents offering

10

8 *Edward McKnight Kauffer, brochure cover, 1938*

9 *Edward Wadsworth poster for the Imperial War Museum originally designed for a Swiss graphics exhibition, 1922*

10 *Zero (Hans Schleger), 1930s*

11 *Gilroy for S. H. Bensons Ltd, 1934*

11

13

their services in *The Advertisers Annual* dropped from 651 in 1940 to 551 in 1945. The Government became the largest single advertiser during the war, through its Ministry of Information set up in 1939 almost as a blueprint of a large centralised service agency, undertaking publicity work for most other Government departments and commandeering the lion's share of the nation's advertising resources, including its talent. British Government publicity assumed various forms, from leaflets to international exhibitions, but its major printed activity at home lay with press and poster advertising. The Ministry recognised the value of posters and in accordance with the established working procedure they enlisted the services of many freelance designers – Clive Gardiner, James Fitton, F. H. K. Henrion, Lewitt-Him, Felix Topolski and Fougasse – employing many of the foreign designers who had emigrated to England in the 1930s, thus bolstering the freelance ranks (Figure 12). In addition to these, the Ministry set up a permanent design section in its General Production Division under J. Embleton. Reginald Mount was in full-time service throughout the war and, in conjunction with Eileen Evans and Austin Cooper, who joined later, this creative division produced the majority of MOI posters. In addition to the freelance designers and this hard core of permanent design staff, S. H. Bensons Ltd was used for MOI poster work because its outdoor department could offer a complete and therefore valuable maintenance service. Otherwise advertising agencies were used only for press campaigns, which were informative and repetitive in nature rather than persuasive. An Advisory Committee was set up for the appointment of suitable agencies for each campaign, and although only a fraction of the nation's agencies were utilised, usually London agencies to boot, the MOI was praised for its impartiality in distributing contracts. Press advertising, however, decreased significantly during the war.[23]

Apart from the MOI, other freelance designers were used by the Government. Abram Games worked for the War Office throughout the war as the only 'Official War Office Poster Artist', with Frank Newbould as his assistant (Figure 13).

Tom Eckersley did poster work for the Air Force, and Pat Keely for the GPO. Other graphic designers went into camouflage work or exhibition design, but although only a few freelances were employed, they all maintained their identity as freelances within a large design organisation, which appears to have positively nurtured creative work. Despite general hardship they worked without restriction; perhaps because the MOI was new and its policies were evolving it was receptive to innovative design ideas.[24] Designers themselves recall this period as, ironically, a happy working time when they joined in an amicable working set-up with a common objective. They designed with meaning for a serious purpose. Tom Eckersley stated later that: 'During the war there were many first class posters because for once the artist was allowed to use his creative ability with little interference.'[25]

Despite the fact that many designers in their idealistic blueprints for reconstruction envisaged one eternal Ministry of Information dedicating publicity to matters of social value such as health, safety and education, in reality this non-profitmaking dream never materialised. Business advertising took several years to get back to normal and although the poster underwent a temporary resurgence, mainly due to newsprint shortages, it never fully recovered its pre-war status. The post-1945 years witnessed a steady and significant expansion in the advertising agency monopoly of available work. British agencies with American financial backing increased rapidly and in the new scheme of things agency services became more complex and self-sufficient. One American agency, Young and Rubicam, listed 24 specialised services in a 1946 advertisement, one of which incidentally was 'Outdoor'.[26] American organisational business methods, which were so studiously emulated by British agencies after the war, were closely allied to quantifiable media and market research. The poster had always been an elusive medium in this respect and it could never be tied up so convincingly. Also it had always taken a back seat in American advertising, which concentrated on the national weekly papers on team work and corporate design. These factors helped to undermine the

British poster's position in the 1950s, as did the Town and Country Planning Act 1947, advances in colour photography and the birth of commercial television in 1955 which, while positively increasing advertising expenditure, altered the patterns of media expenditure. Television's gain can be closely related to the outdoor medium's loss.

The freelance designer had become so inextricably bound up with poster work in Great Britain by this time that when the medium underwent its all-time low due to the combination of these various factors, the freelance designer faded out of the advertising picture almost completely. The successful freelance poster designer, albeit a star, had very rarely made a living from his design work and, just as the early greats had taught to supplement their earnings, so this generation was underemployed after the war, and forced to seek other work. Eckersley and Games went into teaching, Henrion into design practice, and Schleger acted as a consultant to a large agency in addition to freelancing. The early 1950s were such a slack period that an organisation which could afford to pay only small fees had no difficulty in securing work from top designers.

When, in 1961, the British and London Poster Advertising Associations celebrated their centenary, *The Times* marked the historic occasion with a special supplement on posters. It said: 'The past 12 years have probably brought about more fun-damental changes in the poster industry than any other period in its history.'[27]

The temporary demise of the poster, however, was accompanied by a more permanent depression for the freelance. By 1960, 90 per cent of all advertising in Britain was handled by agencies[28] and as the creative element in the business structure became more and more peripheral (by 1970 creative costs in many agencies were less than a fifth of the total), the personal idiom of the designer became less and less noticeable as a result. The reduced amount of poster work at this time was mainly limited to blown-up photographic stills – just one part of a total campaign with the television commercial at the fore.

Graphic design had naturally needed to move with the times; whereas the 1930s had been the heyday of the freelance designer, these working methods became impracticable in the altered conditions of mass advertising post-war. It is remarkable, however, that when British agencies, who had never been renowned for their poster work, took over the designing of this medium the business organisation proved to be a stricture on the intuitive process necessary to successful poster design. When poster work was subsumed by the advertising agencies in the 1950s, it was thus no coincidence that both the truly autonomous poster and the freelance designer were also submerged.

1 Retitled the Institute of Practitioners in advertising in 1954

2 This grew into Industrial Design Partnership in 1935 and formed the nucleus of the Design Research Unit, set up in 1943

3 Harrison, John *Posters and Publicity* London, 1927, 3

4 *Commercial Art* vol 3, London, 1927, 187

5 Candler, Donovan 'The Artist and his Agent' in *Penrose Annual* vol 34, London, 1937, 34

6 Rosner, Charles 'Pat Keely' in *Graphis* 1956, 250

7 *Commercial Art and Industry* London, 1935, 208

8 Candler, Donovan *op cit* 36 suggested six months to one year as a maximum period. Knights, Charles C. and Norman, Frank E. *Commercial Art Practice* Crosby Lockwood & Son, London, 1927, 142 suggested 'several years'

9 Candler, Donovan *op cit* 37

10 Pevsner, Nikolaus *An Enquiry into Industrial Art in England* Cambridge, 1937, 198

11 Critchley, R. A. *UK Advertising Statistics* Advertising Association, London, nd, c1973, 9

12 *Report on the Present Position and Tendencies of the Industrial Arts as Indicated at the International Exhibition of Modern Decorative and Industrial Arts Paris 1925* Department of Overseas Trade, London, 1927

13 *Advertising Lancashire* Manchester Publicity Club second annual advertising Convention, Blackpool, 1926

14 *Posters and Publicity* 1926, 18

15 Defries, A. *Purpose in Design* Methuen, London, 1937, 197

16 Fry, Roger *Art and Commerce* The Hogarth Press, London, 1926

17 Knights, Charles C. and Norman, Frank E. *op cit* 137

18 Set up from 1926–33 to assist the Dominions Office to promote Empire trade in the UK

19 Ullstein, Gabriele 'Jack Beddington' in *Design* no 3, July 1951

20 Russell, Phillips in McKnight Kauffer, E. (ed) *The Art of the Poster* Cecil Palmer, London, 1924, 43-4

21 *Gebrauchsgraphik* no 3, 1937, 7

22 Begley, George *Keep Mum* Lemon Tree Press, London, 1975, 7

23 The total net advertising revenue of the Press fell from £28.2 million per annum in 1935 to £17.1 million in 1943, according to Kaldor, Nicholas and Silverman, Rodney *A Statistical Analysis of Advertising Expenditure and of the Revenue of the Press* Cambridge, 1948, 15

24 Transcripts and translations of Crown Copyright records in the Public Record Office appear by permission of the Controller of HM Stationery Office

25 Eckersley, Tom 'British Hoardings Under Fire' in *Art and Industry* 1949

26 Cited in Brandon, Robert *The Truth About Advertising* Chapman and Hall, London, 1949, 71

27 'British Posters' in *The Times* 20 October, 1961

28 Games, Abram, 'The Poster in Modern Advertising' in *Royal Society of Arts Journal* London, 1962

The beginnings of product design?

the American System of Manufactures and design in America in the 1850s

Hazel Conway
Leicester Polytechnic

The area of product design with which I am concerned is that associated with the mass consumption and mass production of goods produced by mechanical means. In investigating the beginnings of product design, we have to be clear whether these investigations will be concerned primarily with the role of the designer and the separation of the design function from the design process, or the way in which particular techniques of production related to the design of the product, when mass production first became significant.

It is difficult enough to look at patterns of consumption across decades, but if one tries to look at them across different countries and across a century or more, then it becomes well nigh impossible, because the bases of the statistics vary so much that comparisons cannot be made in any valid or coherent way.

If we concentrate on mass production by mechanical techniques, then we have to be clear what we mean by these terms. Terracotta oil lamps were produced in large numbers by the Romans from two-piece wooden moulds. In a sense they were mass produced, but the method of production was a craft-based one with the moulds made and the lamps finished by hand. If we look at woodworking machinery, particularly that introduced during the nineteenth century to speed up production in the furniture industry, we find that machines such as band saws and scroll saws and edge carvers required considerable manual skill, both for their setting and their operation.[1]

Mass production by mechanical techniques means that the operator is not required to exercise judgement in the use of his machine, nor is he required to be skilled in the use of tools, and the items produced, whether of metal or of wood or whatever, have standardised dimensions and are interchangeable with any other part produced by the identical production process. The Americans' lead in this area became apparent in Britain for the first time at the Great Exhibition of 1851, and such was its impact that this system of the production of standardised, interchangeable parts became known as the American System of Manufactures. Such a name implied that nothing of a similar nature had occurred in Britain or elsewhere, and that the Americans' efforts in this area were unique. This was not, however, the case.

One of the earliest large-scale applications in Britain of mechanised production using standardised parts was at the Royal Dockyard, Plymouth, where mass production techniques for the manufacture of ships' pulley blocks were introduced in 1803.[2] The Royal Navy used 100,000 pulley blocks each year, and it was claimed that Marc Isambard Brunel's group of machines, which were manufactured by Henry Maudslay, did the work of 110 skilled blockmakers, using only 10 unskilled men.[3] In the area of machine tools – that is, tools employed in the production of machinery – progress in the standardisation of parts was implied by James Nasmyth when he wrote in 1841: 'Up to within the last thirty years nearly every part of a machine had to be made and finished...by mere manual labour.'[4] In the area of cotton manufacture, Andrew Ure wrote: 'Where many counterparts or similar pieces enter a spinning apparatus, they are all made so perfectly identical in form and size, by the self acting tools, such as the planing and key-groove cutting machines, that any one of them will at once fit into the position of any of its fellows in the general frame.'[5] Of mill shafting he wrote: 'One millwright establishment in Manchester turns out from 300 to 400 yards of shaft gearing every week, finely finished, at a very moderate price, because almost every tool is now more or less automatic and performs its work more cheaply, and with greater precision, than the hand can possibly do.'

So in certain British industries automatic mass production techniques were being applied in the first half of the nineteenth century, and of course in the context of 1851 the Crystal Palace building itself was an excellent example of the application of the system of standardisation and interchangeability of parts, since the girders, columns, sash bars and gutters were produced to uniform specifications in multiples or submultiples of 24 feet.[6] Yet the wider implications of these techniques went largely unappreciated in Britain.

Now it may be argued that all I have said so far is straightforward, well documented history of technology that has little relevance to the history of design. I argue that as product design concerns the development and application of mass-production techniques, then the design and development of the machines and systems of production that contributed towards these are of fundamental importance, though of course they are not the only important factors.

What I want to do now is to look at the American exhibits at the Great Exhibition and at the American System of Manufactures, and to sketch very briefly the outline of the evolution of the system in America and the different social and economic conditions that led to its development and application.

Because American goods for the Great Exhibition were late in arriving, the initial reaction to them was cool, but during the course of the summer several events occurred that drew attention to them, and attitudes began to change. Among the exhibits were corn-husk mattresses, meat biscuits, india-rubber shoes, fireproofed safes, carriages, pianos, woodworking machinery, ice-making machines, locks and Colt repeating pistols. The Official Catalogue noted: 'The absence in the United States of those vast accumulations of wealth which favour the expenditure of large sums on articles of mere luxury, and the general distribution of the means of procuring the more substantial conveniences of life, impart to the production of American industry a character distinct from that of many other countries. The expenditure of months or years of labour upon a single article, not to increase its intrinsic value, but solely to augment its cost or its estimation as an object of *virtu* is not common in the United States. On the contrary both manual and mechanical labour are applied with direct reference to increasing the number or the quantity of the articles suited to the wants of a whole people, and adapted to

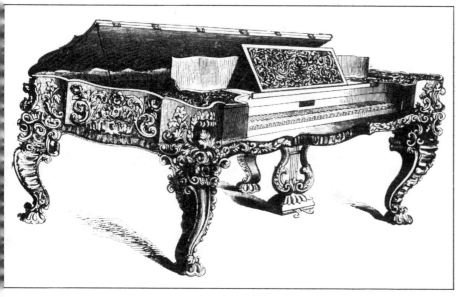

promote the enjoyment of that moderate competency which prevails among them.'[7] The implication that American goods were simpler and directed more towards the needs of people should perhaps be treated with scepticism when one looks at such exhibits as a grand piano 'richly carved and [a credit to] the skill and ingenuity of the workmen who produced it', or at American carriages. Indeed, the *Art Journal Catalogue* commented that 'our American friends with all their apparent dislike of pomp and parade are not insensitive to the luxuries and conveniences of life, is evident from the elegant carriages they exhibit'.[8]

There were three events that had the effect of focusing public attention on the American exhibits. The transatlantic yacht race was won by the yacht 'America' on 23 August 1851. The demonstration of McCormick's mechanical reaper, which was an innovation in Britain although it had been established in the USA since the 1840s, was widely acclaimed – even by *The Times*, which was not noted for being pro-American. And, on the same day that 'America' won the transatlantic yacht race, the American locksmith and lock-picker Alfred C. Hobbs managed to pick Bramah's 'unpickable' lock, which had been on display for 40 years in a Piccadilly shop window with an offer of 200 guineas for anyone

who could pick it. Hobbs had not exactly been working under average burglarious conditions (he spent 51 hours spread over 16 days before he succeeded) but nevertheless the effect of his success was to draw attention to his own locks on display at the Exhibition. When the best lock-pickers (though I'm not sure how they were selected) failed to pick Hobbs's locks the public were naturally most impressed. Hobbs's locks were manufactured on the basis of standardisation of component parts, so that there was maximum interchangeability even among locks of different sizes. Bramah and Maudslay had evolved a range of specialised machinery for producing Bramah's locks, and had used the system of standardisation of parts, but these techniques had not been adopted by the rest of the British lock manufacturers, and the majority of locks were virtually handmade. Hobbs was so impressed by the backwardness of the industry in Britain that he decided to stay behind after the Exhibition and start his own company.

Another of the American exhibits new to this country were Colt's repeating pistols which, like Hobbs's locks, were manufactured using the system of standardisation of parts, since Colt, like Hobbs, found that he could not achieve a sufficient volume of production or uniformity of product at a competitive price using hand labour methods. Because Colt pistols were manufactured by this technique, not only were they cheaper, but complete pistols could be reassembled out of the parts of broken ones on active service. And, like Hobbs, Colt was very impressed by the scope for his product in Britain, returning the next year to set up his own factory.[9]

It was directly as a result of the impact of these exhibits that a British Commission was set up to investigate American machinery and manufactures, and this Commission visited New York in 1853 to attend the international exhibition there and to report back to Parliament.[10] However, the opening of the exhibition was delayed by two weeks, and the Commission decided to use the time to tour around and see for themselves the areas for which they were responsible. They published their findings in the *Report of the Committee on the Machinery of the United States,* with special reports from Mr George Wallis on manufactures and Mr Joseph Whitworth on machinery.[11] George Wallis was headmaster of the Government School of Art and Design in Birmingham in 1853 and had previously been in charge of the Manchester School of Design. His brief was to report on the state of design in the areas of textiles, including carpets and clothing, cutlery, iron and general hardware, jewellery, glass, ceramics, decorative furniture, the position of art education as applied to manufacture, and the copyright of designs.

Joseph Whitworth was the foremost British manufacturer of machine tools and his brief was to report on machines for direct use, manufacturing machines and tools, civil engineering, patent laws and the electric telegraph. He found that in such areas of mechanisation as agricultural machinery and light metal goods the Americans were more advanced than the British, and that new machine tools, particularly milling machines and turret lathes, were being developed for specialised uses. This specialisation and standardisation of parts for specialised uses indicated a major difference in approach between British and American engineers. New American machine tools were more specialised because the parts they were designed to produce were themselves more specialised, and with specialisation came cost reductions. British general-purpose tools were strong enough for the most demanding tasks, but were unnecessarily strong for the majority of them.

When had America started developing this different approach, and why had these techniques not developed so rapidly in Britain? In 1798 the American government gave a large contract to the arms manufacturers Whitney, and the next year they gave another large contract to another firm, North. There was a sudden, sharp increase in demand for small-arms from these two companies, additional sufficiently skilled labour was not available, and under this pressure both firms revolutionised their techniques of manufacture, standardising parts so that they were interchangeable in the final assembly. Whitney described the aim of interchangeable parts as being 'to substitute correct and effective operations of machinery for that skill of the artist which is acquired only by long practice and experience; a species of skill which is not possessed in this country to any considerable extent'.[12] Simeon North said 'I find that by confining a workman to one particular limb of the pistol until he has made 2000 I can save at least one quarter of his labour'.[13]

As early as 1790 Americans had invented machines that automatically bent wire into card teeth and set them in their leather backing, and that automatically cut plate into nails – both early steps in the standardisation of interchangeable parts.[14] In the 1850s and 1860s this method of manufacture was applied to such products as woodscrews, bolts, locks, clocks, watches, sewing machines and locomotives, and such were the advantages in cost and quality of the final product that they could be exported at a very low, competitive price.[15] 'Probably in the United States more people, relative to the whole population, than in any other part of the world, lived in frame houses, with cabinet furniture, stoves, carpets, china, glassware, clocks and watches, rode in carriages, and performed their labours with the facilities of improved machinery'.[16]

The reason most often given for the rapid and early mechanisation of American industry is that it was due to the shortage of available labour, and the high cost of the labour that was available.[17] Because of the plentiful supply of land in America in the nineteenth century, however poor a man was to start with, he could become a farmer – a land-owning farmer, not a tenant farmer with rent to pay. So if industry was to be attractive it had to pay a higher rate than could be earned in agriculture. In contrast, the English agricultural worker did not own his land – he was either a tenant paying rent or else he worked for a low wage – and so industry needed to offer very little extra to be attractive. Yet if it was economically worth while for American manufacturers to replace expensive labour by machines made by that expensive labour, why was it not worth while for British manufacturers to replace the cheaper British labour by machines made by it? And again, why should the pressure of the search for labour-saving techniques result in technical progress, any more than the pressure for methods to save capital and resources? In America labour was scarce compared with land and capital, but why should this difference have provided a greater incentive to mechanise and standardise in America?

The main contrast between America and Britain is not simply between a labour-scarce and a labour-abundant society, but between economies that had their labour scarcities at different periods of their industrial development, with the pressures and incentives that resulted from this. Britain's labour scarcity occurred in the period 1730–80 when the techniques of the Industrial Revolution were being invented and adopted. America's labour shortage occurred in the first half of the nineteenth century, when these techniques were being widely adopted there. During this period in Britain markets were expanding, but the limitations in labour and manufacturing abilities were not sufficient to create the great pressure to try any likely-looking mechanical innovation, which was what happened in America.

The scarcity of labour in America is sufficient to explain why American entrepreneurs sought to save labour by using machines, but another factor of almost equal importance was the rate of American investment, which was much higher than it was in Britain during the first half of the nineteenth century. As the country opened up, the increasing demand for industrial goods took the form of a series of booms, and it was the prospect of expanding markets, combined with the limitations in available labour and manufacturing facilities, that was the feature of industrial development in America at this time. Indeed, the situation was very similar to that in Britain a century earlier, before the 'take-off' of the Industrial Revolution. The standardisation of parts in the manufacture of small-arms is an excellent example of this sudden demand providing the incentive to experiment and apply innovations.

The direction of technical progress depends on the type of problem to which inventors and manufacturers are most alert.

Americans had acquired the habit of concentrating on problems whose solution lay in the invention and application of labour-saving devices. In Britain attitudes were conditioned by plentiful, cheap labour.

This emphasis on labour-saving devices can be seen in areas other than those of industry and agriculture. For example, in *The American Woman's Home,* Catherine Beecher and Harriet Beecher Stowe say that their book will show ways of saving labour, time and expense in the home, so that people of limited means can benefit and so that women will be better able to provide a healthy, industrious and economic (that is, not wasteful) environment. An incentive to apply labour-saving devices in the home was the lack of domestic labour in America. America was the only country where there was 'a class of women who may be described as *ladies* who do their own work'.[18] This was partly due to the range of other work available in a rapidly developing country. In addition there was the example of slavery in the South, and any attempt to treat someone as a servant was condemned as an indignity. Domestic service was not accepted as a 'profession to live and die in. It is…a stepping stone to something higher…Families look forward to the buying of landed homesteads and the scattered brothers and sisters work awhile in domestic service to gain a common fund for the purpose, your seamstress intends to become a dressmaker and take in work at her house…'[19] Thus it was not only in the industrial area that there was a positive attitude towards labour-saving devices.

I would now like to look at the report on American manufactures by George Wallis. The Commission detected marked differences in the development and application of American machinery compared with British practice. Did these differences produce appreciable differences in the design of American products? Because of his background and position, Wallis was familiar both with the state of design in Britain and with criticism of it, and these provided the yardstick against which he measured the design of American goods. From the point of view of the goods produced by the technique of standardisation of parts, however, Wallis tells us little or nothing. Indeed, he stressed that the results of manufacture must be separated from the means of manufacture. He saw originality in the means of manufacture as one of the most remarkable features in American industry, but his particular concern was with the manufactures themselves, and in this area originality was unlikely because 'imitation of European productions has alone been the aim of the manufacturer and the artisan'.[20]

The problem in summarising Wallis's report is that it is very detailed. It covers a wide range of products – textiles, furniture, metalware, jewellery, glass and ceramics – and it does not include illustrations of the goods discussed. All I shall be able to do here is to indicate some of the most significant of Wallis's comments.

From the general point of view of the market in the 1850s for various products in America, the position was that American goods had to compete with those exported from France, Germany and England, and the tone of the market was largely set by the European manufacturers. This European influence was reinforced by the fact that many American workmen had come from Europe, bringing their European conventions with them, and this tended to stifle rather than encourage the development of new forms for ordinary and useful products. In spite of this Wallis wrote, in the context of metal manufactures: 'The American manufacturer is in some respects wiser than his foreign competitor, and in many instances, leaves the ultra-ornate to be supplied from Birmingham and Sheffield, and directs his energies to the development of a better and less exuberant style, which he finds is demanded by the more refined among his countrymen.'[21] In gold and silver plate, and in products made in German silver, electroplate and Britannia metal, workmanship was sound, but lacking the finish, particularly in the chasing, that could be seen in the best English work. On the other hand, American workmen did not seem to commit the more objectionable practice of over-chasing so that the artistic effect of the details was destroyed. In this area of products Wallis mentioned in particular a machine for silver plating spoons and forks developed by Conrad, Bard & Son of Philadelphia, in which two circular dies or rollers were sunk with forms of articles to be rolled out – usually spoons of two sizes, a fork and the side of a knife handle. As the intaglio of one die was accurately adjusted to that of the other, one forming the obverse and the other forming the reverse of the pattern, both sides of the article were produced at the same time, and the rollers achieved the work of a stamp press much more effectively and economically.[22]

Areas of manufacture praised for being superior to their counterparts in Britain included hardware articles for domestic use, 'except where more than an ordinary attempt is made at ornamentation, and then the results are by no means satisfactory'.[23] Military buttons and similar ornamental articles were in better taste than those produced in Britain, by which Wallis meant that 'less effect was aimed at, and extravagant subjects in high relief [were] avoided'.[24] Chandeliers, gasoliers and lamps, however, could not compete with the better class of similar products manufactured in Britain. In America the larger versions of these were used in hotels and saloons, and a showy, cheaply produced article was demanded. Some of the details of the designs were well modelled, but 'there is often a great lack of the congruity in the parts by which a perfect *ensemble* can alone be realised'.[25]

At the New York Exhibition the area of industry that had the greatest volume of exhibits on display was the furniture industry, and here elaborate carving was the rule, much of it the work of Europeans and from French and German designs rather than English ones. None of the furniture manufactured for the Western States of America, which was ordinary, useful and cheap, was on display at the Exhibition and this, said Wallis, was a pity as much of it showed ingenuity and economy of material. 'On the whole, the decorative arts as applied to furniture are vitiated for any present influence on public taste, by an overwhelming tendency to display; fostered to a large extent by a class of persons whose object it is to crowd as large an amount of work into as small an amount of space as possible, and who prefer charging for labour rather than skill and taste. This reacts on the public mind, and habituates it to redundancy and over-ornamentation rather than to purity and simplicity resulting in the really beautiful.'[26]

Wallis thought that the taste of the American consumer was more homogeneous than that of Europeans, and that it was concentrated at the low-quality end of the spectrum. For example, in textiles and fabrics the tendency was to expect an article to last for a short period only, and durability was not wanted. This taste for short-lived articles 'is said to run through every class of society, and has, of course, a great influence upon the character of goods generally in demand, which…are made more for appearance, and less for actual wear and use, than similar goods are in Britain'.[27]

Generally the theme running through Wallis's comments on American design is that there was an underlying simplicity of form and construction that was being swamped by the impact of European goods, and these ornamented and ostentatious imports were in effect corrupting the designs of the American manufacturers and the tastes of both manufacturers and consumers. If one looks for evidence of this in the illustrations given in the *Notes on the New York Exhibition* by Silliman and Goodrich,[28] it is virtually impossible to find, and this is not altogether surprising since the aim stated in the Preface was to encourage American manufacturers by showing examples of European taste and skill and the value of an alliance between art and industry. An article on furniture from this same source, however, strikes a different note. Here, it is argued, the most comfortable chair or bed is the best, as is the most convenient table or desk. 'Usefulness, therefore fitness, or in other words, the combination of ease, fitness, and propriety, is the first and highest qualification of furniture, as well as of every other object, the chief function of which is not to give pleasure to the mind through the eye.'[29]

This attitude has a familiar ring to those who know Horatio Greenhough's writings on Form and Function. Writing a decade later, Greenhough makes a similar assessment of the state of American design to that of George Wallis. Greenhough saw the products from Britain overwhelming American products with embellishments that defy all principles – 'steam-woven fineries, plastic ornaments, struck with the die, or pressed into moulds' – and American manufacturers had caught the disease, because the British understood the market. If, he said, one compared American vehicles and ships with English ones, then one could see how American mechanics with their simplicity surpassed the English artists. 'Far be it from me to pretend that the style pointed out by our mechanics is what is sometimes miscalled an economical, a cheap style. No! It is the dearest of all styles! It costs the thought of men, much, very much thought, untiring investigation, ceaseless experiment. Its simplicity is not the simplicity of emptiness or poverty; its simplicity is that of justness, I had almost said of justice. Your steam artisan would fill your town with crude plagiarisms, calques upon the thefts from Pompeii or modern Venice, while the true student is determining the form and proportions of one article.'[30] I cite this quotation from Greenhough, not in the context of early writings on functionalism, but as yet another example of the American mechanic's reputation for economy and simplicity, used here by Greenhough to develop a criterion for design.

I hope that by concentrating on the *Report of the Commission on the Machinery of the United States* I have been able to indicate some of the factors relevant to this complex subject – the beginnings of product design.

1 Earl, P. E. 'Craftsmen and Machines: the Nineteenth-century Furniture Industry' in *Winterthur Conference Report* 1973, 307–329

2 Rees, A. *The Cyclopaedia of Arts, Sciences and Literature vol 21* London, 1819 (plates vol 2)

3 Gilbert, K. R. *The Portsmouth Block-making Machinery: a Pioneering Enterprise in Mass-Production* HMSO, 1965

4 Nasmyth, J. 'Remarks on the Introduction of the Slide Principle in Tools and Machines employed in the Production of Machinery' quoted in Musson, A. E. and Robinson, E. *Science and Technology in the Industrial Revolution* Manchester University Press, 1969, 474

5 Ure, A. *The Philosophy of Manufactures* 1837, 37

6 Downes, C. and Cowper, C. *The Building Erected in Hyde Park for the Great Exhibition of the Works of Industry of All Nations 1851. Contractors Fox, Henderson & Co* John Weale, London, 1852

7 *Official Description and Illustrated Catalogue 3* 1851, 1431

8 *The Great Exhibition 1851 Art Journal Illustrated Catalogue of the Industries of All Nations* 1851, 166

9 I am indebted to Rosenberg, N. *The American System of Manufactures* Edinburgh, 1969 (introduction) for these details

10 *Report of the Commission on the Machinery of the United States* British Parliamentary Papers, 1854–5, vol 1

11 Reports are reprinted in Rosenberg, N. *op cit*

12 Quoted in Roe, J. V. *English and American Tool Builders* New Haven, 1916, 132

13 Quoted in Clark, V. S. *History of Manufactures in the United States vol 1 1607–1860* Washington, 1916, 420

14 *Ibid* 419

15 *Ibid* 421

16 *Ibid* 436

17 See Habbakuk, H. J. *American and British Technology in the Nineteenth Century* Cambridge University Press, 1962

18 Beecher, Catherine E. and Stowe, Harriet Beecher *The American Woman's Home* New York, 1869, 307

19 *Ibid* 322

20 Rosenberg, N. *op cit*

21 *Ibid* 291

22 *Ibid* 284

23 *Ibid* 269

24 *Ibid* 270

25 *Ibid* 277

26 *Ibid* 295

27 *Ibid* 304

28 Silliman, B. and Goodrich, C. R. *Notes on the World of Science, Art and Industry Illustrated from Examples in the New York Exhibition 1853–54* New York, 1854

29 *Ibid* 182

30 Greenhough, Horatio *Form and Function: Remarks on Art, Design and Architecture* University of California Press, 1969, 22–23. Originally published as Bender, H. *Travels, Observations and Experience of a Yankee Stonecutter* 1852

A voice for whose choice?

advice for consumers in the late 1930s

Suzette Worden
Brighton Polytechnic

The voice of the consumer was recognised as a significant factor affecting industrial design in the 1930s. In *Education For The Consumer,* the first report by the Council for Art and Industry, Walter Runciman wrote: 'The report shows that they have started by approaching the subject from the standpoint of the consumer for, as they rightly appreciate, the decision of the ultimate purchaser has, in the long run, a most potent influence on industrial production.'[1] This report was published in July 1935 and in many respects it reflected interests already present and previously shown in the Gorell Report and in the conclusions given by the Pick Council. This concern had also been illustrated by a spate of exhibitions in the early 1930s, the aims of which had been to make the general public more aware of design.[2]

The Council for Art and Industry's Report mentioned the need for a discriminating public and stated: 'What is required in the consumer is, first, conscious realisation of the possibility of beauty in things of everyday use, and secondly, quicker understanding and appreciation of it when it is placed before him. Once these conditions are realised, British manufacturers will be encouraged – they may even be compelled – to pay more attention to design.'[3]

The Government was therefore hoping that a vocal public could influence design by their choice of products. The usual way that a consumer could make a choice known was through the 'market-place', with information going back to the designer or manufacturer through the retail trade. Yet, by 1944 it was thought possible that the consumer could voice an influential opinion before the product was made, thus almost contributing to the design process itself. The channels for this information included voluntary and social organisations as well as those with roots in the world of commerce.

During the 1930s the consumer was finding that both the products themselves and the variety of goods on the market were becoming more complicated. It was therefore becoming increasingly difficult to make a choice in terms of the usual maxim of *'caveat emptor* – let the buyer beware'. The kind of institutions that the Government looked to for the measurement of public opinion undertook to supply the necessary information to the consumer in order that a wise choice could be made. So that, at the same time as purporting to give information to the manufacturer or designer, the same pressure groups were giving advice to consumers on how to make a choice. By doing this they were setting up standards by which people were encouraged to judge consumer products.

It is worth remembering that, in the 1930s, it was only the upper-middle-class person who could afford to buy most of the domestic appliances on the market, and all but the cheapest furniture was beyond the means of most people. Information was directed, therefore, mainly at that section of society. Also the associations drew their membership from the socially concerned members of the middle class. Averil Sanderson Furniss had written in her book, *The Homes of the People,* in 1920: 'But even more does the responsibility rest on those

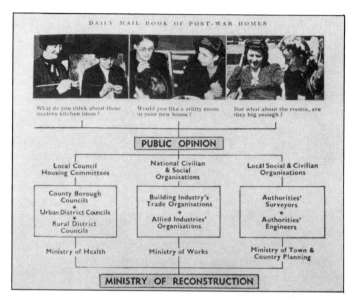

1 *'The Role of Public Opinion' from M. Pleydell-Bouverie* The Ideal Home Book of Post-war Homes *1944, 117*

whose homes are secure, and whose opportunities for education and for leisure are merely roads to selfishness if they are not used as opportunities for service.'[4]

In many cases the same people were directly involved in the running of several associations at the same time. There were also close links between organisations. For example, the Woman's Advisory Housing Council, an organisation which had been started in 1917 by women within the Labour Party, was revived in March 1937. It was supported by 34 societies and its aim was to 'collate the findings of its composite bodies and present them to the Ministry of Health, as the considered opinion of women all over the country'.[5]

The assimilation of the ideas promoted by such institutions and associations would have spread at a quicker rate than the ability to act upon them. Therefore, in terms of the most immediate effect the standards set up would have been the most significant. It is therefore necessary to ask upon what reasoning their judgement was based; that is, was it purely aesthetic or were reasons of efficiency and economy also considered, or was there a mixture of all three?

There were enormous differences in the value systems used to judge, on the one hand, appliances and, on the other, furnishing (within which I include interior decoration). One reason for this was that furnishing had a tradition of the designer being involved in its production and the problems of function had been solved so long ago that their consideration could be minimal up until the early 1930s, whereas appliances were more the work of an engineer; getting appliances to work efficiently was still a problem. This becomes evident if the Design and Industries Association, (DIA) which concerned itself mainly with furnishing, is compared with the Good

Housekeeping Institute (GHI) and the Electrical Association for Women (EAW), two groups which concentrated on appliances.

It is not necessary to go into the history of the DIA in great detail as it has been very well documented.[6] To summarise: the aim was to provide a common meeting ground for manufacturers, distributors, designers and consumers, so that excellence of design and workmanship should be encouraged in industry and mass production. The DIA publicised its propaganda through various journals, year books and *Cautionary Guides,* and periodicals such as *Design in Industry, Design for To-day, Trend* and *DIA News.* Many well-known books written on design in that period were written by DIA members: John Gloag, Noel Carrington and Anthony Bertram are names that immediately spring to mind.

One problem is that, so far, histories of the DIA have tended to come from people within the DIA itself or closely connected with it – that is: from people with a vested interest in supporting the design professions. When the DIA is compared, from the viewpoint of the consumer, with the Good Housekeeping Institute and other similar associations, it becomes evident that although the DIA said that they considered everything by its 'fitness', all information given only referred to appearance. This emphasises a point that is now generally realised, that 'functionalism' as the DIA used the term was very dubious. On the other hand, the Good Housekeeping Institute and the Electrical Association for Women judged design purely in terms of its efficiency; aesthetics did not come into their judgement. Their aims were those of the labour-saving movements in general, and were primarily concerned with improving conditions of health, fitness and hygiene. Courses in cooking, nutrition and household management were run at the GHI and the EAW school (Figure 2). The aim of these courses was to train professional teachers and demonstrators as well as those interested for personal reasons.

An example of this wider concern was the EAW's response to the Government's activities for slum clearance of the early and middle 1930s. They ran an exhibition, in January 1935, on kitchens for working-class homes in the London area.[7]

Advice on choosing household appliances came mostly from groups formed in association with the electricity and gas companies or from magazines sponsored by these companies. In the autumn of 1933 the British Electrical Development Association first published *Electrical Housekeeping* and in the winter of 1936, the first issue of *Fanfare* appeared, representing the Women's Gas Council, an association formed in May 1935. The Electrical Association for Women had been founded in November 1924, on the basis of a scheme that had been formulated by a Mrs Matthews of the Women's Engineering Society.[8] The EAW expressed its views in *The Electrical Age,* which was first published in June 1926. The EAW emphasised the technical side of electricity; it issued a handbook, *The Electrical Handbook for Women,* which first came out in 1934 and had many reprintings, the last one being a completely revised edition which came out in 1971.

The Good Housekeeping Institute was started in September 1924, two years after the first issue of the magazine and was run by the National Magazine Company. The American version had been published two years before the British one. The Good Housekeeping Institute was not impartial, as it serviced the magazine which was, in turn, dependent on advertising revenue. It could not therefore be too critical of the

2 *The EAW school, from Caroline Haslett* The Electrical Handbook for Women *fifth edition 1946 frontispiece*

products of manufacturers paying for advertising space. Even so it was more impartial than its American counterpart.

The magazines sold scientific management through the myth that it would give more leisure. This was the bait used to encourage people to buy more labour-saving devices. George Orwell described women's magazines of the 1930s as having characters 'living several pounds a week above the income of the reader'.[9] This also seems true of the advice given in the magazines described above.

The image of the consumer was the housewife. These magazines did nothing to encourage women to be independent. They reinforced their traditional role of service in the home, away from involvement in production in society.

In April 1924 *Good Housekeeping* wrote on 'the everlasting problem of home management': 'But there is only one really great woman – the homemaker…the task of homemaker is never done…How, then can you overcome them…You never can completely. It is futile to hope for such a thing. But you can make your tasks lighter, your working hours shorter. How? *Good Housekeeping* will help you…it has the necessary facilities and services; it is all a question of using them – when and as often as you need them.'[10]

There was, therefore, a great difference in the aims of the DIA in relation to the GHI and the EAW. In order to examine more closely how they actually judged design I would like, first, to look at the Good Housekeeping Institute for an example of an interest in appliances.

The Institute was run by Mrs D. D. Cottington Taylor until 1940 when Miss Phyllis Garbutt became Director for two years. From 1942 Freda Cowell was Director until 1945 when the present Director, Carol Macartney, took over the post. Mrs Cottington Taylor also wrote cookery books and a book on interior decoration, called *Practical Homemaking,* which was written in the 1930s for Oetzmann's, a large London store which has since closed down. In 1935 she also helped write the British paper given at the Fifth International Congress for Scientific Management. Mrs Cottington Taylor held a certificate of Household and Social Science from King's College for Women and a first-class teaching diploma in cookery, laundrywork, housewifery and high-class cookery. Her successor Miss Garbutt had the same qualifications and was also an associate of the Royal Institute of Chemistry.

The Institute tested all kinds of equipment; a lemon squeezer or a mincer would have received the same meticulous attention as equipment costing from £50 to £60.[11] By September 1934 the Institute had tested 1,050 appliances in 10 years. Each item was observed in use for three months under domestic conditions before it was subjected to specific tests. A list of approved appliances with names of firms able to supply them could be obtained from the Institute for the cost of 2d, which was to cover postage.[12]

No charge was made to the manufacturer and he received a report of the conclusions of the test. If the appliance failed, this too would have been reported back to the manufacturer and, according to the Institute, not infrequently the appliance was modified according to the Institute's suggestions and later resubmitted for approval.[13] The Institute was therefore functioning as a valuable link between the consumer and the manufacturer and was able to pass information both ways.

3 *The Aga model CB, from Herbert Read* Art And Industry *fourth edition 1956, 154*

In doing this the Institute was setting up standards for design. If the appliance passed the tests and upheld the manufacturer's claims then it could be awarded the Institute's Certificate of Approval and the Good Housekeeping Seal could be placed on the appliance. This was, in many ways, an early example of The Design Centre's label.

Knowledge acquired in this way was used in the articles in

Good Housekeeping magazine. Readers could also write in for information to cope with their individual needs. During the month in which the September 1933 issue was going to press the magazine received 2,779 letters of which about half were queries directly concerned with the activities of the Institute.[14]

Readers were able to visit the Institute, which was situated at the top of a block of office buildings near Covent Garden. There were four kitchens used for the testing of equipment and recipes and for the teaching of home management courses. The magazine mentioned that 'Naturally every article does not fulfil the requirements of every household, and we are always very pleased to give further assistance in differentiating between the various appliances and to advise readers regarding choice of what appears to meet their particular conditions most satisfactorily.'[15]

By emphasising the individuality of readers' problems the GHI was not supporting any movement towards standardisation in domestic appliances. Their description of the testing of stoves illustrates this: 'It will be readily understood that with fresh stoves of different types being continually installed in the Institute kitchens for testing purposes, and careful records of the tests being incorporated in our reports, we have, in the course of years, accumulated a tremendous amount of valuable and unique information. Test meals, according to the size of the cooker, are carried out on all stoves, and are designed to check the capacity and economy of the stove for boiling, baking, grilling etc. We undertake more specialized tests if these appear to be demanded. In this way we became aware of differences between cookers, small perhaps in themselves, but sufficient to make one piece of equipment ideal for one household, but not suitable for another.'[16]

What the Institute did notice was progress and a gradual improvement in the design of appliances. The craft of Home Management should therefore take advantage of these improvements. On the design of stoves GHI noted: 'A noticeable feature of many of the newer stoves is the development and increasing use made of insulating materials in order to conserve all possible heat and thus render the stove economical in consumption of fuel.' Economy, efficiency and cleanliness were the watchwords of good design for the GHI.

Reviewing domestic equipment from 1919 to 1935, Mrs Cottington Taylor emphasised economy and efficiency contrasting earlier models with later models, where the design had made them easier to clean and cheaper to run. Of the Aga cooker (Figure 3) Mrs Cottingham Taylor said: 'Although heat storage cookers are often expensive to buy in the first place, the housewife is soon compensated by the saving of fuel and power.'[17] She stopped there but on the same stove, Herbert Read had the following to say: 'But what should be noted here is the way in which these requisites (high efficiency and low running costs) have been ordered into a design of admirable proportions.'[18] He then went on to describe the Aga as an excellent example of architectural principles of design applied to objects in daily use.

On the progress of the design of appliances, which was improving yearly, the movement towards 'streamlining' (I take the word of streamlining to mean *purely* the covering up of surfaces, that is, as design added on) was considered inevitable and American designs were seen as being well ahead of British designs.

Streamlining was seen *just* as progress aiming at efficiency, economy and cleanliness, and not a stylistic end in itself. As

4 *Left: the Flavel 'Kabineat'. Right: the Parkinson 'Renown'. From Michael Farr* Design in British Industry *1955*

6 *'"Good" and "Bad" Ornament' from DIA Pamphlet of early 1940s (undated)*

LIVING-ROOMS: OLD AND NEW

41 The cluttered living-room of the past and a modern example by Messrs Kendal Milne Ltd., with dining table that folds away. Our restless age calls for restfulness in the home. Victorian leisure and domestic staffs could cope with Victorian acquisitiveness and display. We cannot: we must travel lighter.

yet there was no interest in trying to incorporate appliances into furnishing. Mrs Cottington Taylor mentioned two cookers at the Burlington House exhibition of British Art and Industry. These were most probably the Flavel 'Kabineat' and the Parkison 'Renown' (Figure 4). She said that one was so designed that when not in use it resembled a cabinet and might easily be mistaken for a cupboard or a wireless set. She stated that the object of the manufacturer was to provide a cooker that could be used in a kitchen/living-room without striking a discordant note with modern furniture and fittings. So far as the cooker itself was concerned it did not differ from the standard 1935 model. However, Mrs Cottington Taylor would not assess it as she hadn't used it and maintained that that was the only way of knowing the performance of any appliance.[19]

New materials such as stainless steel were also welcomed, but for no other reason than that they were easier to look after. One may conclude that the evaluation of appliances by the Good Housekeeping Institute was entirely in relation to performance in use; good looks were an added bonus.

And now, in contrast, I would like to look at the DIA. The

5 *'Anti-Victorianism in the contrast of "good" and "bad" design' from Anthony Bertram* Design *1938, plates 40, 41*

7 *'The Taste Test' conducted by Margaret Bulley from* Have You Good Taste? *1933. Chairs (correct on right), Bookcases (correct on right), Wineglasses (correct on right), Jewellery (correct on left), Coffee pots (correct on left), Two-handled jars (correct on left), Teapots (correct on right), Voiles (correct on left), Embroidery (correct on left). (Opposite page)*

DIA's judgement of design was very different from the GHI's. Those writing for the DIA looked at artefacts from the point of view of the architect as designer, and this dominated its propaganda. They looked at objects within the context of a total plan whereas the consumer would have looked at new products as single items, to be added to their existing possessions. The DIA had been more inclined to see the answer to problems of design being solved by planning, rather than by the efficient use of an individual product.

The DIA adopted its famous slogan 'fitness for purpose' very early on in its history.[20] But in the 1940s it was still thought to be useful. In 1947 John Grey wrote in an article on the DIA, in relation to 'fitness for purpose', that this doctrine 'always recognised that the job in question might be a practical or an aesthetic one or more often a combination of both'.[21] I would suggest that this balance was not often to be found and that the DIA standards were heavily weighted on the aesthetic side. Its theory said one thing, but the part that the consumer saw would have been a definition of design based on predetermined aesthetic values, thought out in advance and then presented as a *fait accompli*.

The DIA had to solve the problem of how this judgement was to be presented to the consumer. There were three ways in which the DIA encouraged people to look at design in the 1930s. The first was as an orthodox exhibition which was a straightforward object lesson in 'good' (in their judgement) design. DIA members had been active in the organisation of the Dorland Hall Exhibition.

Second, working on a smaller scale the DIA held 'quizzing parties', the invention of J. B. Fletcher of the Birmingham branch of the DIA.[22] Here an assemblage of goods was subject to scrutiny, comparison and written comment.

Third, there was a comparative device in which designs were categorised as 'good' or 'bad'. This was recognised very early on in DIA history as a useful device. In a report of the first general meeting on 27 January 1916, H. P. Shapland was reported to have said, when education of the public was being discussed, that it would be difficult to present the aims of the Association to the public, but one way was to contrast 'good' and 'bad'.[23] An example of this was the DIA exhibition held at Leicester Square Underground Station from 29 December 1936 to February 1937. The DIA report for 1936 described it as an equivalent to the Deutscher Werkbund's 'Beispiel und Gegen Beispiel'.[24] There were many examples of this contrast between 'good' and 'bad' design, but they all had the same message. They were anti-Victorian as shown by Anthony Bertram in *Design* (Figure 5) or they were anti-ornament as in the DIA propaganda booklet of the early 1940s (Figure 6).[25] The GHI had seen progress in terms of evolution, where products only got better; the DIA's idea of progress was one of complete change and a total rejection of nineteenth-century ideas. They wanted an abrupt change of style. More importantly, 'good' design was the work of a designer; a product was not 'good' until art had been put into it.

It is very important to see these judgements of 'good' and 'bad' in their historical context. In some ways they weren't very successful; DIA membership dropped in the late 1930s.[26] This kind of positive versus negative judgement could have been too rigid. Self-criticism first comes in 1944 when Anthony Bertram recognised the danger. In a pamphlet, *Enemies of Design,* he referred to 'Automorphism' where those in a position to influence design were being too dogmatic. That was one 'secret' enemy of design, the second was an excess of logic. Those guilty included designers and architects affected by 'functionalist' doctrine.[27]

The DIA publicised its views in the 'Design and Everyday Life' series on the radio and Anthony Bertram, who was the editor of *Design for To-day*, introduced design on television in 1938. The BBC ran another feature on design which took the form of a taste test. It was documented in *The Listener* and was conducted by Margaret Bulley and Dr Cyril Burt in 1933.[28] This was also about discriminating between 'good' and 'bad' (Figure 7).

During the early 1930s the DIA had supported large exhibitions; towards the latter part of the decade it turned its attention to a smaller, more modest type of exhibition – the fitting out of a showhouse or flat. A great deal of criticism had been levelled at the high cost of exhibits at the Dorland Hall, RIBA 'Everyday Things' exhibition and the Royal Academy Exhibition.[29] The DIA showhouses at Manchester (Figure 8), Birmingham (Figure 9), and Welwyn Garden City (Figure 10) and flats for the Building Centre and for the St Pancras House Improvement Society were all furnished within an established price. For the houses it was about £200 and for the flats it was just under £50.[30]

8 *Parlour House, Manchester, exterior from* Design for To-day *September 1933, 186*

For comparison it is worth mentioning the EAW house at Bristol (Figure 11). This shows clearly the split between appliances and furnishing, as the EAW organised the planning and supply of electrical appliances while the furnishing was dealt with by the firm of P. E. Gane and Co, which belonged to the DIA. In terms of the exterior design the DIA houses were municipal houses, designed to be as simple and cost saving as possible. The EAW house was built privately and with electrical installations cost about £1000. *The Electrical Age* described it as 'modern' but 'not aggressively so'.[31]

Looking at the interiors one can see that the leisure area was considered very separately from the kitchen area by these associations. The kitchen was planned for efficiency. Looking at the kitchen of the Manchester Parlour showhouse (Figure 12) it is evident that the DIA was giving an *impression* of

efficiency – a visual representation of it and *not* an example of a
tested solution. In contrast to this the living area had to show
'good taste' which was in their terms, simplicity of form, and
no ornament (Figure 13 – the living room and Figure 14 – the
parlour). They were also interested in creating an illusion of
space; the accent was on planning. Again the preoccupation of

12,13,14 *Rooms from the Parlour House, Manchester, from*
Design for To-day *September 1933, 187*

the designer as architect is noticeable. The choice of colour, texture and minimum use of pattern were all aimed at getting the feeling of as much space as possible.

The DIA could not consider an appliance until a designer had introduced design into it. So until an appliance had been streamlined – that is, covered up – it could not really fit it into its system of value judgements, which was based on aesthetic considerations.

In conclusion three events were significant in relation to the above account of the DIA and GHI. First, the Government, through the Council for Art and Industry, acknowledged the role of the consumer in *Education for the Consumer*. Second, in 1937, the Women's Advisory Housing Committee re-formed as the need for this kind of channel of communication was recognised. And third, by the mid 1930s, styling had been added to appliances. They could now be considered in aesthetic terms as well as for efficiency. Their acceptance on equal terms with pieces of furniture was beginning.

I would like to acknowledge the help given by the Good Housekeeping Institute.

1 *Council for Art and Industry Education for the Consumer* HMSO, 1935 foreword

2 These exhibitions included the Dorland Hall Exhibition of 1933, the British Art in Industry Exhibition at Burlington House in 1935 and Exhibition of Everyday Things at the Royal Institute of British Architects in 1936

3 Council for Art and Industry *Education for the Consumer* HMSO, 1935, 8

4 Furniss, Averil Sanderson *The Homes of the People* 1920, 49

5 *Fanfare,* vol 2, no 1, 1938, 44

6 The most detailed account is Pevsner's 'Patient Progress Three: The DIA', in *Studies in Art, Architecture and Design,* vol 2, 1968, 227–241. MacCarthy, Fiona *All Things Bright and Beautiful* 1972 and Carrington, Noel *Industrial Design in Britain* 1976 also give extended accounts of the history of the DIA

7 See *The Electrical Age* vol 2, no 19, January 1935, 790–793

8 *The Electrical Age* vol 1, no 1, June 1926 4

9 Orwell, George 'Boy's Weeklies' in *Horizons* no e, 1940, reprinted in *Inside the Whale* 1940 (Penguin edition, 1957, 199)

10 *Good Housekeeping* vol 5, no 2, April 1924, 5

11 'GHI is Ten Years Old' in *Good Housekeeping* vol 26, no 1, September 1934, 42–3

12 'GHI in 1933' in *Good Housekeeping* vol 24, no 1, September 1933, 43

13 *Ibid*

14 *Ibid*

15 *Good Housekeeping* vol 24, no 5, January 1934, 117

16 Garbutt, P. L. 'GHI is Eleven Years Old this Month' in *Good Housekeeping* vol 28, no 1, September 1935, 49

17 The Director 'Domestic Equipment: 1910–1935 in *Good Housekeeping* vol 27, no 3, May 1935, 43

18 Read, Herbert *Art and Industry* Faber & Faber 1934, 154

19 The Director 'Domestic Equipment: 1910–1935' in *Good Housekeeping* vol 27, no 3, May 1935, 146

20 It was reported in the minutes of the DIA Council meeting of 27 January 1916, that Sir Robert Lorimer's suggestion for a motto for the DIA 'fitness for purpose' was received favourably and not formally adopted but left for the executive committee to digest. (DIA archives, DIAP/2/22(ii))

21 Grey, John DIA Pamphlet (reprinted from *Art and Industry,* December 1947) 2

22 *DIA Report* 1936, 6

23 DIA Archives, DIAP/2/24(iii)

24 *DIA Report* 1936, 6

25 Other examples of this contrast between 'Good and Bad' design include: *Design for Today,* August 1933, 148 and 149; September 1933, 168; November 1933, 281; April 1934, 152–153; January 1936, 19–22. The DIA *Cautionary Guides.* DIA 'Register Your Choice' exhibition, Charing Cross, March – June 1953. Carrington, Noel *Design and a Changing Civilisation 1935,* plate V. Bertram, Anthony *Design 1938,* and *Design in Everyday Things,* 1937
Outside the DIA examples include Yorks, F. R. S. *The Modern House* 1934, 17 and 23. Holme, Geoffrey *Industrial Design and the Future* 1934, 34 and 139

26 See Pevsner, N. 'Patient Progress Three: The DIA' in *Studies in Art, Architecture and Design* vol 2, 1968, 236

27 Bertram, Anthony *Enemies of Design* 6–8

28 Holmes, Sir Charles, 'Can Taste Be Taught' in *The Listener* 18 January 1933, 76–82 and February 8 1933, 217. Bulley, Margaret 'A Test in Taste' *The Listener* 27 December 1933, 1001–1002
The test is also documented in Bulley, Margaret, *Have you Good Taste?* 1933

29 For example: 'What are Everyday Things?' in *Studio,* 1936, 285 and *Design for Today,* August 1933, 152

30 See the following articles: 'Cottages at the Building Centre' in *Design for To-day,* September 1933, 185; '3-Bedroom Flat Furnished under £50' in *Trend,* vol 1, no 2, Summer 1936, 114–115; 'A Parlour House at Manchester' in *Design for To-day,* September 1933, 186–7; 'The Designer and Her Problem: (v) Furnishing for £200' in *Design for To-day* September 1933, 175–184; Wright, H. G. 'Two Hundred Pounds: An Experiment in Furnishing' in *Design for To-day* May 1934, 177–183

31 See the following articles: Pheysey, M. E. 'An All Electric House in Bristol' in *Design for To-day* January 1936, 5–8; Newman, Dorothy 'The EAW All-Electric House Building at Bristol' in *The Electrical Age* July 1935, 888–889, and October 1935, 920–921; 'The EAW House at Bristol How the Enterprise was received by the Public' in *The Electrical Age* January 1936, 19–26; 'The EAW House, Bristol: the Owners' Impressions' in *The Electrical Age* Winter/Spring 1936, 338–9

The politics of advertising

Jon Bird
East Ham College of Technology

There seems to be a considerable discrepancy between the descriptions that advertisers offer of the social and economic functions they believe they perform, and their role as perceived by critics of the mass media. However, certain inadequacies also restrict the effectiveness of most critical arguments. In this paper I am interested in exploring the way in which attempts to reveal the cultural significance of public images reveal the conflict in the encoding and decoding of the message. Part one examines positions for and against advertising; part two is an attempt to consider some of the theoretical bases for these positions, to relate them to the broader context of a communicational model, and to suggest what criteria might be applicable for a more thorough analysis of the long-term cultural significance of advertising images.

The history of advertising has been regularly documented, since H. Sampson's *History of Advertising* was published in 1874, to E. S. Turner's *The Shocking History of Advertising,* published a decade ago. That advertising had a 'history' in the 1870s, and that it was considered 'shocking' in the 1960s, says something about the development of the assessment of the 'persuasion business'.

It is not my intention here to pursue a historical analysis, although it is perhaps worth mentioning, in passing, that the two major factors which led to the development of large-scale consumer advertising in this country, in the latter half of the nineteenth century, were the introduction of basic education for all sectors of society – thereby providing the message receivers; and the 1885 Act that abolished tax on newspapers and advertising – thus providing the message channels. The message source, the motivation and the intention all derive from the growth of capitalistic economies. In the West this has reached the point where profit *per se* is no longer the primary aim, but has been superseded by the goal of the well organised (and well ordered) society; the elimination of sharp social contrasts through the satisfaction of needs and desires, which are themselves carefully stimulated and nurtured; and the universal accessibility of goods. Within our society, 'freedom' is depicted as a function of material possession (which is partly true), while what is concealed is that removing all obstacles between the individual and an interesting and enriching way of life requires, not simply this object or that one, but every object. As Eric Fromm sees it: 'The process of consumption is as alienated as the process of production.'

In 1965, Italian radio carried a message of hope for all those to whom washday activities had merely represented the quest for 'whiteness', 'brightness' and 'cleanliness'. A new detergent was on the market which, so it was claimed, 'washed with a sense of responsibility'. I'm afraid that I have no evidence of the effectiveness of this slogan. What is clear is that such messages are part and parcel of societies where the mass media operate to carry information to all social sectors. If we think of advertising as a code mediating between the consuming public on the one hand, and the thing to be consumed on the other, then an attempt at decoding the form and content of the adver-

tising message should provide a way of revealing both its symbolic structure and its ideological function. Before this can be attempted, however, it is necessary to know some of the expressed aims and criticisms of the activity, and the structure and form of communication of advertising messages.

Advertising, as a socio-economic and cultural force, does not want for critics, apologists and interpreters. The range of views expressed extends from outright condemnation, through structuralist and semiotic analysis, to defensive positions both inside and outside the industry. Thus John Berger sees public images as offering a false idea of freedom; the apparent diversity of choice and option extending only to product selection. 'Publicity as a system', he maintains, 'only makes a single proposal...that we transform ourselves, or our lives, by buying something more.' On a similar note, Fred Inglis, in *Imagery of Power,* attacks advertising as a manipulative force in the hands of a powerful minority, selectively describing and shaping reality so that images symbolically represent the dominant group's ideology.

'What we find...is the harmonious interaction of advertising and editorial styles which consistently reproduce the consumers' way of life...The style is also a code of manners and it follows, a structure of values. The values transpire in the objects named and illustrated, and in which they are possessed. Simply put, the values are extreme wealth, sexual attractiveness and rapacity, and competitive success. Attainment of values is signalled by acquiring the appropriate objects, using them, throwing them away and acquiring replacements...What the styles of advertising do is tie the human behaviour which subtends the economic system to the human needs we all feel. Extravagance, greed, careless waste, prodigal consumption, needless change, become both the means to, and the experience of, imperious human wants: to love and be loved, to be safe, to be at home, to have friends, to be wise, to command one's life. At the same time the circle of advertising information is tightly closed to the intervention of such questions as "Who goes short when you produce more? Do we need what you produce? Who pays for you anyway?" Such questions cannot of course be asked, because it is the nature of total systems that they close the circle against alternatives. This is what totalitarianism means.'

The combative position held by Inglis is typical of most critiques of advertising. The language is rhetorical, implying that any satisfaction or pleasure to be derived from material possessions bears no real relation to perpetual human wants and needs. The act of consuming is seen as being enforced rather than natural, and a rejection of advertising messages or the posing of alternatives is impossible. Certainly the images of advertising symbolise social stereotypes, and the more this process becomes culturally embedded, the closer it moves to what Roland Barthes terms 'myth...a mode of signification' whereby it becomes increasingly hard to question its social forms. However, before any attack on advertising is proposed on the grounds of the values it implies, the critic would be well advised to consider that how an object or image signifies for an individual is a direct function of his or her coding of social reality. Consequently the equation Berger, Inglis and others make between advertising and social meaning seems, on the face of it, over-simplified and too reflective of their own ideologies. Although attractive at the level of theory, I would feel less confident about its factual validity.

A fairly standard defence of advertising is to be found in the introduction to an American publication by D. S. Warner and J. S. Wright – *Advertising*. The book serves as an introductory text for students of advertising, marketing and management. The introduction is written by Norman Strause, Chairman of J. Walter Thompson:

'These critics (of advertising) often centre their objections on ideological grounds. They contend that advertisers encourage people to purchase things they do not really need or place too great an emphasis on material values. To make such a statement is to presume to pass judgement on what possessions the common man is entitled to have. It is, in effect, an attack on our consumer-orientated economic system, which for the first time in history promises to make material comforts, and even luxuries, available to great masses of people rather than to the elite few...Advertising's objective is to enable people to imagine themselves as having a more fortunate lot in life, to realise the desirability of things they do not have, and to be willing to work hard to get them. It is this released energy which creates the wealth of nations and distributes it most broadly...It is natural that primary use of income tends to be for material possessions. But these provide only limited satisfactions, and the next move is inevitably towards a better life in cultural terms: expenditures for travel, music, literature and art...the consumption of culture will be our next economic breakthrough. The fulcrum that lifts the economy steadily upward with rising incomes for millions of people and increasing taxes to support governmental investments in public good, is increased consumption. Without the force of advertising to sell our unlimited capacity to produce, consumption would level off and perhaps decline.'

Despite the pre-inflationary context of these utterances, and the consequent economic naivity which fails to equate rising incomes with rising prices, the otherwise level-headed, reasonable and insinuating tone is as indicative of the concealed ideology as is the combative rhetoric of Inglis. It is the language of the copywriter – the language of persuasion. Thus there is the implication that the advertiser sides with the 'common man', protecting him and his best interests against critics who would strip him of his rightful possessions; there is the ethic of hard, 'honest labour' to realise personal comfort and well-being and the chauvinistic application of this ethic on a national scale for the 'good of the country'; there is the recognition that money is first and foremost to obtain basic material essentials, but that, having satisfied the physical self, the spiritual self has also to be catered for; and, finally, all of this is described as a natural and harmonious process resulting from 'increased consumption'. In the language of capitalism, it's 'the way things are'. Finally, the intrusion of big business into the arts has been well documented elsewhere. The advertiser knows full well, as is evidenced in the many juxtapositions that occur in publicity images, the benefit of an association of a brand or product-image with a cultural object. Elsewhere in this book the authors leave the reader in no doubt as to who these critics of advertising are –'the intellectuals' who 'have voiced scorn of the market-place since the days of Pericles'.

Both these positions are exemplified in an attack on an advertisement for Thorn Lighting (Figure 1) by Inglis, and the subsequent defence of the chosen image by the company. The advertisement depicts a furnace worker in dungarees, the light from the furnace behind him creating strong chiaroscuroesque contrasts. He is centrally positioned in the composition, facing the viewer and looking directly at him. The headline states – 'Some places it takes guts to work in', and the body copy leads

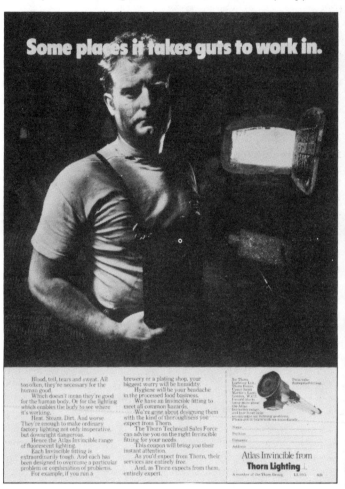

1 *Advertisement for 'Atlas Invincible' range of fluorescent lighting by Thorn Lighting*

into a description of Thorn Lighting with the phrase – 'Blood, toil, tears and sweat'. Inglis has this to say about it: 'The picture of the steelworker seems to me an outrageous insult. It is beautifully taken: the suggestion of inconceivable and satanic power in the rich coincidence of white-orange heat and blackness, the fine face picking up on the far, unexpected side the light, and the powerful forearm glowing golden on the same side, the realistic detail of the sweaty vest, the grimy cheek, the rivulets on the man's strong face strongly marked and clefted, full of a lived, vivid experience. The photographer has learned from Rembrandt these dramatic concentrations of colour and light and he has thrown over the picture that high gloss which romanticizes the subject and puts at a distance the smell, the dirt, the destroying conditions of work. And this, these techniques, this man's life are called in the service of selling industrial lighting in a colour supplement!'

The reply runs as follows: 'If one can't illustrate a factory worker when selling a product designed for the factory, whom may one show? Or does the crime lie in illustrating him well? Or in attempting to sell factory lighting at all?

'Difficult questions, and Mr Inglis's commentary isn't helpful. In one breath he describes the picture as "realistic" (sweaty vest, grimy cheek, etc). In the next, he claims that it romanticizes working conditions, putting smell and dirt "at a distance" beneath a high gloss. A critic's critic might say that he was making *ex post facto* rationalizations of a preconceived thesis, and twisting them to suit his text at that.

'The advertisement is designed to sell Atlas lighting, but the suggestion that it demeans the worker shown, by calling "this man's life" into service, is well below the belt. He isn't being placed in thrall, nor crucified on capital's cross of gold: he is standing in front of a camera for a few hours. And the product is intended to profit him, as well as Atlas, by improving his working conditions.'

Neither argument really convinces. However, from what is implied, but not actually stated, in the arguments, emerge the two most significant factors in any analysis of advertising and its function within society as a system of meanings. These are: first, the encoding and decoding of the image, particularly both the manifest and latent content (what might also be termed the denotative and connotative aspects of the image); and second, the need to consider advertising contextually – that is, not in isolated examples, but the total system and its place within the socio-economic and cultural framework of society. One approach to these complex issues is suggested by Varda Leymore in *Hidden Myth*. She looks on advertising as a modern equivalent to ancient or tribal myths, in Levi-Strauss's definitions as 'the resolution of potential conflicts'. Advertising, like myth, is a conservative force that seeks to maintain established behaviour patterns by proving that the socially dominant ideology is the best. Leymore stresses that the impact of the message on the receiver is dependent upon the total system of advertising messages: 'The message of a single representation will not get through unless it possesses a complete underlying structure.' Furthermore, Leymore recognises the relevance of manifest and latent content in the advertisement, the latter providing the 'key' to the psychological meaning of the message: 'The discourse between advertisers and between advertiser and viewer is carried out not only on the well-recognised surface level, but also on the deep level...while neither is consciously aware of the reality or the existence of this other perception, it is nevertheless there.'

Hidden Myth is based on the assumption that advertising can be regarded as a sign system. This emphasis on totality echoes the comment of McLuhan that 'the medium is the message'! No study of any aspect of the mass media can afford completely to ignore McLuhan, despite the limitations of his overall 'post-Gutenberg' thesis.

Briefly, McLuhan sees advertising as a steady trend towards manifesting the product as 'an integral part of large social purposes and practices'. Advertisements themselves have tended to become increasingly iconic – 'compressed images of a complex kind' – a development which has in turn influenced the presentational format of factual information – 'news' – in journalism generally. McLuhan constantly stresses the psychological effect of advertisements, an effect which he compares with the principles of brainwashing. 'Advertisements are not meant for conscious consumption. They are intended as subliminal pills for the subconscious in order to exercise a hypnotic spell.' Furthermore, the creation of each advertisement represents the combined skills of professional commentators who base their messages on multi-disciplinary research into the formation of public stereo-types or 'sets of established attitudes'. McLuhan's emphasis upon the primacy of the image as the bearer of latent content leads him to dismiss most other critics of advertising for their essentially 'privatist and individualistic' approach based, he believes, on a literary decoding of text: 'The unconscious depth-messages of ads are never attacked by the literate, because of their incapacity to notice or discuss non-verbal forms of arrangement of meaning.' This is antithetical to all advertising messages that present communal life-styles or social codes. (Any contradiction this might imply for advertisements that stress the individualistic associations of products – the 'stand out in a crowd' appeal – is answered by the fact that the message is aimed at a group whose members *all* wish to see themselves as acting individually, but not, as would be the case of the individual, really standing out from the crowd as deviationary and outside social norms.)

McLuhan sees the cumulative effect of the medium as ordering our consciousness in an overall manner which far outstrips the effect of any single image or individual transmission. Within McLuhan's world, individual contents are irrelevant, and his pronouncements on form are, consequently, often criticised as if they expressed a judgement on content. Thus applying McLuhan's conclusions to, say, newspaper or periodical advertising, the style of the advertisement signifies the social universe the paper and its readers actually, or aspire to, inhabit.

It is evident that the arguments against advertising generally stem from a belief in the manipulative resources available to advertisers and their operational effectiveness in the market-place. All advertising has as its final aim some action on the part of the consumer. This can vary from the indirect acceptance of an idea or an attitude towards a company or a cause to the direct action of coupon posting or the purchasing of the product. How valid are the fears of the critics, and how justifiable the claims of the advertisers? Does the persuasive process really work? In order to try and answer this question it is necessary to look at the role of research in advertising and its sources in general communications theory, sociological theory, and psychology.

In general terms, the purpose of research in advertising is the conversion of the advertising process from one-way communication to two-way communication by supplying feedback from the market-place or the consumer to the maker or

Diagram 1

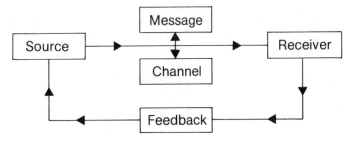

seller. Diagram 1 represents the basic components of the communication process which are:

1 Source – the originator of any message

2 Message – the information and/or the meaning being transmitted

3 Channel – the medium of transmission (newspaper, poster etc)

4 Receiver – the destination of the message (to whom it is addressed)

5 Feedback – the process whereby the response of the receiver to the message is assimilated, either psychologically or behaviourally, by the source

Diagram 2

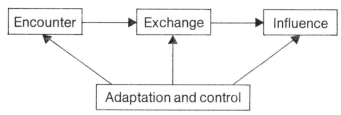

Diagram 2 represents a communicational model incorporating all of the above. Briefly the stages are as follows:

1 Encounter. The initial phase of communication includes all the information available to both the source and the receiver and thus structures the potential encoding and decoding process. In order for the message to be successfully transmitted, the source and receiver must share common codes. Encounter also includes the channels of communication: information is relayed from the source to the receiver through the social (including cultural) spatial and the mass media networks with which they are connected.

2 Exchange. All aspects of the message, specifically the flow of shared meanings from source to receiver through a set of symbols (words, images etc).

3 Influence. The psychological and/or behavioural impact of the communication. This is measured by a comparison of the individuals' attitudes or behavioural patterns to an object or situation before and after stages 1 and 2.

4 Adaptation and Control. The effectiveness over a prolonged period of time of encounter, exchange and influence – of great relevance to advertisers who wish to maintain attitudes or buying habits to branded products for a long time. Because of the extended nature of complex production runs, it is essential that consumer buying habits maintain a consistency and predictability, thus a great deal of advertising seeks to maintain brand loyalty. (For a full discussion of communications theory see N. Lin, *the Study of Human Communication* 1973).

To summarise, the function of all public messages, including advertising, can be seen as attempts to induce individuals and/or groups, to enter into particular relationships with certain products or ideas.

From considering the nature of the communication system in general, I want to turn to the structure of the particular set of messages with which this paper is concerned – the advertising message. Most, if not all, advertisements are constructed according to the AIDCA formula – that is, image and text should fulfil the requirements of:

A = Attention
I = Interest
D = Decisive
C = Credibility
A = Action

In concrete terms these appear in the actual structure of advertisements as;

1 Headline and/or Illustration. The means of gaining the attention of the audience. A great deal of market and motivation research aims to pre-select the main group characteristics of message receivers. Advertisements arouse potential consumer interest by either benefit news or curiosity, or a combination of these. Until recently this was mostly achieved by a headline supported by an image. However, advertisers are now tending to recognise the priority of the image over the text in the receiver's decoding of the message.

2 Amplification of Headline. The bridge from reader or viewer interest to product interest.

3 Explanation of Claims. How the product fulfils the promise offered – why the reader or viewer should be interested in the product.

4 Proof of Unusual Claims. The evidence to support any claim that might not stand by itself, or that requires further elaboration or explanation.

5 ...Further Advantages. In the form of incidental or additional merits of the product.

6 Closing. The idea of interest to the advertiser and, most importantly, a suggestion – implicit or **explicit** – for further action by the consumer.

Not all advertisements follow this complete outline. Outdoor poster sites, because of their limited scanning time, concentrate on points 1 and 6. Their form is usually that of a linguistic message, or headline, in some kind of relationship with an image, or iconic sign. The function of the linguistic message in poster ads is either that of 'anchorage' or 'relay'.

I should mention here that these terms are derived from Roland Barthes' *Rhetorique de l'image* (1964), as well as their analytical function. When I began this research, Barthes' description seemed adequate for the purpose of categorising the primary relationships of text and image in 'l'image publicitaire'. However, I'm now far less enamoured of it, particularly with regard to some recent poster campaigns.

In the case of anchorage, the text operates at the surface level to select from all the possible range of signifieds those which have meaning in the particular context. The text thus clarifies the possible denotations of the image by allowing the viewer to choose the right perceptual level. Simply, it answers the question 'What is it?' At the deep or symbolic level, the text functions not as identification, but as interpretation, serving to limit the connoted meanings of the image. An obvious example would be the Consulate cigarette ads with the headline 'Cool as a mountain stream' which serves, with the image, to remove possible unwanted signifiers of smoking – health hazards, smell etc. Barthes sees the text as the power the originator of the message has over the image (a power which in turn reflects the dominant codes or ideologies, within the society). 'Faced with the projective power of shapes, and the use made of the message, anchorage is a control, it is responsibility; in relation to the freedom of the signifieds in the image, the text has a repressive value, and we can see that it is above all at this level that the morality and ideology of a society enter.' The function of relay is when the text and image stand in a complementary relationship, the text serving to explain, develop or expand on the significance of the image. The text is not among the connotations we might expect to be summoned by the image alone. To return to the six points of advertising structure, points 1 to 5 constitute the body text which acts to convert reader or viewer interest and curiosity already aroused by the headline/illustration into product interest. Body text employs a combination of 'emotional' and 'reason-why' writing. The former stresses the benefits and satisfactions to be had from the product whereas the latter is based on rational or common-sense argument – how the product works, how it is made, how it saves time etc – and supports product claims with specific or 'objective' statistics, case histories, expert opinions, guarantee offers, and so on.

Having considered the concrete structure of advertisements, and an aspect of the decoding process, I want to turn to the use made by the advertiser of motivation research, or the intended psychological meaning of the message. It seems that there is little point in discussing manifest and latent content from the receiver's end only without some knowledge of what was intended prior to the communication.

Advertisers, in common with most public message senders, have long recognised the importance of an understanding of human motives and desires as an aid to effective communication. An example is the play that World War One propaganda made on the fears, hopes and aspirations of the potential recruit and those most likely to influence him – family, friends, school, etc – in terms of 'honour' and 'patriotism'. Vance Packard thoroughly castigated the use of motivation research in advertising in *The Hidden Persuaders* (1957) (see also J. Meerloo *The Rape of the Mind* 1956). Discussing the questionable morality of employing the insights of psychiatry and the social sciences to sell products, Packard hurls Zolaesque accusations at the advertisers: 'What', he asks 'is the morality of playing upon hidden weaknesses and frailties – such as our anxieties, aggressive feelings, dread of non-conformity, and infantile hang-overs – to sell products? What is the morality of exploiting our deepest sexual sensitivies and yearnings for commercial purposes?' And he concludes: 'The most serious offence many of the depth manipulators commit…is that they try to invade the privacy of our minds.'

Packard's fury came long after the 'depth manipulators' first began their devious [sic] tasks. In 1895, Harlow Gale, Professor of Psychology at Minnesota University, was attempting to discover 'the mental processes which go on in the minds of consumers from the time they see the advertisement until they have purchased the article advertised'. Soon after (1903) an early classic was published in this field – Walter Dill Scott's *The Psychology of Advertising*. These early works adopted a tone of high moral fervour married to a strongly behaviouristic approach: 'One of the most unpleasant things that can happen to a bicycle rider, and one of the things that might deter some ladies from buying a bicycle, is this fact that bicycle riders are liable to be chased by dogs. The writer of this advertisement (Figure 2), by means of this illustration, practically tells every possible customer to hesitate before she buys the wheel, because, if she buys it, she is likely to be chased by dogs.'

The copy style of this ad is strongly associated with music hall oratory through the empatic use of alliteration, whilst the product name has an orthographic structure – that is, the deliberate breaking of a rule of language, in this case the misspelling of 'bicycle' as 'racycle' – which gives a distinctive written symbolisation. Despite the obvious historical charm of this example it is, perhaps, significant that both these features are now recognised as advertising clichés. A further example

2 *Advertisement for the 'Racycle' by the Miami Cycle and Manufacturing Co (Copyright: The British Library)*

3 *Advertisement by Thomas Cook & Son, Chicago (Copyright: The British Library)*

from Dill Scott serves to illustrate another primary feature of advertising research and development – the notion of group identity. (He has this to say about the ad shown in Figure 3): 'In the advertisement of Thomas Cook & Son I do not think of the old lady and gentleman as being of my class. They are not my ideals and I therefore have comparatively little sympathy

COOK'S TRAVEL SERVICE

Cruises in Cool Latitudes

NIAGARA TO THE SAGUENAY

Fourteen Delightful Vacation Days, including such points
of interest as Toronto, Alexandria Bay; among the Thousand Islands by daylight and moonlight; down the noble
St. Lawrence and its thrilling rapids to Montreal. Then

A WONDERFUL SIX-DAY CRUISE

on the magnificent steamship "Cape Eternity"—ex-
clusively reserved—to the Saguenay River! Quebec,
Lakes Champlain and George and the Hudson River
conclude a tour of beautiful scenic routes unparal-
leled on this continent. Tours start from Chicago
July 17th and 31st, August 14th and 28th. From
Niagara Falls one day later. Early reservations
advisable.

Ask for Particulars of Escorted and Individual Tours to
CANADIAN ROCKIES—ALASKA—PACIFIC COAST—
NATIONAL PARKS—EUROPE—BERMUDA—SOUTH
AMERICA—JAPAN—CHINA

THOS. COOK & SON, CHICAGO
203 South Dearborn St.

4 *Advertisement by Thomas Cook & Son Chicago
(Copyright: The British Library)*

with them. They are enjoying themselves immensely and
probably never had a better time in all their lives than they are
having as members of this touring party, but as I look at them I
am not pleased at all. Their pleasure is not contagious as far as
I am concerned. I seem to be immune from all their pleasures.
I have no desire to imitate their actions and become a member
of Cook's Touring party.'

In contrast, Dill Scott has this to say about the other
Thomas Cook advertisement (Figure 4): 'The two persons
depicted in this second advertisement approximate my ideals.
They seem to be enjoying the trip immensely. I believe that
they have good taste and if they choose this cruise for their
vacation the same trip would be desirable for me too. In every
case of sympathy we imitate to a certain degree the persons
with whom we sympathise. The action of these young people
stimulates me to imitate their action by purchasing a ticket
from Cook's and starting on the trip.'

The belief in the motivating force of unconscious or subconscious desires over behaviour patterns has resulted in the

various attempts by advertising research to specify primary
and secondary human needs. In many instances this had led to
an over-emphasis upon mechanistic models of social
behaviour. Terms like 'reinforcement' and 'habit' constantly
recur. The analysis of consumer brand preferences, for example, has been conducted on the understanding that continued reinforcement reduces thinking in behaviour patterns,
leading to a stimulus-response automatism. Recent research,
however, has revealed that consumers exercise a wide range of
preferences over brands, the factors affecting any one decision
being both complex and, frequently, unpredictable. Advertisers have come to recognise that the satisfaction of
physiological needs may frequently be delayed or superseded
by social, or other, secondary motives. The broad public that
advertising messages are aimed at are seldom subject to overpowering survival drives. The individual desperate for food is
hardly likely to concern himself with the kind of dish it's eaten
off. In *Public Opinion and Propaganda* (1958) Leonard Doob takes
up this point: 'Some stimulus…makes the individual aware of
the fact that he is hungry. Such a drive, however, does not
function by itself; he almost always has no generalised craving
for food but seeks a particular kind more or less in accordance
with his everyday existence. He wants food, but an attitude-
induced drive must also be satisfied. The goal response – the
eating of the food – is then determined both by the hunger
drive and the accompanying attitude. As an individual, he will
be completely satisfied only when the tension produced by
both drives is reduced.'

The 'tension' related to attitudes that Doob refers to is
derived from the notion of 'cognitive dissonance' in communications theory. As I stated earlier the advertiser is interested in creating a relationship between the product and the
consumer. Consequently, the consumer is seen not just as the
purchaser of the end result of processed raw materials, but as
also, and necessarily, 'possessing' an image of who uses the
product, where it is manufactured and distributed, and the
social values its purchase has for him or her. In order to encode
all of these factors in the advertisement the advertiser, as the
message source, has to be aware of the nature of the communication process. In this context, the notion of tension or
dissonance derives from the need in the individual to maintain
a balance or equilibrium amongst his various cognitive
elements or states. We tend to resist change, particularly if it
threatens or conflicts with our basic beliefs and values. Failure
to do so can result in unpleasant or painful psychological ten-
sions which we seek to reduce. We are selective in our
perception and interpretation of messages, even to the extent
of deliberate distortion or misinterpretation. The advertiser
will, therefore, pre-select the general characteristics of the
message receivers so that the advertisement is so coded to correspond with the psychological make-up of the groups he
wishes to contact, but at the same time this selection will
preclude other social groups for whom the messages create
conflict. These considerations are particularly relevant for
messages likely to create strong dissonances – for example,
anti-smoking or health campaigns. In the case of, say, seat
belts ads, there has not, as yet, been any allowance in the encoding of the messages for differing group models of social
reality. Some people may not wear seat belts because of a
suspicion that the actual act of wearing them somehow
'tempts fate'; psychologically they signify the bearers of ill-
tidings and omens – portents of disaster.

Speaking more generally, it seems that the latent content

of advertisements corresponds to the deep level at which the individual is psychologically constituted. However, it is also the most speculative and hardest to support empirically, although it is the most far-reaching in its implications for the long-term effects of public images. As Barthes says, it is the level at which ideology and morality enter.

Communications theory distinguishes between 'attitudes' – the psychological states of the individual – and 'behaviour', defined as an overt gesture indicating a person's preference and commitment in some observable activity – such as buying a product. The major gulf between motivation research – concerned primarily with attitudes and attitude-change – and market research – the location, extent and buying habits of consumer groups – is that attitude and behaviour do not correspond on a one-to-one basis. I referred earlier to the complex nature of some buying patterns. In *How Do We Choose?* (1976), Mary Tuck compares more recent methods with her personal experience of the informational approach of J. Walter Thompson in the early 1950s, expressed in the belief that it was only necessary for a new product to offer an advantage that other, similar, products lacked, for the public immediately to change brands. The belief that people operated rational systems of choice in their buying habits, shifting from product to product according to the advantages offered by competing advertising was radically affected by research into voting behaviour conducted in the USA in the 1940s and 1950s. The famous Erie County survey on voting behaviour in the 1940 presidential election campaign uncovered the fact that only an insignificant proportion of the population (8 per cent) actually changed their voting intentions, and that these attitude changes were not the result of mass media information, but the influence of families, friends and co-workers. From this and later surveys, emerged a 'multi-step flow model' of communication – that is, ideas flow from the mass media through several relays of 'opinion leaders' who communicate among one another and then to a broad range of 'followers'. Further research into the characteristics of opinion leaders has been of great value to advertisers anxious to know which sections of the public are likely to be most responsive to their messages.

To summarise, then, it is clear that advertisers have, over a considerable period of time, attempted to refine their messages to correspond as closely as possible to the psychological 'make-up' of identifiable consumer groups. If it were actually the case that motivation research made pertinent use of all the recent developments in such areas as the behavioural sciences, cultural and structural anthropology, post-Freudian psychology and so on, then Vance Packard would, in retrospect, seem not only to have got it right, but to have grossly understated his case. Although American marketing journals abound with research papers from all these disciplines and more, the relationship between the theory and its practical application seems, at best, tenuous. There is little research into the effectiveness of actual advertisements, most of it being directed to the analysis of choice, but not to the more far-reaching query underlining the action itself: why do we consumers consume? There are no satisfactory explanations from either the supporters or critics of capitalist economies as to the cultural significance of consumption. There is no return to the state of the 'noble savage'. Mary Douglas, the social anthropologist, has argued that consumer choices represent moral judgements about ourselves, our immediate social environment, and the world at large. 'Consuming', she says, 'is finding consistent meanings.' Earlier, I suggested that advertising seeks to create relationships between product and consumer. This notion can be extended so that goods represent systems of social relationships, and consumption represents the individual's progress towards self-identity and means of self-expression. In this light, the 1960s slogan of 'You are what you eat' has particular significance; but we are not only what we eat, but also how we dress, travel and live – the totality of the way we use goods in our society. And advertising, to a great extent, mediates this process, for it tells us, symbolically, the social, economic and cultural value of the types of consumption in which we are involved.

The context for design history

John Blake
Design Council

I thought I ought to explain that the title of this paper – 'The Context for Design History' – does not really convey what I want to talk about. It came about (as so often happens) because a title was urgently needed for the printed programme, long before I had even begun to think about what I might say.

It would have been more accurate to have called it 'The boundaries of design history', for I want to look at the spectrum of design activity as it occurs today and to discuss some of the implications of this spectrum for your roles as design historians.

I should explain that I feel very much an outsider in this gathering. I am not myself a design historian, and I hope therefore that you will forgive me if I make some assumptions in developing my argument that you may believe to be wrong. No doubt you will not be slow in putting me right.

My work in the Design Council is concerned with the role of design in the industrial society we live in today, and which our children and grandchildren will live in tomorrow. Nonetheless I believe profoundly in the importance of design history, for a greater understanding of the past is an essential input to our understanding of the present, just as an awareness of what is going on now will obviously influence the way in which we look at the past.

We are, among other things, as many of you will know, a publisher of books and magazines on design, and we are beginning to publish a few books on design history. We would like to extend this in the future because we think it will support our work, particularly in creating a more widespread understanding that between the extremes of the two cultures there is a third. This is what Bruce Archer has called the material culture and which in Germany is described as *technik* – the application of abstract knowledge and creative imagination to the practical needs of society. It is often said that it is the low regard in which the concept of *technik* is held in Britain, in comparison with some of the more successful industrial nations abroad, that has been largely responsible for our economic decline during the twentieth century. Our experience at the Design Council supports this thesis, for design is at the centre of the *technik* idea, and we are therefore much concerned with ways of generating a greater appreciation of its importance, especially in educational circles.

And if you were to analyse the work we do at the Council in advising manufacturing companies on the design of their products, you would see we are involved in persuading firms to use, or to apply, on the one hand knowledge and understanding of what is happening in the visual arts and, on the other, information that stems from research in science and technology. In effect all we are doing is to push a little further forward a process which is happening all the time, to help companies to do just a little bit better than they were doing before. Thus *technik,* and therefore design, not only stands *between* the two cultures of the arts and the sciences, but is dependent on and continuously informed or fed by them.

My point is that if design history should take account of what is happening in design today – as I have argued it should – then it must certainly take account of what I would regard as the two most fundamental inputs to the design process: the visual arts at one extreme and the sciences at the other.

Now, I appreciate that the history of design has grown out of the twin disciplines of the history of art and the history of achitecture, and that more recently, perhaps, there has been a growing interest among design historians in the influence of technology and other factors such as economics, social studies, politics, environmental considerations and the like. I also believe that there have been some conflicts and arguments arising out of these different points of view, the ins and outs of which I don't pretend to understand.

What seems to me to be of profound importance is that the history of design should encompass all these aspects so that sooner or later you begin to get a kind of coagulation of ideas into a recognisable body of knowledge which can be unequivocably labelled 'design history' – not as an appendage of the history of art, not as an appendage of the history of architecture, not as an appendage of the history of technology or of anything else for that matter – though with obvious connections with all these things.

But how can this somewhat all-embracing philosophy be translated into a programme of study in which there is some general agreement on where the boundaries lie? There is first the time boundary. You might disagree with me, but I have always felt that, in the sense we understand the term today, 'design' grew out of the Industrial Revolution. Of course, tables and chairs and buildings, weapons, ships and vehicles of various kinds were designed and made for thousands of years before the changes we now call the Industrial Revolution began to take place. There is evidence, I believe, that series production and the division of labour had reached a high level of sophistication even in Roman times. But I guess that so much material from before the Industrial Revolution exists within the histories of art and architecture, and so much since then still remains to be done, that this would not be a matter on which there would be much serious disagreement, though I would be interested in your view.

The secondary boundary concerns the range of subject matter that might be considered appropriate to the history of design. Everything made by man, whether or not industrial processes are employed, must first have been designed – even if the design exists only in the mind of the maker. But it does not follow that everything that is made is therefore legitimate territory for the design historian. Yet there are large and important areas of design activity that, in my view, should form an essential part of the history of design, but which so far have been largely ignored or inadequately treated.

To disentagle this ball of territorial wool, and to help in defining the territorial boundaries of design history, I think we have to look at the nature of design – or the process of designing as it is generally understood today. Let us take a simple example to begin with. A piece of kindling wood chopped from a log has been designed, since the person who makes it must first have a mental plan of its approximate dimensions, which will be related to the dryness of the log and the size of the fireplace. A plan for something to be made is an essential ingredient of design, but it is also an ingredient of other things – a piece of sculpture for example, or a painting – and we must distinguish between design and art.

To qualify as a 'design' an object must, I believe, be useful in a practical sense in addition to any artistic or symbolic qualities it may or may not possess. The piece of kindling wood is useful, and it has been planned, but only in a rough and ready way. Each piece will differ from the next. It therefore lacks definition and is not repeatable with any accuracy. Apart from being a trivial example of little permanent value, these are exactly the qualities you would expect from a hand-thrown pottery jug, or a number of other craft-made objects.

The ability to repeat the production of an object with reasonable accuracy seems to be an intrinsic aspect of our understanding of the term 'design' today, and I would therefore rule out many of the useful crafts in which small, accidental variations are often the very qualities that differentiate them from manufactured items. Note that I said the *ability* to repeat, for there are many items which may be 'one-off' productions, but which are *capable* of being repeated by virtue of the fact that a precise prescription has been prepared – as in a special piece of production equipment, for example.

So design concerns the preparation of accurate plans for useful objects which are capable of repeat production and which may or may not have artistic and symbolic qualities. That still leaves a dauntingly large field, including, for example, the enormous raw materials industries, the pharmaceutical and food industries and others. A rolled out sheet of steel, a quantity of plastics moulding powder, an aspirin, a hamburger, a jelly baby – all fit the tentative definition above, and indeed the chemical formulae for a particular type of steel or a drug are certainly designs of a kind. Are these proper areas of concern for the design historian? They could be, but I don't think they should be. My reasons arise from the consideration of the third boundary and I will therefore come back to this point.

My third boundary concerns the span of knowledge and skills needed to design modern industrial products. I have talked about the preparation of plans. What I believe we have to do is consider how designers go about this task. Let us take a fairly commonplace product like a washing-machine. The designer's problem, one might say, is to design a machine that will wash and partly dry a quantity of laundry. But no sooner have you said this than there is a veritable explosion of questions and ideas. What quantity of laundry? How dry is partly dry? What kinds of laundry? What part of the market? Which countries is it aimed at? What will be the target selling price? What mechanisms are available? Are new mechanisms required? How many washing or drying programmes are needed? How can *our* product compete with other products? And so on.

You can sort these questions into groups. There are economic questions, social questions, market questions, legal questions, technical questions, ergonomic questions and aesthetic questions – and possibly a few others as well. Some of the answers will come from within the competence of the designers and some from other sources – but whatever the origin may be, they will all affect the way in which the designers go about their work. I say designers (in the plural) because for such a product a variety of design skills or competences are needed and these are seldom today encompassed by a single designer. For example, one designer will be required to design the mechanical systems, another will be needed to design the electrical or electronic control systems and yet another to design the casing and controls to meet all the aesthetic and ergonomic requirements – and all must work within the constraints of the company's production facilities and overall cost limits. And they must all work together with an understanding of one another's needs, so that the finished product ends up as the physical expression of a unified idea.

Now if we examine the areas of expertise or skill encompassed by the design team, we will see that two – the mechanical and the electrical designers – have a scientific background. They have to be competent in physics and mathematics and they also require a fairish grounding in chemistry, for they must study the interactions of different washing powders and different types of water with the mechanical wash and dry systems, and the effect of these systems on the particular yarns and dyes used in the materials likely to be washed. They gain such knowledge partly through their aptitude for science subjects at secondary school, but more importantly through their studies at colleges of engineering.

The third designer will have a rather different set of accomplishments. He will almost certainly have been good at art or handicrafts at school, and may also have achieved an average competence in maths and physics. His professional training will have been at a college of art and design at which the emphasis will have been on the aesthetic and ergonomic aspects with sufficient engineering training to ensure that he can translate his particular contribution to the work of the team into practical production solutions.

My point is that all three members of this design team had an important contribution to make to the finished product – and without any one of them the product would have been inadequate in one way or another.

I think we can draw some conclusions about the nature of design from this example. First, as I have already argued, the primary inputs of knowledge in the design process stem from the visual arts, at one extreme, and from science at the other. These can be represented as the opposite poles of a continuous spectrum. Second, by and large, designers operating towards the artistic end of the spectrum work primarily by a form of cultivated intuition and flair; while designers operating towards the other end of the spectrum work from scientific laws and principles to achieve measurable and predictable results. Third, somewhere near the middle of the spectrum there is an overlap where art-based designers work alongside science-based designers, so that they merge almost imperceptably together. Fourth, because it is a continuous spectrum, and because the overlap spans an enormously wide range of product types, it is impossible, in my view, to draw a line at some point on the spectrum and say anything on this side is legitimate territory for the design historian, while everything on the other is not.

And finally— design work in all parts of the spectrum is equally subject to the constraints and influences of economics, politics, law, environment, society and the like, and in turn affects *them* in a thousand and one different ways – thus contributing to a more realistic integration of design history with other historical studies.

I have possibly laboured unduly this concept of a design

spectrum because I suspect that design history has still a long way to go fully to recognise the importance of design engineering in its spectrum of studies, for I am not talking about the influence of science and technology on industrial design, but the evolution of an entirely separate stream of design expertise derived primarily from the physical sciences. I don't know to what extent this science-based designing has been taken in under the design historian's wing, but if it hasn't, I am quite certain that another kind of design historian is likely to emerge from those concerned with the history of science.

For what seems to me the most fascinating and absorbing characteristic of design is the fact that it spans the two cultures in a way which is quite unique in the modern world. It is not therefore two branches of two separate trees we should be aiming for, but a new tree planted firmly in the middle of the design spectrum – a design tree in its own right whose branches will reach out to span the range of design inputs to the process of creating useful products.

The concepts of a spectrum can, I think, help us to answer the question I posed earlier: if sheets of steel and drugs and plastics materials and certain foods are by definition *designed*, should they not be legitimate subjects for the design historian? The answer on the whole is no, because they occur at the extreme edges of the spectrum and are more related to pure science, or maybe to fine art, than they are to design, and will almost certainly be the subject of specialised historical studies of their own – in pharmacy, metallurgy, gastronomy, nutrition and the like.

In any case society, in its pragmatic way, has already sorted out the problem on commonsense lines – so that we don't tend to talk about drug designers or food designers or metal designers, but we do talk about textile designers, furniture designers, machine tool designers and aircraft designers. And to make matters easier for us, the designers of buildings decided to call themselves architects.

So I think we have a few territorial boundaries for design history, even if the boundaries might be a little fuzzy here and there. I would include those areas of the crafts which seem more related to design than to fine art; the whole of industrial design, stretching from those industrial products which have evolved out of the traditional crafts like textiles or pottery to those products embodying new technologies; engineering design, including the three basic skills of mechanical, electrical and electronic engineering but falling short of those products which seem more related to pure technology or science than to design. Architecture I would regard as having so much in common with design for industry that there will be large areas of overlap, though you could argue that it should really occupy a place of its own.

It is a curious fact, bearing in mind the very large number of engineering designers at work in Britain and other advanced industrial nations, that so far as I know, there is no general history of engineering design and comparatively few general histories of engineering. Even more curious, perhaps, is that if you want to become an engineering designer there are only about a couple of courses in engineering design in Britain which you can go on.

This may well account for, or maybe result from, the absence of a discrete profession of engineering design within the wider context of engineering as a whole. As I am sure you know, if you obtain a general degree in engineering there is a wide variety of postgraduate or career options open to you. You may become a production engineer, a research and development engineer, a test engineer, a maintenance engineer, or you might go into management and become a sales engineer or whatever. *Or* you might want to become a *design* engineer – to be involved in the conversion of materials and component parts into products. The only way at the moment in which you can become an engineering designer is to join a manufacturing company and acquire your design skills through experience on the job – a slow and somewhat hit and miss process. Which is why the Design Council has been working to establish a series of engineering design courses – ideally we think at postgraduate level because an engineering designer cannot begin to practise effectively until he has first acquired a considerable understanding of science and technology, for these are the tools of his trade.

Yet far more economic value, far more wealth, stems from the work of engineering designers than from all the industrial designers and architects put together. The Industrial Revolution was essentially a revolution in the development and application of technology – and applied technology *is* engineering design. And while much has been written about the great eighteenth-century and Victorian engineers, there is precious little historical study of the explosive developments in engineering design in the late nineteenth and twentieth centuries, except in areas where they impinge on architecture.

So here it seems is an extensive and largely unexplored piece of territory waiting for the design historian. Without it the history of design is not just incomplete, it is distinctly lopsided. Moreover, I believe that the historian who is concerned with engineering design has a powerful role, not only in helping to define engineering design as a professional activity in its own right, but also in exploring its importance to the survival of our society in the longer term.

There are other aspects, too, which I believe need to be considered – not least of which is the interaction between engineering design and industrial design. There would have been no industrial design, in its true sense, without engineering design, and while, in the earlier years of the Industrial Revolution, engineering design was concerned largely with the creation of machines to produce the kind of consumer products that were previously made by hand, increasingly the end products of industrial activity have been engineering goods in their own right – but engineering goods in which *industrial* designers have had a part to play.

Indeed, I believe that one of the less fortunate aspects of the Industrial Revolution in its later phases was the increasing separation between the specialisms of industrial and engineering design. And while I believe that it is inevitable, because of the explosion of knowledge and the incapacity of the human brain for encompassing it all, that there will be a continuing branching of new design specialisms, it is all the more necessary to create the relevant connections when different specialisms must come together in the same product. An understanding of how this process has come about is an important part of the mental equipment needed to cope with the increasingly difficult and challenging design problems which are likely to arise in the future.

There is one further point I wish to make which seems to me to be of fundamental importance to the design historian, but which I think may have been overlooked. The Industrial Revolution was a key phase in the development of modern societies because it pointed the way to the creation of hitherto undreamt-of wealth – and it did this by producing goods in vast quantities and selling them at a profit.

The alchemist's dream of transmuting base metal into gold was in fact the essence of all modern industrial economic theory – and indeed one might say that the basic role of the designer in industry is to devise means of transforming or converting base materials into products in such a way that the original value of the materials is increased sufficiently to cover all the conversion costs and to add wealth to the company, and thus to the nation. The designer who does not satisfy this requirement is failing in his primary responsibility, and if this happens on more than a few occasions he will be out of a job.

Of course, in reality, the processes of industry do not work in this simplistic manner, but nevertheless the creation of wealth is the underlying objective of all industrial activity, of which design is a crucial part. The economic objectives of design activity are therefore fundamental to any realistic design theory and thus to any realistic view of design history.

But today the economic objectives cannot be separated from the daunting array of constraints and problems for which the designer must accept his rightful share of responsibility. There are many evils that have come about as a result of ignorant and thoughtless developments in technology. But the problems of technology will require better technology to solve them – they will not be solved by modern-day Luddites, or by the cult of primitivism.

These and many other constraints on, and consequences of, design are all part, I believe, of the design historian's canvas, for they all contribute to our understanding of the development of our material culture.

So, to summarise these somewhat rambling thoughts, I am suggesting three things.

First, that the context for design history should increase in width to embrace the entire spectrum of designed and manufactured artefacts and that some priority should be given to what one might call the history of applied technology, since this is a largely neglected field.

Second, that the scientific or technological stream of design development should not be seen in isolation from developments in the art-based stream of industrial design – for although they have become separated in our modern thinking, I believe the interaction between the two streams is of special importance and could reveal much that would inform our present-day thinking.

And third, that the economic context for design needs special attention, though not to the detriment of the social, environmental, legal, political and other aspects, all of which are important. I am not clever enough, I am afraid, to suggest how all this can be accomplished within the meagre resources available for studying design history today. All I can say is that history, as it were, is on your side, and while it may be possible at present only to look at isolated aspects in depth, sooner or later somebody will come along to fill in the gaps and to create the links between different points on the design spectrum.

Stylistic analysis and its possibilities

Stuart Morgan
Brighton Polytechnic

I should like to begin by reminding you of the famous story about Brancusi, Léger and Duchamp visiting the Salon de l'Aviation installed next to the Salon d'Automne at the Grand Palais in 1912.[1] This is Léger's version of what happened: 'Marcel a silent sort of chap – you never knew what he was thinking – inspected the engines and propellers without saying a word. Then suddenly he remarked to Brancusi, "Painting's washed up. What painter could improve on that propeller? Could you, could any of us, make anything as good?" He adored *real* things, so did we all, but not so fanatically as he…' And, Léger adds in an aside, 'Personally, I was more attracted by the engines and metallic parts than by the wooden propellers.'[2]

In looking at the propeller, a genuine, optimistic desire for some democratisation of the art object battled furiously in the artists' minds with the condescension which marked their moment of perception as an act of visual appropriation. Each would struggle vainly to arrive at a point in his aesthetic where an encounter such as this would not be subsumed by previous expectations of art. Even Duchamp, whose later work would attempt a full-scale problematics of objects, felt the need to erect an invisible museum around the propeller in order to make the comparison, so obvious to him if not to us, between engineering and painting.

In one way affectation was involved in even venturing into the aviation section. By accident the paintings had been placed alongside the aeroplanes that year; the three artists were indulging in fashionable 'slumming', and of all the visitors to the Salon de l'Aviation these three had most difficulty in seeing what was in front of their noses. Later, in 1918, Léger was to take propellers as the subject of a painting. It could be argued that his whole career is compromised by the head-on collision of ideas and medium. Later he would make plans for painting entire cities in different colours.[3] Only in his writing was he free. Brancusi was the sole member of the triumvirate who could have made a wooden propeller himself. As the century proceeded, critics began to realise that their picture of him as a modernist in search of Platonic essences was to be undercut again and again by an alternative Brancusi, the Transylvanian shepherd who believed in black magic and who carved tables and furniture for his own studio.[4] Here his characteristic action was either to use these handmade objects in daily rituals such as cooking, or to subject them to that protracted caress which other people called sculpture. By the 1960s his work was once more a major influence – not his birds or his women, as in the 1930s, but his furniture, columns and semi-architectural plans. Duchamp too remained unassimilated until the 1960s, when his art was plundered but, more significantly, adopted as a cultural model – a reaction which shows signs of continuing into the 1970s.[5] If he belonged to that category of artists summed up in Frank Kermode's phrase 'the modernism we neglected', a main reason was his repertoire of reactions to objects and machines.[6] Apollinaire announced that Duchamp's work would heal the breach between art and society, and in some ways he is correct; Duchamp asks the right questions, those which should have occurred to him while considering the propeller.[7] If his answers are obscure or just plain wrong, in his works and in the organisation of his career he discovered a strategy for putting on ice the doubts and ambiguities he felt.

The modernism we neglected is the modernism we put aside. 'These fragments I have shored against my ruins', wrote T. S. Eliot in *The Waste Land*.[8] Ezra Pound provided a sarcastic correction, rewriting the line in his *Cantos*.[9] Not 'shored' but 'shelved' is the term he applies to Eliot's frame of mind. In the course of time the way of thinking which made 'culture' into a library and placed wooden propellers on invisible pedestals underwent a change.

To say it was superseded would be to use a metaphor of replacement which rings a false note; my own allegiances lie with scholars who suggest that the way of 'modernism' was to map out its perimeters, then remain within them in a way best described by the adjective 'post-movement'.[10] Paradoxes were involved in the concept of an avant-garde, permanently reacting against cultural fixity, and there are as many in a picture of a situation without stylistic imperatives – of 'radical eclecticism', in Jencks's phrase, where change no longer has to be described in terms of revolutions and avant-gardes, political and military metaphors, and 'eclecticism' is not 'radical' in any meaningful sense.[11]

The situation I am describing demands descriptive images which do justice to the felt lack of coherent cultural fabric, yet which do not imply deterioration. Venturi and Rauch describing Las Vegas write in this way: 'The Las Vegas casino is a combination form. The complex program of Caesar's Palace – one of the grandest – includes gambling, dining and banqueting rooms, nightclubs and auditoria, stores and a complete hotel. It is also a combination of styles. The front colonnade is San-Pietro Bernini in plan but Yamasaki in vocabulary and scale; the blue and gold mosaic work is early Christian tomb of Galla Placidia. (The Baroque symmetry of its prototype precludes an inflection towards the right in this facade.) Beyond and above is a slab in Gio Ponti Pirelli-Baroque, and beyond that, in turn, a low wing in a Neo-Classical Motel Moderne.'[12]

This collage approach to naming styles was pioneered by Leslie A. Fiedler and before him Parker Tyler, who employed Surrealist juxtapositions from the 1940s onwards. The element of play in such writing is meant as an *aperçu*, the start of an interpretation.[13]

On a more serious level, the metaphors for culture as a whole change in this new situation. Edgar Morin replaces Gombrich's organic structure in which every part is related to every other, like a formalist art-work, with the image of a screen. He quotes Abraham Moles in his *Sociodynamique de la Culture*, who uses as a comparison the random distribution of magazines on a dentist's waiting-room table.[14] As well as absence of stylistic pressures the image draws attention to the impossibility of dialogue between the separate elements that compose the picture.

The trend away from a prescriptive approach, foreshadowed in literary criticism by Wellek and Warren in their *Theory of Literature* of 1942 and defended fully by Northrop Frye in his *Anatomy of Criticism* in 1957, is another aspect of the waiting-room table image. The equal status of all evidence facing the critic, whose task was not felt to imply an hierarchy of value-judgements, led to a situation in which it was easier for the propeller to figure as an object worthy of confrontation on its own merits. A date for this would be unexpectedly late. That artistic 'dematerialization of the object' which Lucy Lippard dates between 1966 and 1972 had as its end result, not the downgrading of the tangible as a focus of critical attention, but simply the acceptance of a greater number and variety of physical manifestations of the art work.[15] Though featured as works of design, the 1931 Bugatti, Buckminster Fuller's Dymaxion car and the STP Lotus Turbocar which occupied prominent places at the Museum of Modern Art's exhibition 'The Machine as seen at the End of the Mechanical Age' in New York in 1968 is a hint that cars were achieving the status of contemporary works of art. A less ambiguous approach is presented years later in Robert Pirsig's bestseller *Zen and the Art of Motorcycle Maintenance*. His view of design objects strains to avoid traditional Western dualisms such as subject versus object, mind versus matter, art versus science, and classic versus romantic. Pointing out that the Greeks never separated art from manufacture, Pirsig argues that by means of the act of work the 'observer' places himself in an active rather than a passive position, close enough to imply, not only a perception of the godhead, but simultaneously a caring intimacy with artefacts on a nuts and bolts level. His subject throughout is 'good craftsmanship', but rather than idealising the work and launching an attack on technology in the accepted polemical style of the early 1970s, he highlights the adjective 'good', returns it to its original moral realm and tries to allow it to suffuse all planes of reality.

Design history exists at that specific historical moment signalled by a post-movement approach, a name for which matters only to the extent that titles betray theories behind their composition. Talk of 'neo-modernism', 'late modern' or 'post-modernism' seems to assume continuity, a sensibility dependent on a previous stage.[16] If circumstances decreed that design history was to be an offshoot of art history, it is worth adding quickly that the nearer the present, the more the methods of art history are subject to criticism within the discipline itself. Two of the most swingeing attacks of the mid-1970s came from the British art historian T. J. Clark and an Australian publishing in New York, Terry Smith.[17] While Smith wrote of 'the dreariness of much contemporary art history, its blandness, conformity, painful obviousness' and 'fake style of certainty', Clark described its state as one of 'genteel dissolution'. In each case remedies were prescribed: Smith felt strongly that the reluctance to rethink methods and an unmistakable distaste among art historians for issues in contemporary art was to blame; Clark felt that unless some means of access was discovered to questions which occupied the founding fathers of the discipline, no improvement could be expected. In their day men such as Dvorak, Burckhardt and Riegel – dim figures, misunderstood and mistranslated – still had powers to open up fields of enquiry closed to present practitioners. Concluding that fear and prejudice keep us from drawing on the early masters, Clark asks 'What kind of a situation is it where my working copy of Riegel's *Spätrömische Kunstindustrie* is a miserable, abridged Italian version?'

The problem of method is there to be shouldered by design historians. They are once more in the position of the three great moderns regarding their propeller, except for added advantages accruing from the edge of that enclosure, the line of demarcation within which the post-movement artists now work. When finally assimilated, that mislaid modernism provided not an antidote but a missing section of jigsaw puzzle, with the addition of which the simultaneous presence of a modernism lasting at least 50 years came into view. The propeller is still there but the context has altered.

Despite a modern respect for fragments or the chance which produces the kind of *objet trouvé* which marks a chic vernacular approach to interior design even to the present – the fashion photographer in Antonioni's *Blow-Up* in 1967 buys a propeller and takes it home – emphasis may more properly be placed on an entire vehicle rather than on one crafted part.[18]

Difficulties accompany any act of analysis and the parallel procedure of fitting the conclusions into a pattern of thought. Does classification take place according to surface features (whether it is a monoplane or a biplane), according to the designer, who may have made six different kinds of aeroplane, but may also have made tables or boxes or electric irons; according to the country of origin or the type of engine that powers it or the principle of powered flight on which it is based (a glider may be found to resemble many types of plane with engines); or simply the date when it was made? Any act of criticism in design history seems comparative. In setting one aeroplane against another it will be found that they differ according to designer or firm or the uses for which they are envisaged. The Sopwith Camel will be designed according to a canon of priorities quite separate from the Jumbo Jet, for example. The nearer the present the date of the object in question is, the fewer the *national* characteristics.

Conscious sorting may go on before or after 'analysis' proper but is obviously a very important consideration, providing a context for the object, a background of expectations. If it happens before, then the analysis will be generic. If it happens afterwards, then a more extensive view will be sought within the definition 'aeroplane', establishing a distance from Leonardo da Vinci, the Montgolfier Brothers and a large duck, on the basis of ideas as distinct from objects, man-powered flight as relative to engines and progenitors as irrelevant or ineligible. Special categories with their own characteristics would be hovercraft or helicopters.

Just how vital this sorting can be is illustrated by one section in this year's 'Documenta 6' exhibition at Kassel in Germany. Under the heading 'Utopian Design' the organisers put on show cars in two categories, by professionals and by artists. The differences are sometimes less obvious than one would expect. The artists have built their utopian vehicles with the expectation of expressing personal feelings about modern life, about cars as fetishes or lethal machinery or embodiments of energy and space. There is a noticeable split between those who work on the basis of an open model like a child's construction, those for whom the car is a miniature room, and those concerned with creating an entirely abstracted, unpowered 'idea' of a car. In other words, there is a range of contexts into which these objects demand to be sorted. Yet the shared ground between art and design is obviously important, on which the tendency towards a 'utopian' situation for creation exists, apart from considerations of money, comfort, durability or use on the one hand and those created with a view to expressing emotions. At least one of the artists, the Belgian Panamarenko, has said that his car is not exhibited as art because it was 'logically' devised. The plans for new models of machines for professional companies, on the other hand, seem futuristic and cold, with the qualities we expect of machines themselves devised by other machines. (In the case of General Motors this is partly true; a computer was used.) The organisers' categories and subdivisions – their equivalent of the 'sorting' I have tried to describe – are reduced to nonsense by the objects themselves. When preliminary sorting is followed by analysis, the question arises of whether it is possible to find a method which would be valid for propellers and paintings, for Panamarenko and General Motors.[19]

The type of analysis traditionally undertaken by art history depends on the idea of style, a term invariably associated with form rather than content. The use of specifically expressive characteristics in speaking of styles leads to particular problems with art-forms where no 'content' is present; the derivation of the word is, after all, from *stilus*, a writing instrument. The process of arriving at an artistic '-ism' involves assuming the *same* content and simply an alteration of manners of expression. In a medium like literature there are immediate problems. Whether or not it is still a general rule in linguistics that every formally different utterance differs in meaning I am not certain, but if this is so, then a term such as 'style' is obviously redundant.[20] One lesson to be learned from this is that the definition of a style involves a process of comparison of individual variations on a basic model. The art historian Meyer Shapiro wrote: 'By style is meant the constant form – and sometimes the constant qualities and expression – in the heart of an individual or group…the style is above all a system of forms with a quality and a meaningful expression through which the personality and the broad outlook of the group are visible.'[21]

If the key words here are 'constant', 'group' and 'system', the static association of all three indicates that the incapacity of stylistic definitions to cope with change may constitute a major drawback. In fact, they manage by interpreting the history of forms as a series of rises and falls, decadences and rebirths. Yet the resulting picture is of only one strand in a more complex interweaving of many styles in a variety of states. Through the confusion may come leading debates – topics which emerge crabwise from between opposing points of view. It could be that in this way new paradigms – Thomas Kuhn's expression – are thrashed out and tested like scientific discoveries.[22] Nevertheless, our means of mapping these, like the method of fixing a style, is to compare similar elements, seeing what they have in common and how they differ.

The suggestion that sorting, 'the means of classification which isolate artistic events into groups and sub-groups for ease of handling', is a mechanism by which myth operates in art history is made by Jack Burnham.[23] A consequence of his idea that art history has a mythic structure is that for this reason 'all objects which possess at least some of the traits of art become art objects'. In his terms, then, the very processes I have been describing serve art history; more than any other device, that of historically orientated stylistic categorisation feeds the myth. 'Newly discovered art objects are, if possible, incorporated into the concepts of object, style and history. When a radical adjustment is necessary, it is made by defining a new stylistic concept, leaving other styles essentially undisturbed.' Burnham calls style the '*bête noire* of art history' and

attacks the vagueness of concepts of style and wilfully ignored inconsistencies. The latter point has to do with the vexed questions of generalisation in history; inconsistencies are unavoidable in any idea of history as an art, not a science. Though Burnham attempts to demonstrate how the reasons for assigning styles are put into operation, in this section he appears to want history to function as a set of strict definitions.

The relevance of the term 'style' is the result of its breadth of application, especially its connection with language. 'Style' remains an equivocal term because of its dual function of suggestion 'heart' and 'manner'. In common usage it also has a normative sense – 'stylish' and 'having style'. The opposition between ornament and substance appears to be uncontrollable, like 'styling' and function in a design discussion. Linking style with 'manner' avoids any sense of applied irrelevance, focusing on the relevant choices open to a designer – pressures of history, knowledge, resources, the brief before him, and so on. But as the *result* of an understanding of style, this will work only by avoiding the individual.

Criticism as a science seems undesirable; the confrontation with objects of daily use does not involve the 'aesthetic' standing-back to which the three men felt compelled when faced with their propeller. However, the scientificity could take the form not of a method directed at isolated works – Burnham's procedure – but an analysis of the way the work achieves meaning, bearing in mind the factors which determine how it can do so. The role of art in society or the use of an object would naturally be emphasised.[24] Three approaches seem to satisfy the requirements outlined, and though they may seem extreme, 'pure' ways of providing co-ordinates for any 'new' object with which we are presented, the main assumptions behind the theories they put forward may be admitted without necessarily pushing each to its conclusions.

The first is semiotics. Saussure's dream of a science which studied 'the life of signs within society' suits the study of design, and the search to find a language outside evaluation in which any object is potentially analysable seems appropriate to a concentration on style.[25] How far a purely formal analysis would lead is more questionable, however.

A second approach is represented by George Kubler in his book *The Shape of Time*, which begins with this remark: 'Let us suppose that the idea of art can be expanded to embrace the whole range of man-made things, including all tools and writing in addition to the useless, beautiful and poetic things of the world. By this view the universe of man-made things simply coincides with history of art.'[26] Kubler, an expert on primitive cultures, treats objects as the debris of history, taking his examples from areas such as pre-Columbian pottery.

The third approach, which I intend to dwell upon at some length, is a more unusual angle and, in the twentieth century at least, a singularly unproductive topic in aesthetics – that of comparisons between the arts.

If style, as stated earlier, involves a 'process of comparison of individual variations on a basic model', one great historical nuisance is that this model changes constantly. This has led some hopeful critics in quest of a single denominator.

Picking up that dog-eared volume mentioned by Clark, Riegel's *Late Roman Art Industry* will return us at once to the age of great debates and to one of the great hopefuls. In his book *Abstraction and Empathy*, written in 1906, the German art historian Wilhelm Worringer made it clear that Riegl was the first man to question the authority of what was then the accepted work, Gottfried Semper's *Stil*. Riegl's innovation was the concept of 'artistic volition', an inner urge throughout history, independent of objects, though directed towards their creation. While Semper's history of art remained a 'history of ability', Riegl's consisted of a 'history of volition'. Differences in style in previous ages could now be understood not as a result of lack of skill but because of variously directed aims. When Worringer claims the psychology of art as an undertaking equal in importance to the history of religion, we are at the heart of a truly heroic conception of what art history can do. At only one point, however, is any entrance provided to what we now understand as design history, and it is exactly at this point that he is most indebted to Riegl. In his chapter on ornament Worringer writes that it offers 'as it were, a paradigm from which the specific peculiarities of the absolute artistic volition can be read off'.[27] Worringer's proposed yardstick will obviously change, since styles change, but will always be 'ornament', an abstraction based on evidence from an area common to art and design.

The weaknesses of Worringer's suggestion can be gauged by a comparison. In his book *Style and Civilizations* A. L. Kroeber presented an analysis of changes in women's dress from 1797 to 1936. He found long periods of high variability alternating with periods of low variability, and connected the high variability with extreme political tension. 'What I call the "basic pattern" of modern Western women's dress style…is a conceptual construct, empirically derived from the phenomena of the history of Western fashion. It is also an ideal implicit in the style itself, a half-conscious value sought for by the style. And intellectually, it serves as a "model" by which to explain and better understand a complex series of happenings.'[28]

Kroeber would be the first to admit that only in relation to fashion would it be possible to employ the 'basic pattern' he goes on to use, a visual lowest common denominator subject to the unceasing variation synonymous with fashion. Worringer proposed ornament as a 'basic pattern', yet the nature of change – in the visual arts, at least – seems more radical, so much so that it would be unreasonable to expect a 'basic pattern' approach. The aims are different; whereas Kroeber is trying to show fluctuations in a single form, Worringer, more ideally, seeks a yardstick by which to establish terms for styles which percolate through every aspect of a culture.

The daring suggestion of a 'reading off' point seems to run counter to common sense. Ornament, he is saying, is where alterations in stylistic climate can be discerned. Yet when such changes of weather come about, the darkness of the sky or the bright sunlight will be evident at more than one small point. When Panofsky indicated the relationship between Gothic architecture and scholasticism he was explaining the concrete realisation of a cosmology, a 'visual logic' by which forms of artistic creation were conceived of as an actualisation of thought processes. The 'logic' could apply equally well to mathematics, music or philosophy. In Panofsky's description Gothic is 'circumstantial, explicit and ornate'. It is a frame of mind as well as a force governing visual appearances.

'A man imbued with the Scholastic habit [he writes] would look upon the mode of architectural presentation, just as he looked on the mode of literary presentation, from the point of view of *manifestatio*…But he would not have been satisfied had not the membrification of the edifice permitted him to re-experience the very processes of architectural composition just as the membrification of the *Summa* permitted him to re-experience the very processes of cogitation. To him, the panoply of shafts, ribs, buttresses, tracery, pinnacles and crockets

was a self-analysis and self-explication of architecture much as the customary apparatus of parts, distinctions, questions and articles was, to him, a self-analysis and self-explication of reason.'[29]

Verbal pyrotechnics are necesssary to recapture some of the exhilaration of such a totally unified aesthetic in which scrutiny of visual artefacts is part of an undifferentiated continuum. Yet despite the longevity of Pythagorean-Platonic thought structures in the Western tradition he is registering no more than a coincidence of patterns of creation within the Gothic style.

In 1972 the magazine *New Literary History* published an essay called 'Periodisation and Interart Analogy' by Professor Alastair Fowler, an authority on numerological examination of Renaissance poetry.[30] Though the issue was planned to explore the topic of comparison between the arts, not even the editors held out any hope that it would constitute a fresh look at the subject. Fowler's contribution seems to me to be a very daring one indeed.

He argues that the 'individual qualities' of a work of art can be recognised only after referring it to its 'social and artistic matrix of patronage, fashion and period tendencies'. Periodisation is not merely an unnatural category, imposed rather than felt; criticism is bound up with cultural history to the extent that it should be concerned 'as much…with contrastive fields and rejections of the norm as with similarities'. In a theory which assumes a complete parallelism of the arts, the perception of an essence is felt to be enough to gauge a period. (Spengler, Wylie Sypher and Mario Praz are critics who work in this way.) Yet it is obvious that there are time-lags between arts. These provide support for opposition to total parallelism, but suggest that perhaps a simple theory will not do. Yet some certainties emerge; literature always precedes the other arts; in Fowler's words, its 'anteriority…seems invariable'. Panofsky stated that no date means the same in more than one country. Periodisation faces the permanent dilemma of whether to classify works by 'their real spatio-temporal dispositions' or by their 'relations within the fictive world of art'. The fault of the first is its arbitrariness, that of the second its taking for granted all kinds of prior critical acts. In practice the two methods intermingle, but Fowler is in no doubt that, although it would be more difficult, periodisation would be more rigorous if it were to 'renounce this option of switching at will between the two methods'. Another problem is provided by E. H. Gombrich's reminder that periodisation is always normative; we always define styles in terms of their departure from norms.

Fowler opts for presenting existing terms for period styles, at least as items to be tested. The only firm ground for interart analogy is style. Analogy involves a metaphor, a translation, and the metaphor has to be sound. Periodisation has to be conceived 'in terms of a convincing model of the artefact'. Period style is there to be replaced as definition proceeds. It is what a work *takes for granted*. Period style is a beginning, therefore, which must be narrowed or revised. Works rather than artists must be discussed. 'Above all, concepts of the artefact should inform every choice of features for comparison…It is astonishing that the general problem of selecting functionally equivalent elements for comparison should seem to have received no attention whatsoever in recent times.'

His worked example is the basis for comparison between literature and architecture in the Mannerist period. Both Drayton and Jonson use the comparison between architecture and poetic structure, more particularly between genre in poetry and type in architecture. It is a short step to the correspondence of rhetoric and ornament; decorum governed heights of style in both building and writing, with schematised 'high' and 'low' levels. Fowler's examples are persuasive, but having established that such close analogies can be drawn, he insists that they can only be valid for a limited period. By the Victorian age a new analogy is needed. 'In short, the notion of a universally valid systematic correspondence between the arts must be regarded as a chimera.' Nevertheless, he acknowledges that for the Mannerist period 'rhetoric seems the most sensitive index to period style, just as ornament is with architecture'.

As an example of what he calls an 'organic' method, Fowler's seems to me to be admirable. As a critical exercise never carried out it is more impressive, however. It extends laterally from Worringer's concept of each period having an ornament to be 'read off' to a much more exploratory area where the word 'design' covers the organisation of spaces, areas, rhythms. This method not only returns art history to the age of the great debates; it seems to avoid many failings of contemporary art history. As a possibility arising from stylistic analysis of design objects, interart analogy is a fertile and unresearched field.

One conclusion is that design historians should guard against the habit of complaining that biography-laden, anecdotal art history offers no theoretical foundations for their own work. 'Art history' must come to terms with contemporary art with identical interests and (sometimes) indistinguishable ways of expressing them. The proximity of some of the methods I have mentioned to recent art – Buren or Burgin or Stezaker to semiotics, Nikolaus Lang, Robert Smithson, Charles Simonds, aspects of Hanne Darboven and in particular Ad Reinhardt to Kubler, for instance, to mix similarities and direct influences – seems to emphasise the urge to come to terms with the object.[31] The possibilities for stylistic analysis may be insufficient as yet, but the dream of a history of things is shared by more than a few critics. Their opinion is summed up by Pierre Francastel in chapter one of *La Figure et le Lieu:*

'The museum is fast becoming an instrument of so-called culture, providing a kind of historical and anecdotal keepsake for visitors who are less and less interested in the art works themselves. It is becoming increasingly rare to find people actually *looking* at a painting. The day is nigh when commentaries will take the place of painting, and paperback surveys and television will have replaced the museums which will then, perhaps, revert to their original function of exhibiting ambiguous works of art of indeterminate significance or value.'[31]

Suddenly we are back again, looking at that propeller.

1 The dating is that of Green, Christopher in *Léger and the Avant-Garde* Yale University Press, New Haven and London, 1976, 84–88

2 Delevoy, Robert *Léger* Skira, Ohio, 1967, 45

3 Léger, Fernand *Functions of Painting* (translated by Edward Fry) London, 1973. xxvii

4 See, for example, Tucker, William *The Language of Sculpture* Thames & Hudson, London, 1974

5 Krauss, Rosalind 'Notes on the Index; Seventies Art in America' in *October* Spring 1977, 68–81

6 Kermode, Frank 'Revolution: The Role of the Elders' in Hassan, Ihab (editor) *Liberations* Wesleyan University Press, Middletown Connecticut, 1971, 94

7 Apollinaire, Guillaume *The Cubist Painters* George Wittenborn, New York 1962, 48

8 Eliot, T. S. *The Waste Land* 1.429 of the first edition text. See Eliot, Valerie (ed) *The Waste Land* Faber & Faber, London, 1971, 146

9 Pound, Ezra *The Cantos* Faber & Faber, London, 1968, Canto VIII, 32

10 Meyer, Leonard B. *Music, The Arts and Ideas* University of Chicago Press, Chicago, 1967. His contribution to Bergonzi, Bernard (ed) *Innovations: Essays on Art and Ideas* Macmillan, London, 1968 contains one version of this concept. Greenberg, Clement *Art and Culture* Thames & Hudson, London, 1973 contains what could be construed as another. Sondheim, Alan *Individuals: Post-Movement Art in America* Dutton, New York, 1977 uses the term 'post-movement' throughout. My note in *Stand* vol 13, no 3, 1972, 42–44 applies Meyer's thesis of 'the end of the Renaissance' to recent fiction

11 Jencks, Charles *The Language of Post Modern Architecture* Studio Vista, London, 1977 employs the term 'radical eclecticism'. On the avant-garde see Poggioli, Renato *The Theory of the Avant-Garde* (translated by L. C. Gerald) Harvard University Press, Cambridge Massachusetts, 1968 and Paz, Octavio *Children of the Mire* Harvard University Press, Cambridge Massachusetts, 1974 The dance critic Marcia B. Siegel announces that the avant-garde is out of date in 1968 (see her *At the Vanishing Point* Saturday Review Press, New York, 1973, 256)

12 Venturi, Robert *Learning from Las Vegas* MIT Press, Cambridge Massachusetts, 1972

13 See, for example, Fiedler, Leslie A. *Love and Death in the American Novel* Jonathan Cape, London, 1967 and Tyler, Parker *Sex, Psyche Etcetera in the Film* Penguin Books, Harmondsworth Middlesex 1971

14 Morin, Edgar *New Trends in the Study of Mass Communication* University of Birmingham Centre for Contemporary Cultural Studies, Birmingham (occasional paper) nd

15 Lippard, Lucy *Six Years: The Dematerialisation of the Art Object* Studio Vista, London, 1973 takes its title from an essay by Lucy Lippard and John Chandler called 'The Dematerialisation of Art in *Art International*, February 1968 in which they talked of the possibility of the object becoming 'wholly obsolete'

16 Hoffman, G., Hornung, A. and Kunow, R. '"Modern", "Post modern" and "Contemporary" as Criteria for the Analysis of Twentieth-Century Literature' in *Amerikastudien* vol 22, no 1 1977, 19–46 includes an excellent bibliography of some of these terms

17 Clark, T. J. 'The Conditions of Artistic Creation' in *The Times Literary Supplement* 24 May, 1974. Smith, Terry 'Doing Art History' in *The Fox* no 2, 1975, 97–104

18 Charbonnier, Georges (ed) *Conversations with Claude Levi-Strauss* Jonathan Cape, London, 1969, 88–100. Kenner, Hugh *The Pound Era* Faber & Faber, London, 1972, 54–75. Krauss, Rosalind *Passages in Modern Sculpture* Thames & Hudson, London, 1977 88–93

19 *Documenta 6* Kassel, Germany (exhibition catalogue) 1977 volume 3, 269–293

20 Hough, Graham *Style and Stylistics* Routledge & Kegan Paul, London, 1969, 4–5

21 Schapiro, Meyer 'Style' in Philipson, Morris (ed) *Aesthetics Today* Meridian Books World Publishing Company, Cleveland and New York, 1961, 81–113. See also Chatman, Seymour 'The Semantics of Style' in Cristeva, J., Debove, J. R., and Umiker, D. J. *Essays in Semiotics* Mouton, The Hague and Paris, 1971, 399–422

22 Kuhn, Thomas S. *The Structure of Scientific Revolutions* University of Chicago Press, Chicago and London, revised edition 1971, 10–12

23 Burnham, Jack *The Structure of Art* George Braziller Inc, New York, 1971, 32–43

24 Morse, David 'Criticism as a Science' in *Twentieth-Century Studies* no 9, September 1973, 32–50. See also Kando, Tom 'Popular Culture and its Sociology: Two Controversies' in *Journal of Popular Culture* vol 9, no 2, 438–486 and 455–103

25 Culler, Jonathan *Saussure* Fontana/Collins, London, 1976, 92

26 Kubler, George *The Shape of Time: Remarks on the History of Things* Yale University Press, New Haven and London, 1962, 1

27 Worringer, Wilhelm *Abstraction and Empathy* Routledge & Kegan Paul, London, 1910, *passim*

28 Kroeber, A. L. *Style and Civilizations* University of Los Angeles Press Berkeley and Los Angeles, 1973 19

29 Panofsky, Erwin *Gothic Architecture and Scholasticism* Archabey Press, Latrobe Pennsylvania, 1951, 58–59

30 Fowler, Alastair 'Periodisation and Interart Analogy' in *New Literary History* vol 3, no 3, Spring 1972, 487–510

31 Francastel, Pierre 'Seeing…Decoding' in *Afterimage* no 5, Spring 1974, 5

The attitudes in this paper were developed during a long experimental course taught jointly with Penny Sparke, whose constant help has been vital

American and British personal transport design in the 1950s and 1960s

Peter Vickers
Trent Polytechnic

Twelve months ago, I became curious about a Vauxhall Cresta parked on the roadside. I knew nothing about car design and proceeded to ask many and various questions.

Everybody I spoke to was perfectly willing to offer opinions and yet it quickly became apparent that most of the information I was receiving was hearsay, folklore, legend or romance, and certainly not substantiated fact.

I gradually began to realise that, once again, I would indulge in some of those delightful discrepancies that exist between an object's reality ('function'?) and its romantic connotations ('fad'?). I say 'once again' because this discrepancy is a recurrent theme. Take, for instance, the rustic Windsor chair, so evocatively portrayed by Arthur Rackham in his illustration of Moley's house in *The Wind in the Willows*.

When I was living in a London suburb, I bought a couple of chairs of this sort in the belief that, by assimilating their atmosphere, I could almost live in the country and tell the difference between, say, a godwit and a greenshank, or a pedunculate and a sessile oak.

Now I live surrounded by the heavy clays of the Trent valley, and, having moved, the floppy, soft armchair in the foreground of Rackham's picture suddenly offered a reality of comfort. After a year, I bought a couple of these over-stuffed, 'vulgar' chairs and sold the Windsors, patina and all.

The romance of the country chair also casts a rosy glow over its making. Take the High Wycombe Museum's re-creation of a chairmaker's workshop. I visited it on a mellow September morning with the sunlight dappling the fretted patterns like roe deer in a woodland glade. But imagine the same workshop on a February morning, or for that matter the position of the men working in the sawpit out of doors. Their lives must have been extraordinarily gruelling, and even when power-driven machinery relieved some of the physical toil, the tedium remained and the danger increased. A woodworking shop at the turn of the century, with its canopy of unguarded belts, appears to our eyes to have been constructed by some offspring of Machiavelli. Indeed, the only resemblance between Ratty and Moley's Edwardian country life and that of the machine-shop workers appears in the latters' coppiced hands, which echo the willows that the wind blows through.

The romanticising of supposedly inanimate objects has not been restricted to rural life. Take, for instance, the wealthy eighteenth-century desire for classic taste and elegance, and how this radically formulated the design decisions involved in, say, Burlington's little country house at Chiswick.

As everybody knows now, and certainly knew at the time, Chiswick House is styled on Palladio's Villa Rotunda. However, features such as the high, domed central hall and cross floor plan to give through draughts, which are sensible in an Italian climate ('function?'), are stylistic visual features ('fad'?) offering little in the way of comfort in England. Obviously Burlington must have been well aware of this, and yet he still insisted on stylistic elegance and not comfort as the premier design criterion.

This is perfectly understandable, but I do find it curious that the rooms in this little country retreat had at least two, and often three, doors. Burlington's wife was not constantly faithful, and yet he designed a home with a multitude of emergency exits for the convenience of an interrupted lover.

The results of designing with too many exits had been recognised for centuries. Sir Balthazar Gerbier in his *Council and Advice to All Builders* (1663), noted that 'too many stairs and back doors make thieves and whores'.

And, in more recent times, the late Mississippi bluesman Elmore James bemoaned inconsiderate designers who had heeded the above advice in a song called 'One Way Out': 'Raise your window baby, I ain't going out that door. There's a man downstairs, he may be your husband I don't know.'

The scale of the American flatlands landscape is vast, and it is hardly surprising that one of the most popular country blues songs, 'The Keys to the Highway', contained the line, 'I'm going to leave here running, 'cause walkin's got too doggone slow'. And Mance Lipscombe, the Texas songster, elaborates the reasons why he has to leave: 'You've been riding around here baby, in your brand-new automobile. With some other man, you don't care how you make me feel.'

1 *'She likes my big Daddy, but I'm crazy 'bout his Pontiac'. Pontiac Silver Streak Sedan, 1948*

The new-found privacy, let alone freedom, provided by the automobile in the American flatlands must have been enormous, and it wasn't long before the new generation of post-war bluesmen realised its potential and incorporated it into swaggering, exuberant songs such as Sonny Boy Williamson's 'Pontiac Blues', probably recorded in the late 1940s, in which he sings: 'We're going to drive on the highway, and turn the bright lights on. We're going to turn the radio on, and get music from up the North.'

It is interesting to note that the only two design features Sonny Boy considers worth mentioning are the headlamps –

2 *Pubertal tail-light buds from the 1956 Cadillac range*

he's out at night with his 'baby' – and the radio, which plays Chicago blues.

Look at Sonny Boy's 1948 Pontiac Silver Streak Sedan (Figure 1). Its forms are rooted in the natural world. The bonnet (hood) looks as if it had been eroded into shape by the action of countless years of running water, or maybe even burnished into existence by a Brancusi. It's the bonnet around which a Hoochie Coochie Man wove his voodoo magic potions, rooted in folklore and legend.

The song 'Hoochie Coochie Man' was written by Willie Dixon and made famous by Muddy Waters in the early 1950s. But what of the young blacks who had never, as Lonnie Donegan put it, 'jumped round, turned around and picked a bale of cotton' in their lives? Their home and culture was that of South Side Chicago and the car town of Detroit, not the share cropper's veranda or the levee. The country image was incongruous until a high-school boy from St Louis, Chuck Berry, put Muddy's Hoochie Coochie Man into V8 overdrive and recorded 'No Money Down' in 1956. It describes Chuck's 'ideal' daydream car:

As I was motorvating
Back in Town,
I saw a Cadillac sign saying
No money down.
So I eased on my brakes
And I pulled in the drive
Gunned my motor twice
Then I walked inside.
Dealer came to me
Said 'Trade in your Ford
And I'll put you in a car
That'll eat up the road.
Just tell me what you want,
And then sign on that line,
And I'll have it brought down to you
In an hour's time'.

I'm going to get me a car,
And I'll be heading on down the road,
And I won't have to worry about that
Broken-down, ragged old Ford.

Well Mister I want a yellow convertible
Four-Door De Ville…

Is it possible that Chuck Berry was here merely about to describe the contemporary Cadillac models? The 1956 model is stylistically very interesting, rather like a tadpole with its legs only half developed (Figure 2). Indications of future forms are recognisable, and yet their origins are clearly evident. Take, for instance, the bonnet: it has similarities, albeit in a more rectangular form, to the rounded Pontiac, with a high central dome surmounting smooth valleys running down to the radiator grille. The tail-light bulbs though are still in their puberty, barely hinting at the mature excitement to come. Their charm is that of the girl next door – pert rather than glamorous.

If the late 1940s shapes evoke the country, those of the mid-1950s belonged to the suburbs. Chuck Berry goes on to paint a portrait of the inner city:

I want a continental spare,
And a wire chrome wheel…

I assume that a 'continental spare' is one carried on the outside of the boot (trunk), European sports-car fashion. To the best of my knowledge, no Cadillacs of this period carried their spare in such a manner – they hardly needed to with their acres of boot space.

Several cars of the period did display this feature, however. In the mid-1950s Fords produced their snappy sports model with the legendary name from the deserts – the Thunderbird. A cut-out in its rear bumper (fender) accommodated the spare. Thunderbirds also provided a 'wire chrome wheel' – it was a snap-on accessory ('fad'?)! In 1962 Fords offered the 'real thing' as an optional extra ('function'?). As for the chrome, even the spare-wheel cover was metal and was, of course, chromed all over.

Strangely enough, one other American car had a 'continental spare' for space-saving purposes. It was the Nash Metropolitan, designed as the family's second, or third, car.

I think it's probably safe to assume that Chuck was incorporating the 'continental spare' into his Cadillac design for its iconographical qualities, and was surely not proposing a Cadillac with limited boot space! He continues:

I want power steering, and power brakes.
I want a powerful motor, with a jet off-take.

Thrust! Hardly a description of a 1956 Cadillac profile! And yet in 1959, three years after Chuck's design brief had been played by the radio stations, Cadillac's new Coup de Ville taxied onto the highways bearing a 'jet off-take' so vivid that even the roar of exhaust flames was solidified into tail-lights (Figure 3).

Wouldn't it be intriguing to entertain the notion, if only for a few indulgent moments, that Cadillac designers had been influenced by Chuck Berry's folksong?

The result is what – banal, socially profound, decadent, powerful, trivial, witty, tasteless, exciting, wasteful etc, etc? Is it the design historian's role to offer such criticism? Should the design historian analyse in the light of today's moral codes, as presented by Vance Packard, Ralph Nader and Victor Papanek? Or should the design historian analyse in the light of the object's contemporary context? Back to Chuck Berry again:

I want air conditioning,
I want automatic heat,
And I want a full murphy bed
In my back seat.

I want short-wave radio,
I want TV and a 'phone,
You know I got to talk to my baby
When I'm riding along.

Cadillacs were constantly incorporating electronic features, and by 1959 the driver was faced with a dashboard not unlike a Boeing's. Not content with this, some Cadillac owners embellished the exterior of their cars with sophisticated communication devices. Such as antennae on the boot and 'road surface sensitisors' quivering to every change of tarmac temperature.

I want four carburettors
And two straight exhausts.

Yet again, the 1959 Cadillac. A rear view (Figure 4) shows a multitude of 'two straight exhausts'. As already mentioned, twin pairs of jet 'exhausts' roar from the fins. Immediately below these, two sets of concentric, annular 'exhausts' flank the long, horizontal 'exhausts' grille. And, almost incidentally, below the fender, two straight exhausts – real ones this time – peep out almost apologetically, naked in their reality. Chuck Berry again:

I'm burning aviation fuel,
No matter what it costs.
I want railroad air-horns
And a military spot.

The 1958 Chevrolet side-light detail combines the imagery of both 'air-horns and military spots'(Figure 5). However, the 1959 Cadillac, as the front view vividly displays (Figure 6), wasn't content with an occasional spot, but emblazoned the grille with a two-tier battery of lights ('fad' or 'function'?). If this armament was critical for improved performance and safety, then the 1956 Cadillac's provision seems dangerously inadequate!

The remainder of the song describes the beneficial financial terms that Chuck negotiates to acquire this daydream car – daydream, that is, in 1956, though a reality by 1959. The Cadillac's appearance had by then been transformed from a domesticated ruminant into an aggressive predator.

Many other American cars had undergone the same transformation; 1959 was the year of the fins, by 1960 they were on the wane as car styles began to touch down. The 1960 Cadillac fin, for example (Figure 7), almost looks as though a designer

3 *Jet off-take tailfin. Cadillac Coupe de Ville, 1959*

4 *A multitude of 'straight exhausts' on the 1959 Cadillac Coupe de Ville*

5 *Two-tier 'military spots' on the 1958 Chevrolet Bel Air*

6 *'A domesticated ruminant transformed into an aggressive predator'. The 1959 Cadillac Biarritz*

7 *'Designers at work' on the 1960 Cadillac Sedan de Ville*

had been at work on it – which is probably more than Chuck rated for his 'broken-down, ragged Ford'.

He wasn't always so disparaging about Fords: a few years later he recorded 'Jaguar and the Thunderbird', and a song dedicated to his '1966 Cherry-Red Mustang Ford', which had 'a 385 horsepower overload'. In fact, he claims that it's so powerful that he's having trouble finding suitable roads for it.

Of course, he's not quite telling the truth. Chuck knew very well about the possibilities of Route 66. And so, for that matter, did the Rolling Stones – the American influence had already reached Britain through films, pop music, television, the GIs, hamburgers, bubblegum and autos.

In 1959 Vauxhall acknowledged this transatlantic fashion and produced their new Vauxhall 6 – Cresta and Velox – range in 'fresh new colours' – and, for that matter, fresh new forms, at least to the British market (Figure 8).

8 *The Vauxhall 6 Cresta, 1958 brochure picture*

9 *1958 Chevrolet Biscayne*

10 *'A barracuda on the prowl'. Chevrolet Bel Air, 1957, headlight detail*

8

9

10

The Cresta's resemblance to contemporary American styles, particularly that of the Chevrolet, is marked. This opinion is by no means a revelation; the similarities are easily recognisable. Compare, for example, the silhouettes of the Vauxhall Cresta and the 1958 Chevrolet saloons (Figure 9). All display a fighter pilot's cockpit bubble giving all-round 'speed cops at seven o'clock' visibility. This menacing quality is further developed as the front wings arch forward, with muscles tensed, to hood the headlamps in predatory fashion (Figure 10). The imagery is so striking that a colleague of mine spontaneously likened the 1957 Chevrolet Bel Air to 'a barracuda that's swallowed a headlamp'. A second passed…'Good grief! They've given it gills too!' And indeed they had, stuck on the wing in just the right position.

'But I thought they were Ferrari cooling vents.' 'No, ejection slots for the spent machine-gun shells.'

6-cylinder, 6-seater Vauxhall VELOX

11 *Elongated Vauxhall Velox, 1958 brochure picture*

12 *Elongated Hudson Hornet, 1955 brochure picture*

The 'machine-guns' are mounted on the bonnet – they are decorative, 'non-functional'. What a silly word 'functional' is. What I mean is that the feature does not alter the performance of the car – although it may well alter the performance of the driver and are very definitely functional!.

Vauxhall's did not employ such obvious pictorial devices as the decorative air vent. However, they did adapt and incorporate the rear fin, and even though the Cresta's 'jet off-take' is perhaps more suited to a Flying Bedstead than Cadillac's Flying Fortress, a 'jet off-take' it certainly is.

The next step was easy: I approached Vauxhall's hoping for 'confirmation of the obvious'. They were coy! Admittedly the events I was interested in had happened 20 years before, and car makers are understandably more concerned about tomorrow than yesterday, but all I wanted was for someone to say 'Yes, there was an intentional stylistic relationship'.

Instead, I was recommended by them to visit the archives at the National Motor Museum at Beaulieu, and it was there that I came across the publicity brochures and photographs.

I was astounded! The Vauxhall 1958 'fresh new colours' brochure did not even mention stylistic derivations once. Far from it; according to the first two pages, the Cresta's appearance derived from an Art College cliché:

'Behold the low and lovely lines of these latest Vauxhalls…a new low hulled shape evolved in the quest for better motoring. Here is form perfectly fitted to function.' It's that word again! To emphasise their design approach, pages three and four showed a 'grid' – well, at least three straight lines in red – superimposed on the side elevation of a Cresta indicating the low centre of gravity – only 23 inches from the ground!

This engineering document was headed: 'Low Overall Height, Low Centre of Gravity; Design Theme for these efficient new Vauxhalls'. Further evidence is provided by a profound night photograph depicting the Velox tackling a cobbled road and gaining 'all the benefits of the new flat-ride suspension. Freedom from roll on corners; freedom from pitch when braking; gliding smoothness on the roughest roads…' And, later on, 'By reducing overall height to 57 inches, Vauxhall designers have reduced frontal area and cut down wind resistance at speed. So this low, functional shape cuts petrol consumption'.

I was confused. Was it really possible that the Cresta's shape had been dictated purely by engineering requirements?

I ventured deeper into the brochure. Just past the centre the Cresta is pictured in a typical setting – a society wedding! Top hats, tails, long dresses and veils! Damn! Not a Juke Joint in sight!

I moped on to the next brochure, a slightly later one I suspect, though still advertising the same Cresta and Velox models. Or were they? They looked different somehow. In fact the whole brochure *is* different – different in character, different in pictorial imagery, and different in copy:

'There is extra value in the very advanced design of this latest Velox/Cresta…value in lasting good looks, performance and comfort. Regular Velox/Cresta equipment includes arm rests on all doors; folding arm rest in rear seat; two ashtrays; dual wind-tone horns; two-spoke steering wheel with chromium plated horn ring; spare wheel in container beneath floor of boot…'

Or maybe we should continue, Chuck Berry fashion:

[I want] Stainless steel mouldings
to windscreen and rear window;
[I want] Chromium plated 'flute'
along side of car;
[I want] Double key locks
to both front doors…

Yes I'm going to get me a car,
And I'll be heading on down the road.
And I won't have to worry about that
Boring, tasteful 'efficient new Vauxhall'.

And yes, it is the same 'efficient new Vauxhall' that's shown in the brochure (Figure 11). The illustrator has, however, literally stretched the truth somewhat to emphasise the 'new low hulled shape'! In fact he has added about two yards to the car. This was standard practice in American car catalogues of the early and mid-1950s, as the 1955 Hudson Hornet illustration (Figure 12) so emphatically shows. Now the Hornet is a big car – *car*, mark you, not stratocruiser – but it is quite impossible for the rear wheels to look only half the size of the front ones! And if Mantegna would have been proud of such perspective, then Rubens would have been more than happy with the model (Figure 13) – voluptuous to hide a fair amount of the Hornet on the front cover!

Vauxhall had taken similar wide skirt, wide smile, and wide belted 'cheese-cake' shots to arouse interest in the Cresta. However, to the best of my knowledge, the youthful glamorous girls were not used in the early advertising brochures. On the contrary, the lady shown lovingly adjacent to the Cresta seems really to be 'Lady somebody or other' (Figure 14). However, a closer look at her smiling face perhaps hints at 'saucy chorus girl origins'.

Vauxhall's choice of female accessory epitomises its design policy dilemma when working in an imported alien style for a market with different economic and social conditions.

Was the Cresta intended to be a respectable family car or was it intended to be a glamorous one? To introduce 'glamour' into the British car industry must have been an enormous problem, since the British car-buying public were not accustomed to replacing cars annually as was done in the States. The American car was a fashion accessory; the new automobile shows were fashion shows, and fluctuating chrome 'hem lines' provided the consumer interest.

By camparison, the British public generally bought new cars on a four or five year cycle. Consider the design problems of creating fashionable items that could accommodate not just one year's change in taste, but four or five.

Or, to put it another way, imagine a woman's turmoil in having to choose a handbag or shoes suitable for five years' fashionable use. The inevitable choice would be a combination of the modern and the timeless – generally called 'good taste' or 'classic design'.

Vauxhall's policy to adopt the fashionable American look, possibly influenced by their parent company General Motors, placed its designers and sales staff in the unenviable position of translating a style generally considered 'tasteless' over here into a product that was 'tasteful' enough to be thought acceptable four years after its introduction.

The result is understandable. The Cresta's overall shape is neither as aggressive nor as flamboyant as its American counterparts (it has restrained tail fins); it shows little use of sculptural devices such as imitation engine cooling vents; and the overall picture was painted in temperate English 'Wedgewood blues' and 'Rose pinks'. And we should not forget the beauty queen turned coffee-morning lady, correctly dressed in a Harrods-style, classic costume.

This American/classic confrontation occurred even more clearly in 1960 when Ford of England produced its Consul Classic, billed in advertising as having the 'Long Low Look' – words certainly evocative of the American highways and automobiles.

However, the brochure's introduction leaves any prospective customer in no doubt as to the car's origins and heritage! 'And then take another longer lingering look! For here with all the traditional understatement of English elegance, is the look of the sixties in British motoring...the clean, the thoroughbred, the classic look. Here's the realisation of an ideal, dreamed and developed by British craftsmen, that makes the Classic far and away the most stylish design in its class on Britain's roads today...'

This patriotic statement is further verified by an illustration depicting the Classic's two-tone interior (Figure 15) with typical English cactii and painted desert countryside viewed through the windows! Ford also had problems in concocting a

13   *Hudson Hornet brochure cover with model, 1955*

14   *Vauxhall 6 brochure model, 1958*

15   *Ford's 'traditional understatement of English excellence' the Consul Classic 315. The traditional English Painted Desert landscape is just visible through the rear window in this 1960 brochure picture*

16 *A suggestion on how to fill the 'cavernous boot' of the Ford Classic*

17 *'My generation's' scooter, sadly without rabbit fur, at Len's Scooter Shop, Shipley, Yorkshire*

suitable relationship between its 'Classic car' and a lady (Figure 16).

Throughout the mid-1950s and early 1960s several other British companies produced cars with various American influences, though most were more tentative than the 1958 Vauxhalls. However, it was not until the mid-1960s that a vehicle appeared on the British roads which had the assertion of the 1959 Cadillac 'jet off-take'. Strangely enough it appeared on two wheels, not four (Figure 17), and its creation was due, not to multi-national companies, but to a confident and mobile youth.

Suddenly the new 'designer' intimately understood the client's needs (they were one and the same person), and stylistic timidity gave way to flamboyant expression in a manner that Vauxhall designers could never have achieved, working as they did to the 'British public common denominator of taste'.

Chuck Berry's dream car took on a new reality and the jet off-take, short-wave radio aerials, continental spare and military spots are all there to see. Obviously the spot lamps and mirrors are not essential to the scooter's performance and may therefore be mistakenly called non-functional! However, even though only one of the lights actually illuminates the road, the remainder shed an even greater light on the character of the owner. In this particular case there is no discrepancy between the scooter's reality and its romantic connotations.

The profusion of automobile iconography that embellished the scooter was not merely advertising men's imagery, but was an actual statement of 'masculine' status. The lamps and mirrors were not bought – they were acquired in more hair-raising ways. They are in fact trophies and spoils of war and indeed the owner of the scooter illustrated here was held in high esteem by other inhabitants of his sub-culture; a sub-culture which had provided the right climatic conditions for an originally imported style to flourish and develop.

British car owners in the mid-1950s were not able to provide such conditions and the Cresta was a commercial disappointment, even though it did look pretty and drove very well.

Did Vauxhalls really imagine they could market a visual style without reference to the life-style that had created it?

Is it really possible to view an object impartially, divorcing its reality from its romance?

I would like to thank the following for their invaluable help: the Secretary, Luke Arnott, and members of the Pre 50 American Auto Club; Len and Staff, Len's Scooter Shop, Shipley; Clients of Len's Scooter Shop, Shipley; Jon Stevens, Editor Scooter World; Dr Dal Herring, Flagstaff, Arizona; Shirley Bowers, Pamona, California; John Morgan, AVA Unit, Trent Polytechnic; the staff of Beaulieu Museum Library.

The Silver Studio's contribution to British wallpaper design 1890-1930

Mark Turner
Middlesex Polytechnic

The first notable mention of the Silver Studio in recent years was by Joseph Darracott in 1968. Mr Darracott, who was at that time teaching Art History at Hornsey College of Art, was instrumental in acquiring the Silver Studio Collection for the college (which is now part of the Middlesex Polytechnic) through the generosity of Miss Mary Peerless, the heir of Rex Silver and the Collection's owner. Joseph Darracott's article 'The Silver Studio Collection and the History of Design' in *The Connoisseur* for November 1968 is an excellent introduction to the work of the Silver Studio over the years of its operation from 1880 to 1964. It gives a good description of the very large contents of the Collection which will be of interest to anyone who wishes to investigate the Studio's contribution to British wallpaper and textile design. Since Mr Darracott wrote there have been one or two references to the Collection, including a passage in Brenda Greysmith's book *Wallpaper,* published by Studio Vista in 1976, and the Victoria and Albert Museum's exhibition catalogue for the Liberty Centenary in 1975. Otherwise the work of the Silver Studio and the Collection at Middlesex Polytechnic have remained comparatively unknown. Yet the Studio was enormously prolific; it did much respectable and sometimes even distinguished work and the visual reference material, library, account and day-books and photographic record of all sold designs which together comprise the Silver Studio Collection would provide material for a very wide range of original research projects. The Collection houses a very wide range of English wallpapers, dating between 1880 and 1960, some Continental examples (notably French) from the period 1910 to 1935, when Rex Silver was supplying designs to the French wallpaper manufacturer Paul Dumas, who printed Poiret's Atelier Martine papers.

The Silver Studio was directed by Arthur and Rex Silver, who were father and son. Arthur Silver opened it in 1880 – appropriately enough in Hammersmith, at 84 Brook Green.

Little is known about Arthur Silver's early career. He came from a prosperous firm of Reading cabinet makers and decorators and he attended Reading School of Art in about 1870. In an interview for the *Studio Magazine* in 1894 he stated that his aim in founding the Silver Studio had been 'the bringing together of a body of men to establish a studio which would be capable of supplying designs for the whole field of fabrics and other materials used in the decoration of the home'.[1] In the same interview he went on to say: 'The problem we must endeavour to solve, is to supply manufacturers with saleable popular designs that even in the lowest class, do not offend the canons of artistic propriety.'[2]

This practical opinion is interesting because although the Silver Studio was formed only two years earlier than Mackmurdo's Century Guild (and although Arthur Silver was a prominent member of the Arts and Crafts Exhibition Society) there is no direct evidence to suggest that he had any of the desires for social reform that influenced the opinions of so many of his colleagues. Nor had he any views on the desirability or otherwise of machine production. He was genuinely interested in design, he was himself a capable designer, he wished to see sound design principles operate even in the housing of the poor, but his motivation was aesthetic, not political. Coming as he did from a commercial background and depending on the success of the Silver Studio for his livelihood, he could not afford to be ultra-fastidious about his clients' demands. But within the limitations of the commercial market he was keen to do good work. And, as the evidence of the collection shows, he was fortunate on two major counts: first, he was working in a period when there were firms who were prepared to risk money on avant-garde designs; and second, he had the services of two highly talented designers – Harry Napper and J. Illingworth Kay, both of whom produced designs very much in the vanguard of Art Nouveau in the early 1890s (see Figures 1 and 2).

There were three exceptionally adventurous wallpaper firms at this time: Charles Knowles, Essex & Co (who produced many of Voysey's designs) and Jeffrey & Co who had produced Morris's papers since 1862 and employed under the direction of Metford Warner the talents of Lewis F. Day, Walter Crane, Bruce Talbert and other well-known designers. Arthur Silver's Studio produced a large number of designs for the three firms, but at the same time they were also able to provide work for more staid and cautious manufacturers such as William Woollams. (Woollams specialised in providing expensive, hand blocked papers with heavy, shaded naturalistic floral designs or with classical motifs reminiscent of the grounds of Walter Crane's wallpapers.)

The Silver Studio was at all times highly adaptable. The only noticeable house-style was the consistent emphasis on draughtsmanship and the exact presentation of the finished design. Both Arthur Silver and his son Rex (who took over the running of the Studio circa 1900) possessed an ability to gauge the requirements of their clients accurately and provide skilful designs (which were often of some quality) which would meet their demands. The work of the Silver Studio was very professional: with one or two notable exceptions it largely reflects the taste of the English middle classes. It was during the 1890s that the Silver Studio built up its connections with Libertys, Sandersons, Warners and other vendors of home decorating and furnishing materials to the English upper and middle classes; and it was firms such as these that consistently bought Silver Studio designs until the 1960s.

When Arthur Silver first began designing wallpapers in about 1885, it was fashionable to treat walls as possessing three separate divisions, the dado, filling and frieze. The dado was the area of wall (usually about three feet in height) from the skirting upwards. It was separated from the next area, the filling, by a moulding or border of some description. Similarly the filling was divided by a picture rail or border from the uppermost section, the frieze. While all three sections could be hung with papers of the same description, quite separate treatments could be used for each. For instance, the dado, which was exposed to the hardest wear, could be hung with

management were firmly avant-garde Art Nouveau productions, but it is important to remember that this was an exceptional period in the Silver Studio's history and that from about 1900 onwards the Studio made a larger concession to popular middle-class taste.

Increasingly popular from 1895 onwards were wallpapers with designs inspired by the French Second Empire, and most popular of all were 'French stripe' papers. There were papers printed with the aid of talc and mica to imitate silk moire. The delightful friezes (see Figure 3) which accompanied these papers enjoyed, as did other forms of frieze, a mere temporary vogue. Mary Clive in her autobiography *The Day of Reckoning* describes her mother's drawing room in about 1910: '...the

walls were papered with white watered silk topped by an exquisite frieze of mauve wisteria. I thought it unutterably lovely and I was aware that it was, as the shops say, a discontinued line.'[3]

French stripe papers, however, never became discontinued and are still available today from firms such as Coles and, in less pleasant form, printed on vinyl coated paper, from almost any wallpaper shop in Western Europe.

linen or a Japanese leather paper, or a heavy embossed paper such as lincrusta or anaglypta. The dado was generally in the darkest colour to camouflage the knocks and scrapes it was likely to receive from furniture and children. So popular was the embossed paper dado, painted in chocolate brown oil paint, that it remained a feature of dining rooms and halls in conservative households until well after the Second World War. The filling, in a house where emphasis was placed upon pictures, would be in a less demonstrative design than the other areas of the wall. The frieze, which in the 1880s was frequently an elaboration of the filling, became increasingly regarded as a decoration in its own right towards the end of the century, the height of its popularity being about 1900.

Arthur Silver died in 1896 at the age of 44. The management of the Studio was given to Harry Napper and later J. R. Houghton, as Rex Silver was only 17. The majority of the designs that emanated from the Studio under Napper's

By 1900 the wallpaper frieze was at the height of its popularity and often regarded as a decoration in its own right, being accompanied by plain walls or an unrelated paper. The increasing popularity of plain walls, which I shall mention again later, was wrongly blamed on the fashion for decorative friezes by A. V. Sugden. He wrote in *A History of English Wallpapers*: 'While it lasted it spared no other style as to motif or manner of expression...everything that had a decorative value was dragged in by the designer to serve its ends and it was not surprising that as friezes became more and more dominant, wallpaper inevitably quietened down until pure design was almost extinguished in the fillings of the period.'[4]

The Silver Studio's contribution to this fashion had begun with a contract made by Arthur Silver through the Arts and Crafts Exhibition Society with the firm of Rottmann & Co. Rottmans imported grass and leather papers from Japan, where they had a factory at Yokohama, and they had been used primarily for dados. However, from about 1893 onwards

*4 Wallpaper produced by Heffer Scott from a
    Silver Studio design c1910*

The Silver Studio designed a whole series of stencil friezes for use on their papers and they were publicised in an exhibition held at Rottmann's showrooms in the City in 1895. This exhibition not only attracted considerable attention and a large number of reviews, but gave impetus to a fashion for stencilled decoration that was to last for nearly two decades. Stencilling was commonly used in Scotland but was less known in England. The comparatively low cost of production in conjunction with the subtle effects obtainable by this method of decoration quickly won public acclaim, and the praise of supporters of the Arts and Crafts Movement for Arthur Silver's honesty in the use of stencil plates, where the joins were not camouflaged and the maxim of Truth to Material seemed fully demonstrated. An anonymous reviewer in the *Daily News* for 8 June 1895 wrote: 'This method is in contradiction to the old one, wherein the ties were disguised or obliterated, to imitate entirely hand-painted productions. Now that the lines of construction have come to be valued for their use in giving balance and force, the newer method becomes the really effective one and represents a close junction of art and craft.'

For the second consecutive year Arthur Silver was interviewed by *The Studio* magazine, this time for his work in the field of stencilling. The article stated that 'One feature... distinguishes Mr Silver's designs from some other English examples, and from most of the multi-coloured Japanese stencilled patterns. In these...the necessary ties of the stencil plates have been utilised to supply the drawing of the design; so far from being ignored, they are emphasised...so that none shall mistake the fact that the result has been secured by stencilling and by no other purpose.'[5]

Rex Silver continued the connection with Rottmann's in his series of Silver Stencil friezes, carried out circa 1904, which proved highly successful. The Silver Studio did a great deal of stencilling work until the vogue for it waned in about 1910. Housed in the Silver Studio Collection is an order book noting the firms and stores which stocked the Silver Stencil pattern book; these include Barkers, Harrods and Warings. Following the Japanese tradition, Rex Silver would also stencil tablecloths, cushion squares and other small pieces at the Silver Studio.

Apart from stencilled friezes, the Silver Studio made but little contribution to wallpaper frieze design. However, the Studio was involved to a great extent in the revival of chintz designs for textiles and wallpapers in the early years of this century – a revival which went hand in hand with a rapidly growing interest in antique furniture and the reaction, which had begun in the 1890s, against heavily furnished rooms.

In the 1890s the Silver Studio had produced some elegant designs inspired by early nineteenth-century French chintz which were presumably regarded as adjuncts to the prevailing taste at that time among the very rich for French Second Empire decorating. However, by 1912 English floral chintz papers were among the most successful of British wallpaper designs and the Studio sold large numbers of designs in both England and France, for use on both cotton and wallpaper, inspired by English, rather than French, chintz (see Figure 4).

In order to explain the increasing popularity of lighter, more delicately patterned wallpapers, it is necessary to turn our attention to what was happening in British interior decorating at the turn of the century. In little over twenty years from 1890 to 1910, the British upper middle class completely revolted against the use of heavily patterned wallpaper in favour of undemonstrative wall surfaces. Following the advice of Norman Shaw[6] and other important vernacular-revival architects, walls became regarded as being unobtrusive backgrounds to the objects the room contained. It was as if a suitable British style of decorating had to be found to match the exterior of the houses that were being built by such architects as Lutyens, Guy Dawber, Bailie Scott, Voysey and their many imitators. You could dismiss the end-product as 'Stockbroker Tudor' perhaps, but its influence was felt strongly on the Continent, if only in the gradual elimination of clutter; while the confidence and flair with which the British upper classes began to combine glazed chintz, antique furniture of all different periods, oriental rugs, porcelain and paintings was to have great repercussions on twentieth-century decorating as a whole. Through decorators such as Elsie de Wolfe, who took inspiration from the English and French country house, and Sybil Colefax, Syrie Maugham and Ronald Flemming, all of whom were familiar with such an environment, a style of decorating was created, albeit dependent on the possession of money with which to buy the essential ingredients, which has as much claim as any other to be called an International Style.

The late Victorians were enormously interested in the furnishing and decoration of their houses, as the proliferation of books and articles on interior decorating from 1890 onwards reveals – a proliferation equalled only by the large number of ways in which one's house could be decorated. Styles available ranged from the design-conscious, avant-garde Arts and Crafts interior of plain walls and expensive hand-made furniture reminiscent of eighteenth-century 'country' furniture, to opulent Second Empire Boulle, marquetry and ormolu, in conjunction with the watered silk wallpapers mentioned earlier. Middle-class interiors, however, were normally cluttered assemblages of inherited furniture in conjunction with elements of currently popular taste.

Many reasons can be cited for the rapid clearing and lightening of rooms towards the turn of the century. Partly it was simply the reaction of a new generation who wanted to be able to move around a room without knocking into things, and who no longer felt the need for such an obvious show of prosperity. Certainly the growing awareness of hygiene led to the removal of much superfluous drapery, as dust and germs were synonymous in the mind of the late Victorian housewife. This might also explain the interest in fabrics such as glazed chintz and the decreasing popularity of velvet and plush.

Certainly the same process happened on the Continent, but at a somewhat later date. The Silver Studio sold many light sprigged chintz designs to France from 1900 onwards, and Elsie de Wolfe's decorations for the Colony Club in New York were inspired by the French use of *treillage* and chintz. In Germany, too, one finds that enlightened Englishwoman, Countess Elizabeth Von Arnim, with her love of conservatories and Thoreau, pouring scorn on her German neighbours' dark paint and lace curtains: 'The floor is painted yellow, and there is no carpet except a rug in front of the sofa. The paper is dark chocolate colour, almost black; that is in order that after years of use the dirt may not show, and the room need not be done up…There are a great many lovely big windows, all ready to let in air and the sun, but they are as carefully covered with brown lace curtains under heavy stiff ones as though a whole row of houses were just opposite, with peering eyes at every window trying to look in, instead of there only being fields, and trees, and birds. No fire, no sunlight, no books, no flowers; but a consoling smell of red cabbage coming up under the door, mixed, in due season, with soapsuds.'[7]

There can be little doubt, too, of the influence of the Aesthetic and Arts and Crafts movements on this process, for both placed great emphasis on simplicity. No doubt sensible British women soon noticed that genuine antique furniture was cheaper, particularly if it was 'country' rather than Chippendale or Hepplewhite, than the largely derivative products of the Arts and Crafts movement, and in many cases cheaper even than machine-made reproduction furniture. It also had the advantages of being hand-made and British, and its age hopefully ensured its discreet good taste.

In about 1900 illustrations of these 'new interiors' began to appear in books and periodicals devoted to the decorative arts and interior decorating. The architect Gerald Horsley recommended in 1906 (in an article in *Flats, Urban House and Cottage Homes* edited by W. Shaw Sparrow) that: 'A room with walls of a light plain colour never looks smaller than it is…the room looks larger and makes an admirable setting for furniture and coloured hangings…Persian rugs, the colour of flowers and chintz, of brass and copper, of deep mahogany and oak, are accentuated by their surroundings.'[8]

5 *Wallpaper produced by Sanderson c1925*

6 *Chintz c1935 from a design by F. Price of the Silver Studio*

7 *Wallpaper by Heffer Scott from a Silver Studio design c1920*

By 1910 chintz wallpapers were the most popular for the middle classes. The designs available ranged from French vine and trellis to straightforward copies of eighteenth and nineteenth-century printed cottons. Most popular of all were large patterned Chinoiserie Bird, Tree and Vine designs which the Silver Studio began to produce in large numbers and which were to become increasingly popular in the 1920s for furnishing textiles (see Figure 5).

From 1920 onwards it becomes increasingly difficult to find wallpaper mentioned or illustrated in books devoted to interior decorating. Yet a paradoxical situation exists, because we know from mill records that the 1920s was a period of great activity for the wallpaper industry. In the years following the First World War it would seem that it was much cheaper to use the cheapest wallpaper than to use emulsion paint, and hardly more expensive, though needing more expertise, than using distemper. Paper produced by photogravure printing could be varnished, which gave it an even longer life in kitchens, halls and bathrooms. It would seem that the wallpaper industry concentrated its attention on the cheaper end of the market and its designs were no longer for the design

of the past and then sees the paper coverings used today! Of course, there are some good papers, but they are lamentably few and difficult to find. The manufacturers of papers have turned their minds to mass production with a result that is worse than in any other decorative trade and they do not seem to realise that there are people who want beautiful papers, and who by not being able to buy them, have been forced to distemper and paint. There are fine designers today, but the makers seem content with the mediocre.'[9]

Rex Silver temporarily abandoned working for wallpaper manufacturers in 1931. He was being asked to make dull re-adaptations of existing papers, which gave his Studio little scope for either imagination or draughtsmanship (and probably paid badly). Despite a continued series of economic crises in the 1920s and early 1930s, there was still a considerable amount of money available to be spent on interior decorating. Mayfair was already pioneering a Regency and Early Victorian revival. Liberty's and firms such as G. P. and J. Baker required many new designs for textiles in a variety of modes, and for them the Silver Studio supplied elegant neo-Adam designs for chintz (see Figure 6), soft fauvist-influenced dress silk designs in gentle colours and, to a lesser extent, somewhat unhappy Cubist-inspired designs which were sold to the Edinburgh Weavers and Foxton's, who also produced work from better-known British designers such as Minnie McLeash, Marion Dorn and Duncan Grant.

While Basil Ionides firmly places the blame for the deterioration of wallpaper design in the 1920s and early 1930s at the feet of the wallpaper manufacturer, one feels that they can hardly be held responsible for appealing to less educated palates when interest in wallpaper design had declined so greatly at the opposite end of the social scale.

One of the more remarkable features of wallpaper and textile design in France immediately before the outbreak of the First World War was the rapidity with which the more decorative elements of avant-garde art were absorbed: nowhere is this more noticeable than in the rich colours and soft forms of Paul Poiret's Atelier Martine. In England, too, the colours and forms of the designs for the Russian Ballet, which first performed in London in 1909, were noted and rejected by a writer on wallpapers in the *Studio Year Book of 1915:* 'Recently we have seen a demand which originated on the Continent, for violent colours and strange designs. But this has not found any response amongst the designers of English wallpapers, nor is it reflected in the taste of art lovers for the decoration of their walls. After all, nothing can replace those patterns which are sound in construction and drawing, harmonious in colouring, and which have been designed by British Artists for British homes. Moreover, they have stood the test of years amidst the passing of many fashions.'[10]

However, the vogue for a decor that combined the elements of contemporary French decorative art with those of the Russian Ballet did eventually establish itself here, though it did not have any real influence on English decorative art until the First World War was over: Mayfair then soon publicised a temporary vogue for brilliant colours and fauvist and cubist forms. Its influence in the early 1920s was (amongst other things) to brighten the colours used on wallpapers of all designs. As early as 1920 the Silver Studio produced a wallpaper design combining brilliant tango orange with midnight blue and deep green. This particular design (see Figure 7) also has the heavy black outlines which were a characteristic of English modernist papers in the 1920s.

conscious but instead reflected popular fashion. Because of the poor quality of the paper, few samples of wallpaper from this period have survived, but the Silver Studio Collection is fortunate in possessing over 40 pattern books from the 1920s and early 1930s together with several hundred samples.

Such was the poor standard of wallpaper design by 1933 that Basil Ionides wrote in *Colour in Everyday Rooms* that: 'The walls of a modern house make one despair that they will ever become nice again. When one thinks of all the beautiful things

For the very rich and fashion conscious, there was no reason why French papers should not be used; so during the early 1920s Coles imported wallpapers from Paul Dumas in large numbers. In 1924, Poiret opened a shop in Mayfair to sell his papers and textiles. This was soon followed by that most design-conscious of stores, Galleries Lafayette, with Maurice Dufrène in charge of their design department, which opened a branch in Regent Street.

Contrary to popular belief many English designers were very aware of French decorative art. Rex Silver had papers by Henri Stephany and the Atelier Martine in his Studio and spent a week at the 1925 Paris Exhibition of Decorative and Industrial Arts. He was also receiving sample dye colours from French manufacturers from 1921 onwards.

Shortly after the First World War, however, cheap wallpaper manufacturers could be found supplying papers characterised by what can only be described as a lurid exoticism, reflecting the popular British taste at that time for a romanticised view of China, Arabia and the Mediterranean (preferably by moonlight). The colours were misinterpreted versions of the gaudier ones used by Bakst for the Russian Ballet – black in conjunction with red, blue, green, yellow and, above all, orange. The reaction to these colours in the late 1920s was rapid and total: porridge grounds became ubiquitous, enlivened by brightly coloured cut-out wallpaper friezes, corners, panels and dados. The origins of this rapid, and peculiarly British, suburban development are virtually unknown. Illustrated examples of its use would seem to suggest that the idea was to treat the wall as if it were a Japanese print, with sprays and blossoms or leaves in the corners and with panels, borders and dados supplying extra decoration. Possibly it was a continuation of the old dado, filling, frieze idea, and the brightly coloured cut-out leaf, flower and scenic papers were a whimsical adaption of this. Some were fairly naturalistic in design. It was possible to have a whole herbaceous border as a dado and a positive orchard of cherry blossom as a frieze. As late as 1952 a writer in *Model Housekeeping* was still feeling it necessary to condemn their use: 'I must issue a solemn warning against some of the terrible things that can be done with wallpaper in the name of decoration. Some wallpaper manufacturers have produced the most deplorable collections of ornamental strips, floral cut-outs, medallions, birds, butterflies, galleons and so forth,

intended to be applied as friezes, borders, elaborate and meaningless panels, and scenic effects. Once you have started sticking things on your wall, the process is liable to go to your head. The urge to fill a blank space with just one more clump of humming birds may finally land you with a complete herbaceous border, a teeming jungle, or a perpetual view of the whole Spanish Armada in full sail.'[11]

Cubist elements seem to have made their first appearance in Silver Studio wallpaper designs circa 1926–27, and it is likely that Rex Silver had seen the work of Sonia Delaunay and others in Paris in 1925: but the colours used in English wallpapers at this time, in reaction to the first half of the decade, were subdued in tone and closer to those favoured by the Bauhaus. Also English wallpaper manufacturers liked any cubist element in a design to be tempered by sprays of naturalistic flowers or fruit — a somewhat unhappy combination, although the idea of avant-garde art penetrating suburbia with the rapidity with which it did, even in a diluted form, is an interesting one.

Although the written records and a mass of samples show that the Silver Studios produced many hundreds of designs for wallpaper during the 1920s, the firm ceased to design wallpaper in 1931, concentrating, until the last war, on textiles. Though no reason for this is explicitly stated in the Silver Studio's diaries, it seems clear that Rex Silver lost heart in the constant struggle to find buyers for design work which he and his team of designers found both limiting and uninspiring. Much of their work around 1930 consisted of mere adaptation and alteration of existing designs. The manufacturer would send a sample of the paper he wished to have altered or adapted with a piece of paper attached giving guide-lines. Typical indications were as follows: 'It is a kind of *general* design but always useful for shops.' 'This is a simple kind of thing but can be very *difficult*.' 'This stripe much too hackneyed – try something much more snappy.'

Faced with such an absolute stagnation of ideas and constant, vague, muddle-headed correspondence from manufacturers who hardly knew what they wanted (only it must be like last year's selling lines and needed to be cheap) it is hardly surprising that a design studio which had always tried to do good work gave up and concentrated on design for textiles, where middle-class money was still available and where critics still showed interest in what a designer did.

1 'A Studio of Design' in *The Studio* vol 3, 117–122

2 *Ibid*

3 Clive, Mary *The Day of Reckoning* London, 1964

4 Sugden, A. V. and Edmondson, J. L. *A History of English Wallpaper* London, 1926, 186

5 'Stencilled Fabrics' in *The Studio* vol 5, 1895, 181–184

6 Blomfield, Sir Reginald *Richard Norman Shaw (Architect 1831–1912)* Batsford, 1940. Blomfield wrote: 'Shaw had very definite views on wallpapers. He insisted that they should be "backgrounds pure and simple – that and nothing more".

7 Von Arnim, Elizabeth *Elizabeth and Her German Garden* London, 1898

8 From an article by Gerald Horsley, in *Flats, Urban Houses and Cottage Homes* Hodder and Stoughton, London, 1906, 115

9 Ionides, Basil *Colour in Everyday Rooms* London, 1933

10 Warner, Horace 'Wallpaper Designers and Their Work' in *The Studio Year Book*, 1915, 170

11 Smithills, Roger 'The House Beautiful' in *Modern Housekeeping* London, 1952

Henry Wilson's Welsh church

Cyndy Manton
Brighton Polytechnic

I want in this paper to give a brief, illustrated survey of the varied career of the designer and architect Henry Wilson (1864 to 1934), followed by a close examination of a single building of his – St Mark's Church, Brithdir. Wilson's attitudes to architecture and his working methods will be looked at in relation to the finished building to provide a detailed insight into the birth of a church.

One of the most constantly intriguing things about Henry Wilson is the difficulty of compartmentalising him. The power and originality of his designs and writings conspire to put him outside any labellable 'box', such as 'Arts and Crafts', 'Art Nouveau' or 'Pre-Modernist', and reveal an architect and designer whose work is consistently striking, but who is sometimes apparently contradictory in his attitudes. On the one hand we find him publishing a translation of the Futurist Manifesto and writing to his brother about how exciting he finds the 'noise and rush and skyscrapers' of New York.[1] Yet on the other he is still the 'live Arts and Crafts' supporter who could solemnly exchange letters with Gimson about the tribulations of finding villages where *real* Double Gloucester cheese was still made.

Partly because of the problems of 'identifying' him, and partly because of his own persistently stressed debt to his old master J. D. Sedding, I think Wilson himself has been somewhat underestimated. To an extent he seems typical of his generation, trying to reconcile old craft ethics with a modern world – and certainly his attitudes do change as his career develops. Yet Ashbee's opinion of him was clearcut: far from being a 'typical' designer, Wilson, he declared, was an 'arch individualist', and, quite simply, 'England wasted him.'[2]

Wilson's career included a wide range of activities, from building, sculpture, woodwork and metalwork to jewellery, stage design and illuminated manuscripts. He was born in 1864, the son of a clergyman who kept the school at Cleobury Mortimer in Herefordshire. He attended Kidderminster School of Art, where he received a traditional training in drawing and design, and was then articled to a Maidenhead architect, E. J. Shrewsbury. In 1883 he moved to London, first as an apprentice to John Oldrid Scott, and then, 18 months later, to John Belcher. After a further two years he became chief assistant to J. T. Sedding, collaborating with him on several important buildings such as Holy Trinity Church, Sloane Street, London. After Sedding's death in 1891, Wilson continued the practice. He completed many of his master's commissions, and carried out several architectural and design works of his own, working initially from Sedding's Oxford Street office, then from his own studio at 17 Vicarage Gate, Kensington, and later from the house and workshops he built at St Mary Platt, Kent, in about 1902.

St Peter's Church, Ealing, was one of the buildings left unexecuted by Sedding (Figure 1). Work only started on Sedding's original plans in 1892, a year after he himself had died. Wilson was left with the responsibility of putting them into practice and adapting them where necessary. The buttressed

1 *St Peter's Church, Ealing, showing buttressed west window and external arches connecting piers*

west window and the external arches connecting the piers along the length of the church are particularly noteworthy features, and give the interior an unusally airy, Gothic feel.

The Church of the Holy Redeemer, Clerkenwell, is another example of Wilson revising and completing Sedding's designs, which were originally drawn up in 1887 and reworked by Wilson in 1892. Wilson's association with the church was a long-standing one, and included the campanile, clergy house and parish hall; an extension behind the baldachino to accommodate the Lady Altar; a side chapel; and finally the Eyre Memorial of 1927 (Figure 2). (This memorial, which now surmounts the baldachino, is a golden figure of the young Christ. It is a replica of the statue that Wilson originally designed as part of the memorial gateway for Tonbridge School in Kent, erected in memory of former pupils killed in the Great War – hence the youth of the figure.)

St Martin's, Marple, is another 'shared' church, built by Sedding, but with additions and decorations by Wilson

2 *Interior of the Church of the Holy Redeemer, Clerkenwell, showing baldachino surmounted by the Eyre Memorial*

3 *Detail from the plasterwork frieze in St Martin's Church Marple*

4 *Pulpit, St Bartholomew's Church, Brighton*

5 *Tomb of Bishop Elphinstone, from a photograph taken while work on it was still in progress*

(Figure 3). His Lady Chapel, with its very fine plasterwork, dates from 1895, and the Christopher Chapel and the font, with its pronounced Art Nouveau tendencies, from 1909.

Some of Wilson's most striking work is inside Edmund Scott's remarkable Byzantine Church of St Bartholomew, Brighton, built in 1874 (Figure 4). Wilson's fittings date from 1899 to 1908, and include the octagonal green marble font, the beaten-silver Lady Altar, the green marble pulpit which stands on pillars of red African marble with carved white alabaster capitals, and the baldachino. This massive and breathtaking structure, 45 feet high, again combines red, green and black marble with white alabaster details.[3]

However, an obituary by F. W. Troup in the *Journal of the*

Royal Institute of British Architects thought it probable that Wilson's 'reputation and claim to distinction will...rest ultimately upon the superb monument which he created for the reconstructed tomb of Bishop Elphinstone, King's College, Aberdeen', commissioned in 1912 and erected in 1926[4] (see Figure 5).

Wilson believed that, in accordance with medieval precedents, the sculptor and even the architect should have served an apprenticeship as a metalworker, and in pursuit of this ideal he himself had worked in a bronze foundry for two years. As his career progressed he tended to move away from architecture and to concentrate more on the expertise he had developed as a metalworker and the associated skills of jewellery. In 1903 his book *Silverwork and Jewellery* was published in the 'Artistic Craft' series, and in 1910 he was working as the goldsmithing instructor under Lethaby at the Royal College of Art. One of his most important metalwork commissions was for a casket that was presented to Joseph Chamberlain in 1903 in recognition of his services as British Colonial Secretary. It is architectural in concept, with imagery appropriate to the Colonial Office, and made of silver, gold, enamels and semi-precious stones.

In 1922, Wilson emigrated to France, thus ending his term of presidency of the Arts and Crafts Exhibition Society, which he had held since 1915. For one year during his term of office, in 1917, he had in addition been Master of the Art Workers' Guild, and these jobs give some indication of the important role he played in promoting the public face of the arts and crafts. As well as being a prolific writer and an eloquent lecturer, he was also famous as an exhibitor abroad and as a leading figure in the organisation and design of some major arts and crafts shows – notably the Burlington House Exhibition of 1916, of which Troup again remarked: 'In this elaborate scheme the somewhat sombre rooms were completely transformed into a series of interconnected halls;...Wilson was the only man who could have brought into this great decorative scheme the work of such distinguished artists of different schools and of such varied temperaments.'[5]

Wilson continued to work from his new home in Paris through the 1920s, and his last commission was completed only a short time before his death in 1934 – the huge, heavily symbolic bronze doors for the Cathedral of St John the Divine, New York.

I have decided to concentrate in this paper on a small Welsh church – St Mark's, Brithdir. This is one of Wilson's major works, and one which encompasses in a single building the most important of his attitudes to architecture, design and working methods. Its interest derives from the way in which Wilson's conformity to conventional Arts and Crafts ideology is displayed alongside aspects that demonstrate his divergence from familiar beliefs – a theme that pervades much of his work.

Brithdir church was consecrated in September 1898. The building had been started in 1895 when Mrs Tooth, widow of the Rev Charles Tooth, commissioned Wilson to build a church on some land she owned near Dolgellau, North Wales, as a memorial to her late husband. The Rev Tooth had for some years worked as a vicar in the Midlands, but because of ill-health had moved to Italy and founded St Mark's English Church in Florence.

Describing the foundation plaque (Figure 6), Wilson explained to Mrs Tooth that 'the lion of St Mark would have wings inlaid with pieces of opal pearl and an eye of selected iridescent shell. This will give gleam and interest to the plate which it might otherwise lack.'[6] Here and throughout the building, Wilson showed a clear view of what the finished church would look like. The foundation plaque is situated fairly low on the west wall, behind the font, and is only dimly lit. He added 'the expense is inconsiderable', and gave the price of cutting the pearl as 'about 1 shilling a piece'. The problem of cost was a constant consideration in the building of St Mark's, and when corresponding with Mrs Tooth Wilson rarely mentioned any development without telling her how much it would amount to. For all his idealistic, even visionary, attitudes to architecture, he was still acutely aware of the realities of the prices of labour and materials.

The lion of St Mark used here is incidentally a good example of the sensitivity Wilson retained throughout his career to traditional symbols and images, which is especially noticeable in his metalwork. Even in his last work, the cathedral doors of 1934, the lion of St Mark forms one of the panels.

Because Brithdir church in a sense had its origins in Florence, Wilson paid close attention to Italian sources. In June 1895 he wrote: 'I have had constantly in mind one or two of those delightful simple churches just south of the Alps, where all the effect comes from the management of the light and the proportions of the roof and walls.' (see Figure 7).

Wilson constantly stressed the 'simplicity' and 'studious severity' of St Mark's, and the fact that it was a very important commission to him. He was quite resigned, he said, 'to making everybody's life miserable until the work is done...I have been so much interested in the work that I have spent more time on [it] than usual...the chief merit of Brithdir is that it is *personal*,

8 *St Mark's Church, Brithdir, from North*
9 *General interior view of St Mark's Church*

and not immediately derived from some existing original.'

Mrs Tooth's constant scrutiny of Wilson's every move, combined with the need for stringent price controls, made his task at times a difficult one. He replied quite sharply to one of Mrs Tooth's queries about delays in the work: 'I want you to please believe a little that I have put of my very best into the work, the more as I have taken as long as possible over it. The rapid rate of production in modern times is absolutely destructive of *real* quality...Moreover it prevents any possibility of getting the artist's best.'

Wilson insisted on personal involvement with the construction as well as with the conception of St Mark's. 'Most men I know delegate all the most important part of their work to others. I have not the conscience to do that, and what ever work I undertake I must do myself.'

He makes frequent references to the work he is doing in his London studio towards the church, and to his busy visits to the site. On one occasion he rejected some inferior timber. On another he writes: 'I propose not to use the assorted slates generally in use...but to select myself from the quarry the natural tints and colours of the slates, and...use these on the roof, and...produce a building which should harmonise continually with its surroundings.'

However, he did make careful use of assistants in carrying out the project. One of his pupils was 'to see after' the joinery and the woodwork, another the masonry, and a third, whose home was in North Wales, was to stay for three or four weeks at a time to supervise the work. Wilson felt confident that these measures, together with his own visits and the presence of Mr Williams, the proprietor of the Dolgellau building firm employed to do the basic construction work on the church, would ensure that his ideas were accurately carried out.

The design of the church was dominated by the importance Wilson attached to using Welsh workmen who, like his Welsh pupil, would have a natural understanding and affinity with the methods, materials and landscape of the district. 'In order that the work may be done locally I have omitted anything like carving or elaborate masonry, and am relying for effect entirely on the colour of the stone, the method of building, and the proportions.' Unfortunately, Wilson's optimistic faith in Mr Williams was somewhat misplaced; he caused delays even before the first stone was laid, since he was unable to interpret the plans. The difficulty of explaining his requirements must have been exasperating to Wilson, who certainly seemed to know as much about building as Williams himself. He complained to Mrs Tooth that 'Mr Williams does not quite understand that we want to make the roof at the same time as the walls, so that the timbers may have time to season and take their bearing before they are forced together;...he has no more knowledge of building than a cat, and has been persistently misrepresenting my methods and proposals.'

Strict guidance was clearly necessary if Wilson's plans were to be faithfully executed. He was determined, for example, to have the church built of stone in large blocks, and Mr Williams's assumption that the stone was to be 'tooled', or smoothed, had to be quickly corrected by Wilson: 'In the ordinary walling the stone is to be left unworked with its natural quarry face shewing.' As he shrewdly remarked, an added bonus besides that of visual effect was that rough meant cheap. 'Not squaring all the stones with mathematical accuracy...will not only be an improvement in their looks, but an economy as well, a rare conjuncture!' (Figure 8).

The completed building would rely for its impact on mass rather than finish. Wilson wrote, with evident satisfaction, 'Every time I see the church it gives me greater pleasure...it is so massively built, and almost Egyptian in its solidity.' The comparison is a curiously exotic one to apply to a remote Welsh church, but is particularly interesting when we discover that, after moving from Vicarage Gate, the Wilson family lived for a time at Alma Tadema's house at Fairseat while awaiting the completion of 'The Thatched House' at Platt.

Whatever diverse influences went into St Mark's, Wilson constantly had in mind the ideas of matching the church to its context, and the right use of materials. He therefore adamantly opposed Mrs Tooth's suggestion that the roof should be tiled: 'If tiles were used on that design it would utterly spoil it and strike an inharmonious note in a most beautiful landscape. Tiles, it seems to me, are quite a foreign element in a slate country...The rocks and stones, the grass and trees, are all part of the...scheme, and are intimately connected and influenced by each other – and the art of a place must be *of* the place, not imported into it.'

When the church was completed, Wilson was confident that an authentic and compatible effect had been achieved: it had taken root. 'The church pleased me very much. The masonry is wonderful, and it all looks as if it had sprung out of the soil instead of being planted down on it.'

The church is a significant expression of Wilson's philosophy of architecture – an exercise in environmental 'truth to materials' – and an expression, too, of his own originality. 'I am not giving you a church turned out of a mould: I have built it as simply as I know how, and have been looking forward to embellishing the interior in an individual manner.'

Just as the link between North Wales and Florence is a surprising one, so too is the transition between the quiet, severe exterior and the striking interior of St Mark's. The first impression the visitor receives is one of bright, vibrant colour. The scheme is carefully planned, and the effect is very dramatic. It also provides an interesting example of how the very process of building could act as an influential factor on the finished church. The strong, deep colours were specifically calculated to supplement and interact with the architecture – very pointedly in this case because Mrs Tooth had previously insisted on extra windows which Wilson had been reluctant to add, partly because they would disturb the balance between window and wall space, but mainly because they would make the interior too light. (Figure 9).

The decoration was carried out by a man whom Wilson had just been employing to colour the inside of another church near Chester, and who had once worked for Morris. There is, too, an interesting correlation between the colours used at Brithdir and those at St Martin's, Marple, where the same basic colours are used, but in gentler shades. Thus the 'rich warm red' and 'dark blue' of Brithdir's chancel, together with the 'warm cream' of its nave and the leaf green of its cornice, reappear as the salmon pink, powder blue, white and hazy green of Marple's Lady Chapel.

If the overall impression conveyed by the inside of St Mark's is of all-enveloping colour, the focal point in both a liturgical and compositional sense is the altar (Figures 10, 11 and 12). Later in his career Wilson worked primarily as a jeweller, and it is interesting that the church functions almost as a piece of architectural jewellery, with the altar as the gemstone and the building as its mount. In one letter, Wilson actually spoke of the whole church as 'the simple beautiful *setting* for the altar'. Wilson gave an explicit description of the design and making

10 *The altar*

11 *Detail of The Virgin Mary*

12 *Details of the child angel and lettering*

true. He had, he said, experienced a difficulty which, 'though real enough and worrying enough, sounds a little ridiculous. The model who sat for the child angel was so restless that the sittings had to be indefinitely multiplied, a little being done each time. I could not change the model because he was just the type I wanted.'

Over the altar is a panel of raised copper with a vine springing from a chalice and an inscription from the Vulgate: 'This is the cup of the New Testament in my blood.' At each side are patterns of bluebells springing from the monogram IHS.

The pulpit (Figure 13) was being worked on at the same time as the altar was being cast. Mrs Tooth suggested that it should be framed up in wood to 'improve' its appearance and ensure that it did not rival the richness of the altar, and all Wilson's powers of argument were summoned up to oppose the idea. He wrote indignantly: 'Really the pulpit does *not* look like a pot at all… Logically to frame a metal panel in wood is wrong; and aesthetically also. The *strength* should be in the *frame*, and the eye, however strong the frame may really be, always gives more importance to metal. Moreover, there is no possibility, in a framed pulpit, of avoiding the idea of something seen before.'

Another confrontation with Mrs Tooth arose over the door giving access to the pulpit, which again Wilson fiercely defended. Almost snappishly he insisted 'The door was put there because it fills a void from the church, and is in that way like all the attached wall pulpits in France and Italy…From the beginning I designed the door there. I attach great importance to it. You see, if I had done the ordinary thing, everyone would have accepted it and been pleased.' Mrs Tooth clearly bowed to Wilson's irresistible persuasion, for the pulpit was erected just as he had envisaged it. In the centre of each panel is a wreath encircling a bunch of grapes, beaten up from behind, and an inscription from the Vulgate: 'Now gird up thy loins and say to them the things that I deliver thee.'

Wilson certainly argued his cases here with conviction,

of the altar: 'The whole altar and retable would be sheathed in copper, and the front of the altar would be beaten with a diaper of flowers. On this diaper the figures of the blessed virgin and the angel would be raised…under my superintendence. The effect in the church would, I think, be very splendid.'

There were some unexpected difficulties in the execution of the altar. No space was originally left for the lettering, and it had to be fitted in as the work progressed – very satisfactorily as it happened, since the writing became part of the composition. In explaining to Mrs Tooth why the altar took so long to complete, Wilson gave an excuse so unlikely that it must be

animals hidden in their nooks and crannies. He reassured Mrs Tooth that, although they looked 'dull' in the packing cases (they were made in London, not on the site) nevertheless they would just *'make* the chancel' since they were specifically designed to be seen from below, when the half-hidden animals would come to life. Among the others, which include an owl, a rabbit, a tortoise, a dolphin and a kingfisher, the mouse is especially reminiscent of the old misericord tradition, where designs are fitted creatively and compactly into the space available. The tail turns round and can be seen at the side of the curving Art Nouveau 'SM' insignia of St Mark's at the end of the stalls (Figures 14, 15, 16).

13 *The Pulpit*

Details of the carved choir stalls

14 *Tortoise*

15 *Mouse*

16 *'SM' insignia, with the mouse's tail just visible at the base of the M*

though he had conceded some points of design to Mrs Tooth in respect of local styles and customs. For these reasons he had given up the idea of a rood screen, and the angel heads that were to have been inserted into the wet plaster at each end of every roof beam. But he conscientiously struggled to avoid wrongful compromise. Whenever the proposed adjustment seemed detrimental to the spirit of his design, he would assert his own inspired feeling for what was *right*. He consequently opposed Mrs Tooth's suggestion for a cruciform groundplan as vehemently as he fought her idea of tiles for the roof: 'Quite apart from the individuality of [my] arrangement, it is a peculiarly Welsh treatment. The cross-shaped plan descends at once to the ordinary level...and destroys what is most valuable in [this] design, the long-waisted look, to use a rather inappropriate but exact comparison.'

Wilson speaks of proportion, too, as a vital aspect of the wooden altar rail. 'I have made it more solid than usual because the common rail is so flimsy and feeble that it imparts an air of weakness to the whole church. The common brass ones are not one quarter as good looking. Moreover they have the disadvantage of needing constant cleaning.'

Simplicity is the keynote of the Spanish chestnut choir stalls which, as Wilson pointed out, 'are practically nothing but framed-up seats' with little ornamentation except carved

17 *One pair of inlaid doors*

18 *The lead font basin, with the foundation plaque behind it*

The plain wooden lectern, of consciously simple design, was cheap to produce and aptly fitted its surroundings, but the two pairs of doors facing each other on the north and south walls are more lavish (Figure 17). Their brass handles and contrasting bands of wood show Wilson's pleasure in rich materials and inlay. Their shell insets, too, recall the detailing on the foundation plaque, and again hint at the techniques of jewellery.

The last two major items in the church's furnishings – the organ and the font – were carefully tailored to suit the atmosphere of St Mark's. Wilson deliberately left these until last because, unlike the pulpit and the altar, which are almost part of the structure of the church, they are isolated objects that could give a fragmentary or intrusive effect if badly managed. He wrote to Mrs Tooth: 'so many otherwise beautiful churches are ruined by commonplace or ill-arranged organs', but he gave close attention, not just to the appearance of this one, but also to the practicalities of performance, raising it up slightly to give resonance and carrying power.

Finally, the font basin (Figure 18), set on a plain octagonal pillar, was designed by Wilson, modelled by a pupil, Arthur Grove, and cast in lead by a Mr Dodds. It has a simple country

air about it, and echoes the dark metal of the foundation plaque nearby. Wilson may have had the local leadmining industry in mind when he designed it; but it is certainly another instance of his search for innovation within tradition. Leadwork was currently undergoing a revival, and *The Builder* of March 1900 contained an illustrated article on recent examples, in which St Mark's font was featured.

By the time the church was completed, the estimated cost had increased from £900 to £1450, despite Wilson's meticulous attention to economy. He was quick to counteract Mrs Tooth's complaints. 'I do not understand how the work has run up so. It is not as if it had been very elaborate in design…The only thing I know is that I believe it is going to be one of the best bits of work this end of the century! If that be any comfort.'

He saw the price of the finished church in more than purely financial terms: 'I cannot tell you how I have thought about it, or what it has cost *me*…' but he was sure, too, that its value would be a lasting one. 'Now I have no hesitation in saying that what is done at Brithdir must live, because it has come out of my own life; and I feel a certain amount of pride in knowing that good work is there.'

1 Wilson Archive, Royal College of Art. Letter to Edgar Wilson, July 1927

2 Ashbee, C. R. *Masters of the Art Workers Guild from the beginning till 1934 (ms)* 315–316

3 A detailed description of the fittings of St Bartholomew's may be found in Taylor, Nicholas 'Byzantium in Brighton' in *Architectural Review* April 1966, reprinted in Service, A. (ed) *Edwardian Architecture and its Origins*

4 Troup, F. W. 'Obituary' in *Journal of the Royal Institute of British Architects* 24 March 1934

5 *Ibid*

6 All subsequent quotations are taken from the correspondence between Henry Wilson and Mrs Tooth held in the Brithdir Collection, Gwynedd Archives Service, Dolgellau, whose staff I should like to thank for their assistance

The photographs were taken by G. Harris

Towards a design history bibliography

Anthony J Coulson
Open University Library

Architectural history has traditionally always dominated writing on the history of design. In his very influential book *Industrial Art Explained,* John Gloag advances the thesis that 'The architect is almost the only professional man in the community who is trained to think lucidly about design.' Very many important designers of the last hundred years were trained as architects, and architecture has generally been rated as the mistress art – or design. However there is now a well established and developing interest in the history of other aspects and areas of design.

Consequently, it now seems a good time to take stock of the situation and try to work out an introductory bibliography to the History of Design in Great Britain, covering approximately the last hundred years. This is essentially a preliminary study for a lot more systematic and detailed work to follow. A definitive bibliography is just not possible at the present state of the subject and its documentation.

For the past few months I have been wrestling with the problems and detail of this research and have gathered in a considerable mass of partly digested information. As I am still locked in the struggle to bring some shape from this material I hope you may find it helpful for me to run over the difficulties and some of the methods and plans I am using.

By removing architecture I felt that I might have reduced the labour to slightly more manageable proportions, but I soon realised that I had removed the peg – provided by a well developed body of historical writing – on which most design history has depended. However, there is a vast body of design, and now design history writing, quite separate from architectural writing and so the next problem was to try to establish some focus for the bibliography. Consequently I decided to concentrate my research on four main lines of enquiry:

1 The history of institutions, educational changes and the evolution of concepts of design presented in a chronological way
2 Distinct areas of design activity, such as Graphics, Printing, Interior Design and Furniture
3 Product design in specific materials, such as Glass, Ceramics, Leather
4 Activities of particular designers

This final category I set aside for two main reasons: it is always easier to trace a name or an individual through indexes, library catalogues and other records (biographies are generally far easier to locate than subjects); the Design History Publications Sub-Committee hopes that some form of biographical dictionary may soon be produced.

To return to my remaining three lines of research, it was clear that a bit more selection was necessary to make the task at all manageable. Consequently I have set aside a number of areas of activity that have developed coherent if embryonic literatures in their own right and are well served by indexes and interest groups. On these grounds I have excluded photography and most design associated with the performing arts. Also – and very reluctantly – I decided that I would have

to leave out many aspects of technical engineering design. Consequently I have not been able to tackle such fields as computer aided design, circuit design and many aspects of mechanical engineering design. Unfortunately these can only be researched at present by careful analysis of current or near-current literature and then followed back in specific detail through very specialised resources. I had hoped to deal with these subjects in a general way, but a preliminary search of some of the more general indexes, such as *British Technology Index* and *Engineering Index,* soon showed that this would not be feasible unless I could check thousands of specialised facets. All too easily I would be working up a general bibliography of the history of technology.

Even with these limitations how did I break into the apparent no man's land between art on one side and technology on the other? Clearly I had to rely on the major bibliographical tools generated by the largest library collections. For retrospective searching there were the subject catalogues of the British Museum, Library of Congress and the National Library of Art. Other useful sources are the library catalogues printed by G. K. Hall of the Library of the Graduate School of Design, Harvard University, the Research Libraries of the New York Public Library, the Library of the Museum of Modern Art New York and others. For more accessible British material there is the *British National Bibliography.* For articles I drew on the *British Humanities Index, British Technology Index* and their predecessor *Subject Index to Periodicals* as well as the more specialised *Art Index* and *Art Design Photo* which I will discuss later. As well as these fairly obvious works there is the motley range of individual library catalogues, research lists and smaller-scale bibliographies. The problem with using these general works is that only fairly broad searching is possible and this leads to an abundance of marginal and ephemeral material which is very often difficult to check. Terminology and outdated ideas of subject classification make many early subject catalogues very difficult to use. The popular tendency to group works under 'Art and Industry' or 'Art and something else' rather than 'Design' and more specific applications tends to generate a lot of confusion. There is also the vast problem of the patchy and imperfect indexing and cataloguing of many areas of nineteenth-century writing. Without years of patient checking and great good fortune the bibiliography could not hope to be more than the most selective listing – charting landmarks and attempts at historical writing rather than all the documents needed for research. Sadly many indexes, such as the *Bibliographic Index,* which should be ideal for bibliographic research, almost completely ignore design in any form. Consequently there are not many short cuts available.

Even turning to the more specialised indexes that have a clearer interest in design I found the ICSID *Design Abstracts International* to be very selective with only very occasional articles in the historical field. The more general art indexes *Art Bibliographies Modern* and *Art Index* are a bit more helpful though mainly concerned with the decorative arts. *Art Design Photo* has a slightly wider coverage of graphic design but has not been going long enough to make a lot of difference. Unfortunately the problem is the same here as it is with the more general indexes – only the larger circulation journals get indexed time and again. So many important historical journals, such as *Furniture History* and *Journal of the Printing Historical Society*, are not covered by the larger indexing systems.

Technical indexing services are even harder to use because history and often design are generally minor facets and the information cannot be extracted even by computerised search unless the enquiry stems from a very specific subject. Unfortunately this situation is often complicated by the inclusion of trade literature, particularly house journals where the historical articles indexed are often of a chatty and very ephemeral nature. Certainly there is a lot of useful historical material contained in a detailed and long-established set of abstracts, such as those published by the Printing Industry Research Association, but the material will only come to light through prolonged and very specific search.

The whole situation soon became alarming when a check on the bibliographies contained in some long-established works revealed a lot of material that had seemingly gone unrecorded anywhere in the bibliographical net. The problem is then one of checking as much material that still exists for further clues. Then we meet the problem that there is really no one central design history collection in Great Britain. Libraries that have been constituted recently cannot hope to catch up on the backlog of older materials now out of print and rapidly increasing in price. Even in the older collections many of the more ancient books have been lost and never replaced. Too often writings on design have been of subsidiary importance to the body concerned and so they have not been bought at times of budget cutbacks. The result is that material for the bibliography might be all over the place or nowhere at all.

Consequently all I could hope to do would be to try to draw up some sort of fairly representative listing from the material available with some notes on the obvious gaps or more localised problems in parts of the literature. Even when I had extracted a fairly large body of references the picture is still that of a subject trying to establish itself even in areas that boast quite a body of published work. This is clearly the reason why there is a very substantial body of carefully researched studies of historical costume but a shortage of serious analytical writing on changes in fashion.

Perhaps it may now help to delineate some of the characteristics of the literature as I see it.

1 First, and most obvious, a lot of really important writings are just not available. Many important documents, such as the memoirs of Mackmurdo and Godwin, have never been published. Many many more works are out of print and almost completely unobtainable. With cheaper reprint and microfilming methods I don't see why quite a few items could not be reissued in the same way that architectural monographs are now being reissued. But is demand sufficient at the moment?

2 Second, the historical writing that does exist is still very patchy. There are detailed studies of Victorian sheet music covers and buttons, but the detailed history of the Society of Industrial Artists and Designers is yet to be published.

There are many detailed studies of particular areas in progress, but actual publication is still very much dominated by the interests of the collector and the coffee table rather than the serious historian. Consequently we seem to have a glut of books on silver, but not very much on aluminum. Even now many areas of historical enquiry are swamped by a seemingly endless tide of picturebooks of very questionable quality, often trotting out the same old posters or well-worn prints. For most publishers plates dominate text except in a few areas geared more directly to the limited scholarly market. Even here current market forces predominate. Unless there is a greater degree of direct sponsorship from the firm or body concerned many studies will never get published. Here the difference between publication in the design history field and history of technology field is very marked. In the case of technical history it always seems to have been easier to drum up funds from the company or parent body for a commemorative study.

3 The third characteristic of the literature follows from this situation. Too much really important writing appears in small journals that command a small circulation and so will never reach a wider audience. Unless there is a drastic change in present indexing arrangements this will only encourage duplication of work and lead to the increasing isolation of specialist groups.

4 The fourth clear characteristic is that literature begins to breed literature and so there is now probably a disproportionately large body of writing in a few well documented areas whilst other fields, such as most aspects of earlier design education apart from the Bauhaus, are almost completely overlooked. In common with any newly emergent subject area it will take time and the reconstitution of very many scattered records before a more balanced view emerges. Even so there are distinctive problems inherent in many of the materials for design history that may never be overcome. Quite apart from commercial fears of breach of design copyright there is the sheer difficulty of checking trade literature and even old journals just not kept by many libraries or archives. Unless a much more careful check is organised, valuable primary and secondary evidence will continue to be dumped as companies and organisations fail, move or clear their lumber rooms. Some of the better-known collections do reach the notice of the Historical Manuscripts Commission, the Business Archives Council or even the local archive or library, but still a lot of material is destroyed unrecognised.

Another key difficulty with the literature of design history is its dependence on short-lived evidence in the form of exhibitions, trade fairs and their associated literature. Very often these events have been poorly documented or recorded in only the barest outline. Good collections of catalogues have been built up by the Victoria and Albert Museum and other long-established libraries but they are only ever likely to be a selection. Short print runs and limited circulation make it often very difficult for libraries to collect them and record them. Consequently a lot of very valuable material is soon lost.

I am sorry if this has all sounded a rather familiar diatribe, but it really brings us back to the guiding principle behind my attempt to construct a bibliography of this period – the need to assemble some form of unified body of information about design history in Great Britain. Ultimately this must lead to some form of resource centre to collect information and materials to feed further investigations. As more records of all kinds and even studies of records disappear, the more important it becomes to establish this centre as soon as possible. A necessary first step must clearly be some form of list of what already exists in published form and here I hope my bibliography may be some use.

Design history: process or product?

Roger Newport
Wolverhampton Polytechnic

The subject of design history in Britain is, as we all know, traditionally descended on the one hand from the Fine to the Applied or Decorative Arts, and on the other hand through Architecture.

When Diploma of Art and Design courses were first run in 1963, the limits of the subject were brought into question, but in professional terms it was still very much circumscribed by the people who taught it. For most of the first DipAD student designers, the history of their subject consisted principally of the history of architecture, with an obligatory and largely unexplained element of the history of art.

While there can be few, if any, arguments that these subjects are not educational in a broad sense, as well as in the more immediate terms of a general design education, most students, after wandering in a slightly bemused fashion back to the studio, had no other option but to forget them and to get on with their work.

It is this dichotomy between what design students do when they are designing, and the sort of information they are presented with in the name of the history of design that I want to explore in some detail.

The discipline of design history is, of course, larger than that element which is taught to designers; but I would like to consider this element alone, and see whether it does not, after all, contain something of importance for the subject as a whole, and maybe of importance for the health of design, which is after all our core subject – our host as it were.

As the discipline stands at the moment, I am of the opinion that we are not only in danger of becoming less relevant to our core subject than successive Government reports have hoped, but we are in danger of enabling design historians to talk a completely different language from designers; in danger of setting permanent precedents for our subject which will enable criteria for criticism to specialise away from criteria for performance.

Some movement to isolate a new specialism is necessary, and this particular movement is perhaps not critical if the audience for design history is the student design historian. But the situation becomes more and more untenable if our audience includes the student designer, and if this specialising movement is away from designing.

We are now, 14 years after the establishment of complementary studies elements in design courses, far better equipped and far better informed than we were to teach the various subjects we include in the history of design. But very few go any further to bridge the gap between conventional approaches, which develop general statements about the appearance and environment of generic groups of artefacts, and what concerns the designer.

We still find it almost impossible to see present-day design and production as part of our subject. There still seems to be a professional gulf between the most recent designs that we are willing to talk about and what people are designing now.

There are probably fairly good reasons for this, which we must all have speculated about. One is that we realise historical illustration cannot be a precedent for immediate practice without an understanding of the philosophies behind both, and the connections between them. But this is often extremely difficult: the traditional crafts, for example, had no accompanying literature of philosophy; and the philosophy of present-day designing is very largely unwritten, and in any case still very actively developing.

The 'Art-based' movements on the other hand, with their accompanying literature and well preserved evidence, provide us with both illustration and philosophy, and therefore the easiest way to circumscribe our history of design.

Another reason is perhaps becoming even more important. Historical assessment of design has in the past been undertaken with reference to art patronage and its associated bias towards the rich and influential, whereas recent developments in the means of production have moved designing towards technology and the anonymous – trends which the training of design historians has not followed at all closely.

Lathes and sewing machines, microscopes and astrolabes are perhaps more important to the history of our well-being and understanding than is their contemporary artistic endeavour.

When we show only the results of the design process and say nothing about the process itself, we cannot be too disappointed if the only people who can make use of what we purvey are illustrators and advertisers, whose job it is to portray as well as to design, or craftsmen or designers with a somewhat unfortunate bent towards vicarious historicism. But a historical crib-sheet of tradition, style and motif is the very least we should aim at, and in many ways the very worst.

On the one hand we have designing, which is arguably the only way that man decides his material future; and on the other its history, which we pride ourselves on judging by criteria that are historically accurate, but which are comparatively inapplicable in the modern context.

We show, by and large, the iconography of successful innovation and privileged indulgence, in a situation where 'designing' demands the creation of alternatives and, consequently, where concepts of failure and compromise are of more importance. We are in the unexpected company of the consumer lobby when we study the objects and say nothing about the activity.

It is perhaps one of the bases of our problem – one that we have inherited through our educational system – that the Victorians drew so dangerously strong a line between work and family, between industry and culture – and ultimately, therefore, between technology and design.

Before I begin to talk about the process that confronts the designer when he gets back to the studio from his design history lecture, perhaps I ought to define some of the words we commonly use a little more closely. For example, if we go through even this short talk and every time I say 'designer', one of us thinks of a studio potter, another of a textile designer, another of an engineer and so on, then I do not think that we can hope to reach the end of it in any kind of agreement.

'Design' is an incredible container of a word. It conveys all the artefacts of many different skills, as well as the generalities and tools of the process. At the same time it seems to me quite evident that we haven't got the terminology to describe what actually goes on.

In May, I noticed a caption to a photograph in *The Times* which read 'Harry Norris (left) Wimpey Finance Director "Discussions against shareholders' interests". Right, Godfrey Bradman, Tax Avoidance Designer.'

At the other extreme, the second verse of William Cowper's famous hymn 'God Moves in a Mysterious Way' reads 'Deep in unfathomable mines/Of never failing skill/He treasures up His bright designs/And works His sovereign will.'

I presume that we all discount the history of tax avoidance, and most if not all of natural history, when it comes to deciding what we shall teach as design history; but on the other hand, the term is recognised by people 'in electronics' as well as 'in Christmas cards'.

In schools it has come to include art, craft, environmental studies, technology and home economics, or at least parts of them. The Atomic Energy Authority, polymer chemists, even members of parliament recognise the word as describing part of their job: polymer chemists 'design' new plastics; members of parliament 'design' a bill for the House. The dictionary will support their claim, in that the definition it provides is 'mental plan', 'scheme of attack', 'purpose', 'end in view', 'adaptation of means to ends' and so on.

The way we as a profession fight back upstream to what we teach is presumably via the rather sweeping assumption that everything made by man manifests some if not all of these facets of determination – these facets of design – and that some facets are more worth talking about than others.

The way we decide what to talk about, and the reasons we talk about it, are what I think we need to be more purposive about. As Pevsner put it in his note of dissent from the 1970 Coldstream Report: 'It is clarity of thought and expression, it is unbiased recognition of problems, it is the capacity for discussion and it is ultimately understanding they must achieve. But to understand one must know the facts, and to choose relevant facts one must command a surplus of facts. That is the unpalatable truth.'

Pevsner was talking about our students. The same must obviously apply to ourselves. At the same time, if we consider that all man-made things must, by definition, contain an element of predetermination – an element that all the 'designing' professions would recognise – then of course we never can command a surplus of facts.

When we choose what to talk about and how to talk about it, we have to look for the facts with a view to their relevance – we have to select our illustrations with a view to their meaning – and we can only do that if we 'know about' what they have to relate to.

We have really got to disentangle what we mean from the words we usually use, and one of the main things we have to do is to differentiate product from process – designs from designing – in much the same way that Antoine Lavoisier distinguished process from materials with the classical alchemist's experiments. It was only with distinctions like these that alchemy gave way to chemistry, and I think we ourselves have got to work out the same distinction.

I want us first to consider a craft activity, because craft is so readily assumed to be just a sub-section of design. If we imagine any craft activity, we see that here the end product is an integral part of the process of designing. The craftsman works immediately with the end product, but he doesn't work like a machine. He compensates for errors and inaccuracies, for inconsistencies in the material; he changes his mind as he goes along, considers what he has already done and responds to it.

In terms of perception and action, he maintains a feedback loop with the object he is making; and we see that this simple description fits most of what goes on in art colleges. The description fits the sculptor, painter, potter, blacksmith – everybody who makes something. It fits because it doesn't say anything about intention, only about method. In this use it is very similar to 'skill', except that 'craft' doesn't imply that you are any good at it.

When the designer sits down at the drawing board, he maintains an immediate craft relationship with a model of the thing he is designing – he cannot do so with the actual end product, because it is the other side of a production process, the other side of the expenditure of time and effort, and probably the other side of compromise with other people. Instead, he sits down with a drawing of the end product, or some other kind of model of it.

He doesn't carry out the manufacturing process in the same breath as he considers how the thing shall be, but he does have to consider it as part of the design work – along with many other sorts of consideration.

A piece of craft work that gets reproduced doesn't turn the original into a work of design. This isn't just a minor shift in emphasis, it is a major distinction in the way you proceed. It means in effect that the craftsman is limited to what he can cope with in his head, and limited to what he is skilled enough to make himself – and the designer isn't.

The drawing isn't an end in itself – a 'work of art' as it may be for the artist – it is a tool, an artefact that enables him to do something else.

The craftsman's relationship is with the end product; the designer's is with a model of it, or more usually a model of only one aspect or one part of it. The difference is like that between performing as a concert pianist with a symphony orchestra and writing the music for them to perform.

As Professor Archer and Ken Baynes put it at the 'Design for Need' conference in 1976: 'The core subject of the discipline of design is the set of languages used to describe, evaluate and adapt the world of things. The term "modelling" is applied to describe this set of languages. A model is something which stands for or represents something else. Modelling is the making and using of models. A model could be a drawing, a plan, imagery, a form of words, a chemical or mathematical formula, a diagram, a complex construction in wood or metal – anything which is used to stand for or represent something else.'[1]

There is another qualification of the designer's use of the model though, because if we just leave the definition of 'designing' at 'the usage of models', then our subject becomes the history of all literature, language, music, planning and painting and nearly everything else.

The designer's main task is not to model existing fact as do the sciences – although he may do in order to record, describe or analyse – and it is not to model fiction, as the design is useless unless it can be transcribed into fact.

The main type of modelling he undertakes is that of the future, or better still, of 'likely future' or 'possible future', and we can identify two main types. One we can term 'exploratory', which involves extrapolating from recent and present facts to a 'likely future'; the other is 'normative', which involves identifying a desirable 'likely future' or goal, and then specifying how to get to it.

With the craftsman's activity, there need be no separate designing activity, because the decisions are taken – the craft is manifest – when the object is being made. We cannot look at the design process as a separate entity of, say, the waggon maker's art, because if there was one, it took place only in conversation with his customers or fellow craftsmen.

Even devices that are considered revolutionary, like the Newcomen engine, can be explained in terms of assembling existing traditional craft skills and mechanisms. The engine house was in the builder's tradition; the beams and pulleys in the carpenter's; the cylinder in the cannon founder's; the pipework in the plumber's and the boiler in the distiller's. And one can read other devices like Tull's seed drill and the early motor car in the same way.

Within the art college, the craftsman can of course, and frequently does, design. The potter and the jeweller draw or model what they are going to produce, and we can differentiate this design activity from their subsequent craft activity.

We can even see this pattern with the sculptor's maquette and the painter's sketch. But here the craft activity is more likely to model fiction or abstraction; and if it does so in sufficiently thoughtful a manner, we are probably fairly happy to label it 'art' if not with a capital 'a'. It is worth pointing out that we currently accept art that has been produced by both the design and craft activities, and that the art object of course has itself to be a model, if it is to work at all.

The appearance of a 'designed' object need not model or symbolise anything. It may do so, as an aid to the prosecution of its own function, but only when it is necessary to maintain communication with people or other systems which can recognise its meaning and respond to it. I am thinking here of things like the signs and symbols we might use on a control panel to facilitate its operation.

It has been suggested at this conference that perhaps design history should limit itself to, for example, the outside of a motor car, and perhaps not try to deal with other elements like the engine. Besides the thought that Ettore Bugatti and Georges Roesch would turn in their graves, it is perhaps a proper art historical attitude which does not see how it can function with artefacts that do not have an 'art' element, do not model anything and do not intend to symbolise anything.

It is at this point I think, if at no other, that we can identify the complete breakdown of links between art and design – and indeed between the approaches of art history and design history. Although these distinctions are recent, they do exist in the attitudes if not in the minds of our students, even if not in the minds of the historical figures we talk about.

Leonardo Da Vinci wrote: 'If you despise painting, which is the sole imitator of all the visible works of nature, it is certain you will be despising a subtle invention which, with philosophical and ingenious speculation, takes as its theme all the various kinds of forms, airs and scenes, plants, animals, grasses and flowers, which are surrounded by light and shade. And this truly is a science and the true-born daughter of nature.'

Incidentally, he also considered sculpture to be a lesser art, because the artist is not in control of the light, only of the form which it illuminates.

In our terms, this explanation of painting is not absolutely satisfactory, because of course what Leonardo did was much more than merely use paint to record light as photographic film does. He did not just portray what was in front of him, did not just portray fact; he also constructed and portrayed events that he either believed had happened in the past, or that he believed were myth. He also of course drew what he imagined could be fact in the future.

Once we have made these tentative distinctions, then it becomes easier to see any particular activity, which we must still label with the vernaculars 'art' and 'design', as consisting in varying proportions of both activities, but necessarily involving a craft activity. Don't let's concentrate alone on what the producer was called – 'commercial artist', 'engineer' or 'draftsman' – let's concentrate on what he did, and consequently on how we are able to make sense of what he did.

Let's go back to the situation where we imagine how a student designer tries to make use of the information presented to him by design history. Deciding on how things should look is only one part of the process.

When the student designer is presented with a design problem, the extent to which the problem is defined determines the amount of freedom he has, the number of alternative solutions he has at his disposal, whether he realises them or not. There are comparatively very few problems that can be so tightly defined in terms of an artefact, its manufacture and all the details of its future use that there is only one best answer with no alternatives and no choice.

The designer's problem is to work out what the constraints entail, and then to reconcile the conflicting requirements. As David Pye put it: 'The requirements for design conflict and cannot be reconciled. All designs for devices are in some degree failures, either because they flout one or another of the requirements or because they are compromises, and compromise implies a degree of failure.

'...It follows that all designs for use are arbitrary. The designer or his client has to decide in what degree and where there shall be failure. Thus the shape of all designed things is the product of arbitrary choice. If you vary the terms of your compromise – say, more speed, more heat, less safety, more discomfort and lower first cost – then you vary the shape of the thing designed.'[2]

With any design there are arbitrary choices to be made; and the designer's compromise starts from the idea that a device, for example, should ideally weigh nothing, cost nothing, disappear when you don't need it, be absolutely beautiful and work 100 per cent efficiently. And after all that, the student designer still has to work out what to do with his freedoms – his arbitrary choices. If he is designing a nut and bolt to a set of standards, he won't have many. If he is designing a decorative door-stop or the pattern for a carpet, he has very little else.

Let me take an example where externally imposed constraints are few. A potter may be told that the jug he is designing needs to contain just over a certain volume, and needs to pour at a certain rate. The rest may be up to him – up to his philosophy, which in turn will be bounded by his knowledge and skill.

Concepts of 'truth to materials'; knowledge of manufacturing techniques; ideas about beauty; decisions concerning what aesthetic or what feeling he should evoke; determining which models best reproduce his intention – all these are the concern of the designer.

All of the facts that are implied by the brief, and the facts from which he constructs his philosophy, presumably have to be available to him either through departmental study; through the experiences he generates for himself in terms of the 'hindsight' he accumulates; or through the study of design history.

You will notice, however, that these attempts at a clearer resolution of the activity say nothing about the way it is briefed – about the way it fits into society. Nor do they say anything about what are usually termed 'design methods' – black boxes, transparent boxes, their communicating networks and how you struggle from one decision to the next.

How then can we, the historians with an overriding interest in design, help the student designer? First, it might be more effective to show how we do not.

The history of Victorian furniture, for example, will not necessarily help the student of furniture design. If he is designing a chair with a moulded shell, and is thinking of covering the plastic foam upholstery with a stretch fabric, it will not help him any more than it will help the student abstract painter.

It will not make him conversant with anthropometrics or increase his critical appreciation of form and proportion any more, and in fact considerably less, than will his craft relationship with the models of his own work.

It could help the student who is working in the vernacular tradition; that is, if the furniture we show is in that idiom, and if we show it in enough detail.

It is more likely that the furniture we show will be highly decorated, handmade pieces, unmistakably the work of one of the rapidly increasing number of designer/architects. But their philosophies, even when they are recorded and accessible, will probably have little relevance to our student and his chair.

The furniture we show may even be some of the mass-produced, steam carved majority which brought design within the reach of the general public instead of confining it to a minority who could afford the handmade product.

As the American catalogue of exhibits to the 1851 exhibition expressed it: 'The expenditure of months or years of labour on a single article, not to increase its intrinsic value, but solely to augment its cost or its estimation as an object of virtue, is not common in the United States – on the contrary, both manual and mechanical labour are applied with direct reference to increasing the number and quantity of materials suited to the wants of a whole people.'

Perhaps the main point we can make here is that the excesses of high Victoriana – and their long-lasting effects – are presumably what you can expect when you confine a designer to the drawing board as the only respectable form of modelling and expect him to do nothing else, because of your assurance that the artisan and his machine will produce whatever he draws (Figure 1).

And if we can say nothing else relevant about Victorian furniture – about philosophies, production techniques, materials, craft traditions or the process of designing – then and only then do I suggest that we fall back on teaching the identification of formal tradition, style and motif, even if we cannnot say anything about the processes of their conception.

In terms of a designer's working philosophy – in terms of any investigation of, say, 'truth to materials', which is not completely uncritical – the Greek adaptation of wooden forms to stone, or the Victorian adaptation of stone forms to cast iron and wood, must be seen in the same light as streamlining

things that don't move, the modern silversmith reproducing a machine-accurate finish with a planishing hammer, the graining of plastic to look like leather, or the reproduction of Adam fireplaces in glass fibre reinforced plastics.

The object that combines function with unrelated appearance – the object of 'dual identity' – is perhaps but the epitome of this conflict between meaning and function, on which the student takes his stand by choosing to be designer, craftsman or artist – whatever material he is working with.

A designer's philosophy interacts with, and is determined by, the stand he takes on issues such as these, and it is only with a clear understanding of the relevant facts that he can take a stand rather than just find himself in one by default.

Another part of Professor Archer's paper defines the history of design as being that 'which like natural history, represents not only the study of design phenomena in the past, but also a systematic account of how things came to be the way they are'.

What else can we do besides provide material for alternative modern design philosophies? My principal theme is the language of models, and this perhaps is where we can not only trace their historical development, but also make useful distinctions within the process at the same time.

We know that the very first models available to us record the most important facets of the life of early man – hunting and childbearing – in the form of stone and clay miniatures and wall paintings. These signs developed into pictograms; symbol systems like cuneiform developed, and both modelled facts or ideas rather than sounds, which our alphabet models.

Recently, in the United States, chimpanzees have been taught to communicate with their keepers by deaf and dumb language. They have been found not only to chatter among themselves and make up their own words like 'water-bird' for 'duck' and 'hurt-food' for 'mustard', but they have even been proved to lie to get out of anticipated trouble.

One, presumably as a result of these new stimuli, has not only begun to draw representationally, but also tells us what it is that he has drawn. It will be interesting to see whether they too can model the future, besides being able to anticipate it.

But models as versatile as language and pictorial representation are only as good as the ideas they model, and the evolution of these ideas is of course part of the explanation we have to give of how artefacts 'came to be the way they are'.

Religious ritual, for example, is as important to understanding the concepts that make cathedrals or Navajo hogans the shape they are as it is to understanding how the Japanese smith controlled the making of the Samurai sword (Figure 2).

If we can now make steel without an associated Shinto ritual, make buildings higher than the highest Gothic cathedral, and construct dwellings that do not have to have the front door facing the rising sun, it is purely because we have improved the veracity of our ideas – improved the model of the world that all of us learn and carry around in our heads, and which can be termed our 'cognitive" model of the world.

There is an important group of artefacts whose sole purpose it is to improve on man's perceptual abilities, and so give us more and better information with which to develop those theories we need to bridge the gap between what we know to be true (our cognitive model) and what we discover to be true; and others whose purpose it is to model those theories, so that we can test them. Telescopes, astrolabes, electron microscopes, cameras, amplifiers, radar sets, techniques like thermography and maps of every sort, (Figure 3) all improve the range of what we know.

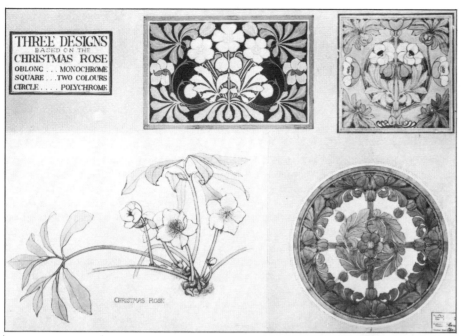

CHRISTMAS ROSE

1 *ACT examination sheet 'Three Designs based on the Christmas Rose' by Charles Hawkes, a 21-year-old 'decorator'. Dated 1909*

2 *'The Swordsmith Munechika forging the blade "Little Fox" aided by the fox spirit in the form of a youth' by Ichiyusai Kunigoshi, c1835*

3 *Detail from the 'Mappa Mundi' showing the British Isles, c1300. Original in Hereford Cathedral*

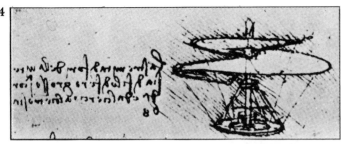

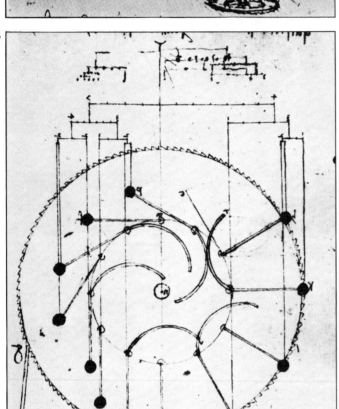

Our cognitive model is, of course, the first model with which we test our ideas about the future; and with some of us, that's as far as we get because we do not know how to get the idea out of our heads and into a form where we can study it as an entity in itself, whether our idea is intended fact or pure fancy (Figure 4).

Even if we do know how, we may not be able to model our idea well enough for it to help us much – we may, for instance, not be able to draw well enough for a sketch to help us decide whether the idea we have will work or not. On the other hand, drawing in itself may be unable to tell us what we want to know.

Ladislao Reti tells us: 'For Leonardo, drawing was a kind of language, in images that were more immediate and telling than the word itself. Often, in his notebooks, he switched from the written word to sketches to make his point graphic or even as a means of debating with others or himself.'[3] This might not surprise us very much, but he not only used the languages of writing and drawing; he used maps, plans and elevations, sections, musical scores, perspective, diagrams, figures and mathematics (Figure 5).

Some of his sketches prove that his cognitive model wasn't foolproof – or rather, prove that it couldn't have been working with the right information. But they also prove that the factors we see as difficult or impossible were not modelled in a way that tested them (Figure 6). He also drew test rigs which tested what his sketches could not (Figure 7).

Not all designers, however, are capable of using the languages that would be most appropriate to their work. James Brindley was engineer to the Bridgewater canal among a great many other things, but he was capable of reading and

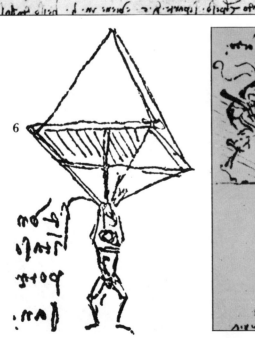

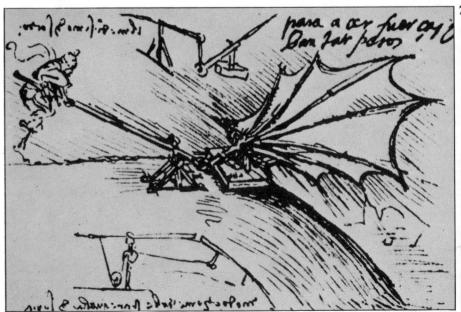

writing only with great difficulty. We are told that when he had mathematical problems to solve he developed the habit of retiring to bed until he had solved them.

When confronted with the problem of convincing the investigating committee in Parliament of the feasibility of his scheme for the Barton aqueduct (Figure 8), he made his first submission verbally, but finding that his sketches and technical phrases were incomprehensible to the committee, he next explained by carving a whole cheese with a penknife into a model of the aqueduct, complete with a barge on top. This, and practical demonstrations with clay, sand and water on the Commons floor, made his point and ultimately gained approval for the scheme.

We are told that Benjamin Baker not only illustrated the principle of his Forth railway bridge to the Royal Institution by means of an almost anthropomorphic model (Figure 9), but some say he also devised it this way as well.

Samuel Smiles quotes James Nasmyth as saying: 'Following up this idea, I got out my "scheme book", on the pages of which I generally thought out, with the aid of pen and pencil, such mechanical adaptations as I had conceived in my mind, and was thereby enabled to render them visible. I then rapidly sketched out my steam hammer, having all clearly before me in my mind's eye…In little more than half an hour…I had the whole contrivance in all its executant details before me in a page of my scheme book.'[4] (Figure 10).

This design incidentally, cut the time required by certain processes by a factor of 160, and was so controllable that it could be made to crack an egg without damaging the wine glass that held it, as well as forge anchors and all sorts of other things (Figure 11).

8   *The Barton aquaduct on the Bridgewater canal designed by James Brindley and completed in 1761*

9   *'Living model of the cantilever principle' of the Forth railway bridge by Benjamin Baker*

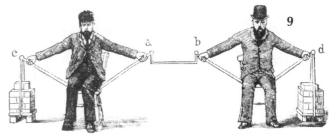

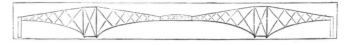

10   *First drawing of the steam hammer, 24 November 1839, by James Nasmyth*

11   *Engraving of 'Steam Hammer in Full Work' from a painting by James Nasmyth*

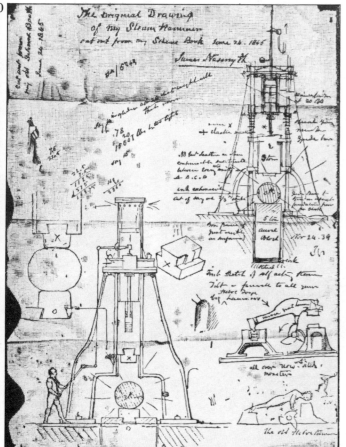

All these modelling techniques, and even the lack of them, only serve to highlight how important the subject is, and to illustrate the enormous range available to the working designer. If we look at other cultures we find illustrations that are even more revealing – like the Kashmiri carpet makers who do not work to a visual plan, but to a chant which is voiced at the same time as they work.

Whatever the designer's ideas are, he can model them, and in modelling them he will produce further ideas. For example, he can sketch it to see roughly what it might look like. But a sketch is too specific to model, say, social problems like bad housing or vandalism; and conversely it is not exact enough to tell if parts are too large or too small to fit together.

He can draw up his idea using measured perspective to see almost exactly what it might look like. He can talk about it to other people to gauge their reaction. Talking about it is a very cumbersome way of, say, describing formal considerations, but a very good way of generating ideas about the extent of the problem area or about less conventional solutions.

He can draw a diagram – like a map of the London underground – to sort out the main ideas involved, or to pass them on, and of course, diagrams lead on to Set Theory and computer logic, and to techniques like Critical Path Analysis.

He can make an accurate scale model – like an architect's model – to see if his ideas about dimensional proportion or the location of parts and forms was right, but it will not tell him much about the acoustics, circulation, plumbing or heating unless it has been specifically constructed for the purpose.

He can draw a measured elevation and plan to see if the various parts fit together as he had imagined, but it might be very misleading if he is inexperienced at judging (say) three-dimensional proportion with them.

He can use maths, geometry and trigonometry as 'languages' if he wants to measure and calculate line, area, volume and many other quantities.

There are many other, more specialised models. He can model a component in transparent plastic, stress it and view stress contours with the aid of polarised light. He can model the amount of light coming through the windows of a room, and display them as a plan of intensity contours on a digital computer's VDU. He can statistically model the average size of chair user, and the probability that he will use a particular chair for a given length of time.

One of the designer's most important tasks is to choose a language to fit the problem in hand. A project aimed at producing a designed artefact usually starts off in writing, probably couched in circumspect terms. It is then processed through several kinds of model, and ends up as an extremely specific engineering drawing – a model which even specifies how much tolerance is permissible either side of 'spot-on'.

If the history of design is incomplete without the history of designing, then our major task is to learn to read these models as they were used, and that involves us in learning how to interpret them – knowing how to read the languages.

As Bernard Myers shows so clearly in his lecture *Aesthetics*, it is no use looking at objects of art or design if all you read into them are vague comparisons of style and ethos. If you are comparing say, a mid-nineteenth-century American steam locomotive by Matthew Baldwin and a British one by Daniel Gooch, then each can be interpreted in terms of factors like the ownership of land; the cost of the different civil engineering problems involved in laying track; the length of journey, and the ability to predict when you were going to arrive; and the

12 *Model of the dome of St Peter's, Rome*

quality and availability of fuel and water. Each visible part can be explained in terms of the social, economic, geographical and historical factors governing its design.

Interpreting models, of course, involves learning how to read them in the same way as you have to learn to appreciate music or painting, read a landscape if you are going to mine it, or a river if you are going to navigate it.

When Thor Heyerdahl set sail in 'Ra', the voyage ended in near disaster because reconstruction of the reed boat from ancient illustrations did not include a rope tied to the stern section, but for which none of the builders could see a reason.

Perhaps this extract from Luigi Barzini's description of the 1907 Peking to Paris race best illustrates my point: 'At a village we stop for water. The car is thirsty and so are we. A good-natured crowd surrounds us, gives us clear, cool water, and starts upon a minute examination of the lower part of the automobile. They discuss; they draw nearer; some bolder youths bend down to the ground to look better at the flywheel. Then all bend down. That flywheel evidently puzzles them. We also look, vainly trying to discover what it is that so attracts their attention. The scene is decidedly ludicrous. At last one picks up courage and, more by signs than words, asks us for an explanation. Ah! At last we understand. They are asking "Where is the beast?" The horse, which is not in front, must surely be inside. "Indeed" says one, pointing at the radiator with an expressive piece of mimicry, "Indeed, it drinks water through a hole!'" but it is difficult to see how and where the un-happy animal is confined. Ettore [their chauffeur] tries to enlist their enthusiasm by a demonstration lesson, and opens the engine-cover to show the cylinders. But the people continue to look underneath with the greatest persistence; and we depart leaving them still perplexed.'[5]

We may well be able, with the relevant facts, to interpret Victorian and Edwardian design and engineering by learning to read the end product. But we cannot hope to say anything at all of what design activity was involved, or is involved in more modern design fields like aerospace or electronics, unless we learn to read the complex models involved not only in their design, but also in their explanation.

Not all modern design decisions are taken in the relatively accessible terms of the primitive steam engine or motor car; and it is perhaps worth pointing out that even these are only recognisable, let alone 'readable' or identifiable, because of cultural familiarity as well as accessibility.

A Shaker, Benjamin Young, wrote: 'In building a house, or constructing any machine, each part naturally lies in apparent confusion till the artist brings them together, and puts each one in its proper place; then the beauty of the machinery and the wisdom of the artist are apparent.'

Hogarth, in his *Analysis of Beauty*, wrote: 'Fitness of the parts to the design for which every individual thing is formed...is of the greatest consequence to the beauty of the whole...In ship-building, the dimensions of every part are confined and regulated by fitness for sailing. When a vessel sails well, the sailors call her a beauty, the two ideas have such a connection.'

James Nasmyth in his evidence to the Select Committee on Arts and Manufactures in 1835, said: 'Usually, the most economical disposition of the materials coincides with such a form as presents the most elegant appearance to the eye.'

Some things have changed.

Inside the shiny box there can lurk just about anything. The box need not be self-consciously beautiful, but it may conceal an important work of design – one that may not be visible to the naked eye, even with the lid off.

We cannot look at the outside of a clock, a Bulleid locomotive, Concorde, a radio or a computer and necessarily find ourselves enabled to say anything meaningful about what it does or the way it was designed.

If we limit ourselves to the way things look, we limit ourselves to what in today's terms is, in effect, the iconography of successful salesmanship – we limit ourselves to trailing several steps behind *The Hidden Persuaders*.

If we limit ourselves to the way things look, then we limit ourselves to understanding and commenting only on a small part of the designer's job.

As I have heard designers say, when people insist on talking only about the derivation of what a thing looks like, 'That's not the point; that's not what it's about'.

My argument, then, hinges on the assertion that in choosing our design historical facts, we must choose with relevance to design, not only in the hope of enabling our students to be better designers, but also in the hope that the specialism of design history has more than a redundant association with designing.

By relying on criteria that have been accepted in the past, by retreating into a perhaps mistaken impression of what the subject is about, we do an injustice to design history, to our students, and ultimately to the quality of the material our successors will have to work with and make sense of.

I suggest that design history is important enough to remain as flexible as design itself. The study of history is not a manufactured product to be stored on the supermarket shelf; it should respond to the relevance that its particular audience demands of it. Design history is a process as well as a product.

I would like to end with one of Dr Christopher Dresser's many useful quotations, because I think it sums up my attitude to the whole problem: 'The principles discoverable in the works of the past belong to us, not so the results.'[6]

1 Bicknell, Julian and McQuiston, Liz (eds) *Design for Need – The Social Contribution of Design* Pergamon /ICSID, 1977

2 Pye, David *The Nature of Design* Studio Vista, 1971

3 Reti, Ladislao, *The Unknown Leonardo* Hutchinson, 1974

4 Smiles, Samuel (ed) *James Nasmyth, Engineer – an autobiography* John Murray, 1885

5 Barzini, Luigi *Peking to Paris – a journey across two continents in 1907* Alcove Press, 1972

6 Dresser, Christopher *Principles of Decorative Design* Cassell, Petter and Galpin, 1873. Reprinted Academy Editions, 1973

Art and design history: the parting of the ways?

Clive Ashwin
Middlesex Polytechnic

The study of the history of art and the history of design in British colleges and departments of practical art is not a completely new phenomenon. The National Diploma in Design (NDD), which was the principal advanced qualification in practical art and design from 1946 until its supersession by the Diploma in Art and Design (DipAD) in the early 1960s, entailed an examination in the theory and history of every candidate's specialism. In 1949, for example, Dress students were confronted with the following: 'Fashion changes in the past two years have indicated clearly that the corset is by no means a static article of dress. What do you know of changing corset shapes from the sixteenth century onwards? Give your answer in the form of sketches with brief descriptions.'[1]

However, the current extensive provisions for the study of the history of art and the history of design in British colleges – and universities – is largely attributable to the policies pursued by our national Ministry of Education (later, Department of Education and Science) since 1960. These policies were initially formulated with specific reference to the so-called 'public' sector of art education – the colleges and schools of art and design – as distinct from the 'autonomous' sector of the universities. But there can be no doubt that the rapid expansion of the teaching of and research into the history of art and design which we have seen in our universities since 1960 is at least partly attributable to the demand for qualified staff occasioned by the subject's development in public-sector institutions.

It would not be appropriate to recount here the complex general history of art educational policies over the course of the past two decades; my intention is rather to focus closely on one or two issues which I regard as of pressing importance. However, I think it would be useful to note some interesting features of the terminology adopted by official documents with regard to the history of art and design and the assumptions which, I feel, they betoken.

The *First Report* of the National Advisory Council on Art Education (NACAE), published in 1960 and popularly known as the first Coldstream report, stipulated that the study of the history of art should be an obligatory component of all the new DipAD courses. Every course, it laid down, 'should cover the history of the major arts in several significant periods in time'. It also declared that 'each student should learn the history of his own subject'[2] – fashion including the history of costume, furniture the history of furniture, and so on. The history of specific design subjects was, the report argued, often adequately taught by specialist studio staff as an extension or reinforcement of studio work. 'History of design' did not appear as a term in the 1960 report, and I think it would be reasonable to assume that no very great importance was attached to it as a distinctive feature of the new courses.

The *Second Report* of the NACAE, which concerned itself with the vocational sector of art education, envisaged courses in 'design appreciation' intended to elevate the taste and discrimination of vocational design students and 'stimulate a general awareness of aesthetic values'.[3]

When the National Council for Diplomas in Art and Design (NCDAD), the executive body recommended by the NACAE, reported in 1964, it generally adhered to the principles and terminology of the NACAE. There was no specific mention of the history of design. The section devoted to the history of art noted evidence of a degree of resistance to art history in the colleges, and the assumption that it was 'some tiresome extraneous discipline which was being imposed on the natural body of art studies'. The report urged that, 'somehow, the atlas of historic time has to be made vivid and comprehensible to the art student', and it called upon the services of 'the professional art historian' to perform this feat of cultural salesmanship.[4]

The language of these early reports reflects the kind of art history that was being taught, or attempted, in colleges during the mid-1960s. Its backbone consisted of units based upon the major periods of fine art interest together with, in some cases, peripheral offerings in the history of design. Yet the majority of students for whom the courses were intended were training to be professional designers, not fine artists, a situation which still obtains today. Of course, one can justifiably argue that it was, and still is, highly beneficial for the designer of, say, textiles to know something of the imagery of the modern movement in painting and sculpture which did so much to determine the character of contemporaneous design; but the real reason why textile students found themselves sitting through lectures on Cubism, Futurism and Dada was not that these movements had some important bearing on the design of textiles (which, of course, they have) but because they represented what staff by and large felt able to offer.

The first token of recognition of the history of design as a feature of course experience occurs in the Report of the Joint Committee of the NACAE and the NCDAD, published in 1970, which expected to see 'historical, scientific and philosophical methods being applied to the history of art and design and to their relationship to society'. The Report continued: 'We are in no doubt that every student's course must include some serious and relevant studies in the history of art and design.'[5] The *Second Report* of the NCDAD, also published in 1970, noted under 'History of Art and Complementary Studies' that 'in the field of the history of design, the limitation of specialist staffing resources is still serious; but where teaching has been possible, it has been of great value to students'.[6]

Since 1970, the history of design as an academic discipline has acquired an increasingly distinctive identity. The most recent edition of the *Directory* of the Council for National Academic Awards (CNAA), the body since 1974 responsible for administering most advanced courses in practical art and design, claims that, 'History of art and design is a compulsory study in all art and design courses...' The CNAA also validates a small nucleus of new courses in which the history of design plays a substantial part, and one of which is a named honours degree in the History of Design.[7] We may reasonably safely predict that this growing presence of the history of design as a distinctive academic discipline will continue to be extended laterally, in the form of additional provision at first-degree level, as well as vertically in the form of the provision of postgraduate studies.

I think it would be fair to say that the justification for the introduction of art history into practical art and design education has never been fully explained or understood; it seems to have been assumed as axiomatic that such studies would inevitably make a valuable contribution to the art college curriculum. Many of the reasons that continue to be quoted in defence of its provision do not bear scrutiny. For example, one might agree that every course at first-degree level should entail the exercise and demonstration of a certain level of articulate reasoning in written and spoken English, but art history is only one of many academic disciplines that would foster these accomplishments, and some of them might well perform the task much better.

Similarly, there is little evidence to support the claim that a knowledge of the history of art makes a valuable contribution to performance as an artist. On the contrary, it could be argued that the extensive historical knowledge possessed by artists such as, for example, Poynter and Leighton proved to be a positive disadvantage to them, providing them with a burden of theoretical impedimenta which they were ill-equipped to carry. The knowledge of past art that was of value to their greater contemporaries, Whistler and the Impressionists, was not the kind that could be found in treatises on the history of art, but empirical evidence drawn from direct encounters with the work of their historical mentors, who included Velazquez, Goya, Delacroix and Hokusai.

However, the fact that we might find it difficult to establish a clear justification for historical studies as an integral part of practical art and design education does not necessarily mean that the policy of their introduction was a mistaken one. In education, as in many other provinces of human endeavour, some of the most enlightened innovations are adopted on the basis of little more than goodwill and intuition. With all its problems, I think that the broad strategy proposed by the Coldstream Committee and pursued with certain amendments over the past 17 years has produced substantial benefits for the colleges, their students, and society at large. But equally I feel that we can no longer proceed on the principle of ad hoc adaptation to circumstances that has characterised the provision of art and design history in the context of the DipAD and, latterly, the BA in Art and Design of the CNAA. New forces are at work which must be recognised, and which make it imperative that we ask some fundamental questions about the rationale and intention of theoretical studies of any kind in colleges of art.

One of the most important of these new forces consists of the radical changes in institutional structure that have taken place since the early 1960s. The traditional college of art tended to see itself as composed of a small cluster of related art, craft and design pursuits. Inter-departmental and inter-disciplinary dialogue was confined to a limited number of possibilities between, for example, painting, drawing, illustration and 'commercial art'. The absorption of colleges into large and highly diversified units, notably the polytechnics, has completely transformed the possible range of alliances. Nowadays many design departments have easy access to a high level of professional and academic provision in natural science, social science and technology. The establishment of new alliances

and the withering of old bonds between design practice and fine art practice has led to a corresponding and understandable questioning of the value of the history of the fine arts to the design student. The disciplines of design practice have in recent years acquired a new confidence and autonomy; a natural corollary is that they should demand an independent account of their origins and history.

Almost imperceptibly, the claim that fine art practice provided 'those fundamental skills and disciplines which underlie and sustain any form of specialisation', made in the *First Report* of the NACAE[8] and endorsed by the NCDAD, has been quietly abandoned. In 1970 the NCDAD recorded with regret 'a closing of doors between one area and another'. In particular, it observed that 'it is notable that recently very little but lip-service has been paid to the notion that there should be a fine art element in design study. Relatively few colleges have continued to provide fine art as a service to other areas'.[9] It was inevitable that the hairline cracks which appeared between the old domains of art and design practice would, in time, open into fissures, and that these fissures would send secondary radiating lines of cracks into the related domains of art and design history.

It would be difficult to refute the charge that art history as it has been taught and studied in our colleges and universities has hitherto neglected the serious study of design in favour of concentration on painting, sculpture and a certain amount of architecture. The chair upon which Rubens sat, the type-face from which Rembrandt read, the steamer in which Gauguin travelled, have normally only been recognised as attaining significance when they impinge in some identifiable way upon the style, technique or iconography of a painting. But, it is claimed, a balanced programme of study of the fine arts automatically provides the student with the background of knowledge and the intellectual skills necessary for the intelligent study of artefacts and design. There is reason to doubt the truth of this assumption: the study of design often requires an economic, technological or sociological mode of analysis which plays little or no part in conventional courses in the history of art. Of course, the art historian teaching in an art college can always supplement his training in these directions by continuing self-education; but that is quite different from claiming that these cognitive skills have been acquired in any specific way from his training as an art historian.

The truth is that more often than not the art history graduate regards his hard-earned breadth of knowledge in the fine arts as a kind of investment upon which he feels obliged to draw interest by teaching it. In the resulting state of inertia the question becomes not what the course or student needs, but what will be accepted from a predetermined range of expertise – predetermined, that is, by the material encountered by the lecturer during his own period of formal education.

In recent years a more serious charge has been added to the claim that conventional art history provides an inadequate account, or none at all, of the history of design. This is that it has misrepresented or distorted the history of design in order to make it conform to the assumptions and methodology of art history. Even Nikolaus Pevsner's *Pioneers of Modern Design*, for four decades the most widely read introduction to the history of modern design, has been attacked on the grounds that it provides a romanticised and over-simplified account of the evolution of design; an account which, it is claimed, presents the reader with a succession of designer-heroes of epic proportions – Morris, Shaw, Voysey, Mackintosh, Gropius – who successively transform the practice of design in a manner analogous to the transformation of nineteenth-century painting at the hands of Goya, Turner, Delacroix, Manet and Cézanne.

The history of design conceived as the history of 'pioneers' is, it is claimed, particularly attractive to the art historian because it allows him to account for the evolution of design in terms of the unique personal insights of individual designers, rather than in the more complex terms of technological change and socio-economic transformations. Consistent with this view of the history of design is the policy of ignoring or minimising the importance of vernacular or functional design in favour of artefacts with 'decorative' or 'aesthetic' qualities. One critic of *Pioneers of Modern Design* has written: 'In actuality, a careful reading of Pevsner's book shows that he was well aware that machinery and utilitarian functional forms played a major role in the thinking of at least some of his pioneers; but by emphasizing the artistic creativity of individuals and further relating it to contemporary painting, and by giving no examples of machine design or anonymous vernacular design, he leaves the reader with a fragmentary and distorted picture of the history of design in the nineteenth century and the beginning of the twentieth century.'[10]

The art historian's preoccupation with style and symbolism leads, it is claimed, to an excessive concern with superficial aesthetics and 'decoration' at the expense of function: 'In the way that design history is being written and taught today the material considered is often limited to what is "beautiful" or "decorative", and the main function of the objects is frequently just that: to be "decorative". The main point for consideration generally seems to be the form and decoration, and the way they relate to other objects, especially fine art objects. This means that the question of style is treated on a comparative basis, as in art history, and the discussion will centre, for example, on the development from Art Nouveau, through Deutscher Werkbund, Futurism, Constructivism, De Stijl and so forth, to Art Deco. This is not design history. It is applied art connoisseurship.'[11] Even more radical than the claim for drawing a distinction between art history and design history is the proposition that the assumption that design history is a province within the domain of art history is an exact inversion of the truth. 'On the contrary', it has been claimed, 'the history of art is a subsection of the history of design, albeit a very important one with a longer history of its own...'[12]

I believe that the impetus towards the establishment of the history of design as an autonomous discipline is rapidly gaining momentum. Already there is a proportion of staff in our larger colleges who are able to spend their time entirely upon the teaching of aspects of design history. Many design departments are large enough to generate and sustain their own courses in the history of design, independently of any parallel provision which might exist in the same institution for the history of art. Soon the first graduates in the history of design will be moving into the field of teaching, and perhaps they will be as reluctant to teach the history of Realist and Impressionist painting as their art history-trained colleagues have been to teach the origins of photo-mechanical reproduction and the development of the Colt ·45.

It would be mistaken to conclude that the problems of historical studies in the context of practical art and design education can be reduced to the single problem of the relationship between the history of art and the history of design. There are many other contingent issues which I am unable to afford more than a mention in the present context. For example, there is the general question of academic standards: my work brings me into regular contact with graduates from many centres, and I must confess that I feel far from confident that they all have a good grounding – or any grounding at all – in any definable aspect of the history of art or design. I should be happy to be proved wrong in this evaluation, but so far as I can see the machinery for making such an assessment on a national basis does not exist. The unregulated provision of course options creates the risk of an ill-assorted pick'n'mix of historical and pseudo-historical course units, providing the individual student with neither intellectual substance nor logical continuity. The pill of history may be so thoroughly sugared that it is no longer recognisable as history at all.

I suspect that many of the staff who experienced the trauma of 1968 were so demoralised that they retreated, perhaps for ever, from a recognisable teaching position. They became reluctant to assert the values they knew their subject embodied and, like Manzoni's character Don Abbondio, who felt like an earthenware pot forced to travel among a lot of iron ones, dedicated themselves to a life of unarmed neutrality. Attractive as many of the new policies may be, such as the abandonment of formal examinations, the popularity of continuous assessment and the phobia of stand-up teaching, we can attribute their introduction to a catastrophic loss of nerve and not, as it is popularly rationalised, to a desire for educational liberalism.

The little research that has been done into the condition of historical studies in the art college suggests that beneath the calm, superficial stratum of 'business as usual' there exist a growing number of doubts, problems and confusions which need attention as a matter of urgency.[13] What is required is a clear articulation of aims together with the establishment of principles for course design. Part of any systematic review of the provision of history of art and/or history of design in colleges and departments of art and design must take the form of a new rationale for the construction of curricula, and I should like to devote the remainder of this paper to a proposal for determining what kind of course might be appropriate to students working in different areas of specialisation and at different levels. I believe that if we can establish a reliable basis for the construction of courses, then many other problems such as the functional relationship between design history and art history will be solved as a matter of course.

If we examine most syllabuses in art and design history we will see that they normally consist of a list of names of periods, movements, regional and national schools, and individual artists and designers arranged sequentially, with or without options. Occasionally, they further define their area of interest by, for example, specifying a certain genre of artefact within a period, as in the case of 'Painting of the Nineteenth Century', or 'Twentieth-Century Furniture'.

Now I think it would be generally agreed that such headings, or a sequence of headings constituting a syllabus, tell us very little of the real character of the courses they denote in terms of educational value. It is, of course, important for a student to acquire a repertoire of factual knowledge about the subject he is studying, and although one might disagree on priorities of detail, I think we would all agree that a student who completed a course on nineteenth-century design but had never heard of the Great Exhibition of 1851 would be lacking in a rather fundamental piece of useful information. Similarly, we would expect of such a course a reasonable knowledge by acquaintance, enabling the student to identify with confidence a range of characteristic works produced during the period in question.

But although a course that aimed to do no more than provide its students with an inventory of names, dates and places, and an acquaintance with the appearance of a selection of key works, might make an excellent chronicle or catalogue, it would not add up to the history of anything. In order to qualify as history some attempt must be made to select, arrange, relate and explain facts in terms of a proposed pattern of historical causality that shaped and determined the character of the art works and artefacts under investigation. These causal factors are many and varied, and include technological and economic conditions, religious beliefs, social and political aspirations, and the biographies of individual artists and designers. But we must never forget the fundamental distinction between these two components of historical study. On the one hand, we have the facts – the objects and their associated records and documents – which are given to us by sense experience and to which we may return for confirmation or with further questions. On the other hand, we have the theories, the hypotheses, the explanations, by means of which we attempt to make historical sense of a confused mass of data, and which we must never fail to recognise as intellectual inventions with a life-span only as long as they appear to serve their purpose.

What I am arguing is that any unit of study in the history of art or the history of design has two dimensions. The first, the inventory or chronicle of works, we may call the *object of cognition:* this comprises the thing or class of things upon which the attention of the percipient is focussed. The second, the explicatory propositions, we may call the *mode of cognition:* this consists of the strategy adopted by the subject in order to bring conceptual order to the object of cognition.

The full extent of the first dimension, that of the object of cognition, can be defined as the totality of man-made objects. It includes the stone age axe and the Boeing 707; the Toby jug and the *Oath of the Horatii;* Bramante's Tempietto and Gatwick Airport. Not all of this vast range has been deemed to be of interest by the mainstream art historian, who has, on the whole, confined his attention to objects with some claim to aesthetic status and, more specifically, without functional connotations. This class of objects (those with aesthetic appeal and without functional purpose other than as objects of disinterested contemplation) we generally refer to as works of fine art.

The second dimension, the mode of cognition, is more difficult to conceptualise. As with the first dimension, we must define it inductively, by the systematic accumulation of identifiable historical strategies; but as we cannot rule out the possibility of the invention of new modes of historical cognition such a list could never be regarded as definitive or complete. In other words, while the totality of objects created during, for example, the nineteenth century must remain the same (or even diminish owing to decay and destruction), historians' attempts to make sense of that corpus of objects will inevitably increase in both number and variety as long as the nineteenth century remains a source of interest to them. This corpus may be extended by the 'discovery' of a 'new' work as the result of a revised attribution or by the removal of an obscuring agent such as a layer of whitewash; but in a literal sense it was, of course, there all the time waiting to be discovered, and was certainly not invented by the perceiving subject as is the case with a new mode of cognition.

The historiography of art history demonstrates that the most important reforms in the character of the subject have been brought about not so much as a result of the discovery of new objects (as is frequently the case with archaeology), but by the formulation of new strategies for analysing, evaluating and relating already familiar or well-known objects. This generalisation can be illustrated by reference to, for example, Vasari, Morelli, Wölfflin and Gombrich. The strategies we now employ to bring order to the infinitely complex history of art and design are composed of a synthesis of methods, all of which have been devised and developed at some time during the long history of the subject as an intellectual pursuit.

Let me now illustrate the dimension of the mode of cognition with some examples – not, I should stress, a comprehensive list or in order of priority. Confronted with the evidence of the individual object of cognition (art work, artefact, design etc), the historian may claim that it:

1 reflects the spiritual/political/social beliefs of the milieu of its origin (eg religious symbolism in painting)

2 provides evidence of the level of technological development at the time/place of its origin (eg building technology as reflected in architectural examples)

3 reflects the economic circumstances of its origins (eg the extravagant use of ornament as a token of superfluous wealth)

4 contains evidence of its originator's biography (eg originator's state of physical or mental health, travel, contact with formative influences)

5 possesses a distinctive and identifiable morphological character (eg belongs to a certain 'style' which relates it to works of the same or different genres)

6 represents a link in an evolutionary chain of works (eg is a 'transitional' work falling at a time of stylistic change)

7 exemplifies the level of technical expertise of its originator and/or his milieu (eg skilled or clumsy use of materials)

8 possesses an inherent aesthetic quality (eg is 'charming', 'perfect', 'magical', 'subtle', 'mysterious', 'bold', 'overpowering', 'crude', or their opposites)[14]

And so on.

Needless to say, these and other modes of cognition are often employed simultaneously and synthetically, in which case the historian has the added responsibility of attaching differential weightings to them.[15]

If we were to draw up these two dimensions of the object and the mode of cognition to a workable degree of detail, it would then be possible to use them as the two axes of a matrix (say, object on the vertical, mode on the horizontal) within which we could represent the problems of course design. Let me illustrate how such a matrix might help by considering two issues which arise frequently in the discussion of objectives and content in course design.

The first issue I wish to consider may be called the 'body of knowledge issue'. It is often asserted that the study of any discipline necessitates the acquisition of a so-called body of knowledge, a basic groundwork of information without which any form of constructive thought or reflection is impossible. What, for example, do we regard as the essential minimum of useful knowledge for the student of, say, typographic history? Is it possible to define such a minimum foundation? How much of the 'atlas of historic time' should he be able to sketch from memory, or at least fill in the names on a blank outline map? I appreciate that the 'body of knowledge' approach is somewhat unfashionable at the present time; there has been a tendency to question the worthwhileness of defining such minima. However, I feel sceptical of this view. Could one really feel happy about a graduate in graphic design who was unable to locate Baskerville in the correct century? Or a student of painting who knew nothing of Cubism? All such questions can be defined in terms of the vertical axis of our proposed matrix, that of the object of cognition. Attempting to establish such knowledge criteria might sound like a rather banal exercise, but I do not see that we can avoid it if we are to understand the full implications of the courses we plan and teach.

It might be worth adding here that one consequence of the separatist view that art history and design history should be taught and studied independently is that such a policy would require not one but two matrices, albeit incorporating elements of each other.

The second issue is that of cognitive skill. It is often claimed that the criterion of success in academic study is the acquisition of cognitive skills – the ability to think logically, to use evidence scientifically, to synthesise information and to communicate findings coherently. Sometimes these ends are advocated or pursued in opposition to the 'body of knowledge' approach: knowledge per se is disparaged as redundant or inert – so much ballast to be acquired only when the subject feels the need for it, and abandoned as soon as that need disappears. Give the student the cognitive strategies, it is argued, and the facts will take care of themselves.

Here, you will see, we are working along the horizontal axis of my proposed matrix, that of the mode of cognition, and once again I take the opportunity of reverting to the question of the relationship between art history and design history. Will one scale of cognitive modes, one axis, one matrix, satisfy the needs of both? If the strategies available to and employed by the art historian are not identical to those needed by the historian of design, how big is the discrepancy? Again, is it possible to conceive of a matrix flexible enough to accommodate the needs of both? I am not arguing that a systematic approach to course planning would immediately provide us with answers to these questions, but it would at least enable us to answer them in an orderly and rational way.

1 Ministry of Education *Examinations in Art, Question Papers 1949* HMSO, London 1949 List A, Test II 2. See also Clive Ashwin *Art Education: documents and policies 1768–1975* Society for Research into Higher Education, London, 1975, 82–92

2 Ministry of education *First Report of the National Advisory council on Art Education* HMSO, London 1960, para 25.

3 Ministry of Education *Vocational Courses in Colleges and Schools of Art* (Second Report of the NACAE) HMSO, London, 1962, para 27

4 National Council for Diplomas in Art and Design *First Report* HMSO, London, 1964, paras 50, 51

5 Department of Education and Science, Joint Committee of the NACAE and the NCDAD *The Structure of Art and Design Education* HMSO, London, 1970, para 39

6 National Council for Diplomas in Art and Design *Second Report* NCDAD, London, 1970, para 22

7 At Manchester Polytechnic. See *Directory* of the CNAA, 1977, 103

8 NACAE 1960, para 20

9 NCDAD 1970, para 18

10 Schaefer, Herwin *The Roots of Modern Design* Studio Vista, London 1970, 1

11 Wilkins, Bridget 'Teaching Design History' in *Bulletin of the Association of Art Historians* no 2, February 1977

12 del Renzio, Toni 'Mistaken identities in the history of design' in *The Times Higher Education Supplement* 4 February 1976, 7

13 See, for example, the report by Maurice Whitbread 'Art and Design History in Polytechnics and Art Colleges', in *Bulletin of the Association of Art Historians* no 3, October 1976, 11–13

14 All these adjectives are used to describe architectural examples in Pevsner, Nikolaus *An Outline of European Architecture* Penguin Books, Harmondsworth, 1943, seventh edition, reprinted 1964, Chapter One 'Twilight and Dawn'

15 The mode of cognition has, of course, much in common with what is commonly referred to as 'methodology'. It should, however, be pointed out that most historical methodologies are composed of a synthesis of several modes of cognition. A methodology which confined itself to the exercise of one exclusive mode of cognition (eg iconographic interpretation, socio-economic analysis) would be attractive because of its simplicity, but stultifying in its effect